S0-ADT-322

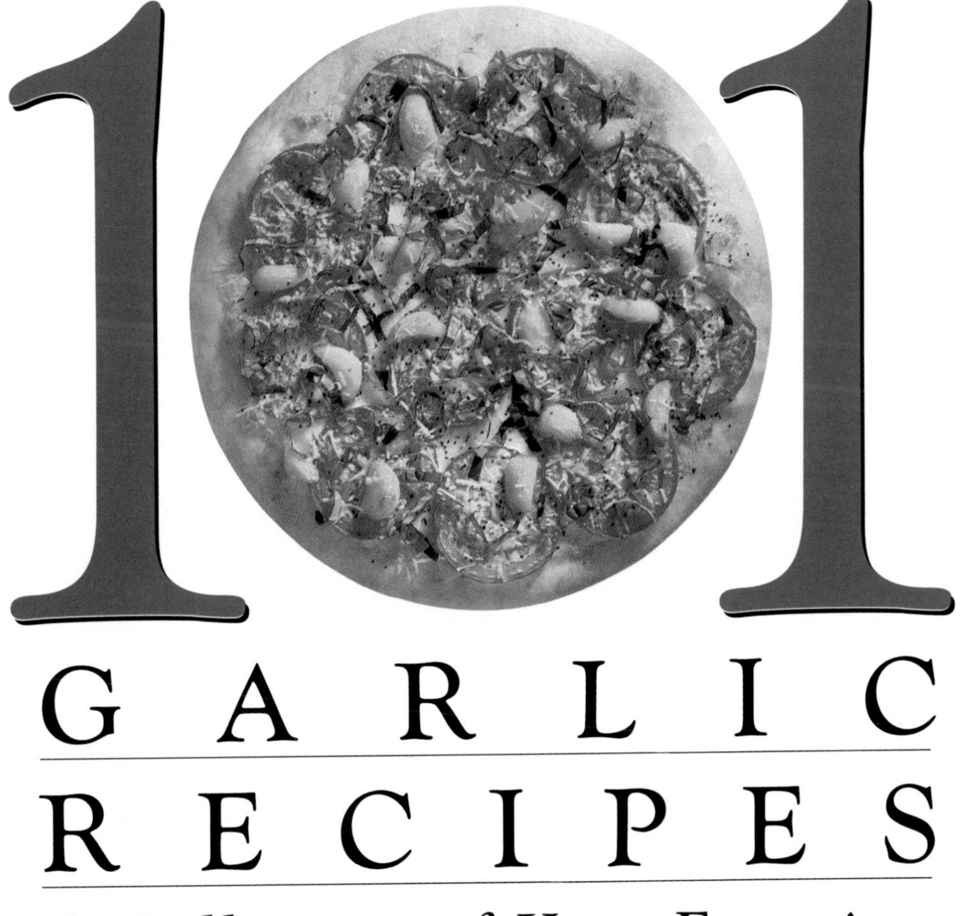

GARLIC RECIPES

A Collection of Your Favorites

PUBLICATIONS INTERNATIONAL, LTD.

Louis Weber, CEO
Publications International, Ltd.
7373 North Cicero Avenue
Lincolnwood, Illinois 60646

Some of the products listed in this publication may be in limited distribution.

Front cover photography by photo/Kevin Smith.

Pictured on the front cover: Roasted Garlic & Fresh Tomato Pizza *(page 39)*.
Pictured on the back cover *(from left to right)*: Spinach-Stuffed Shells *(page 54)* and Herb-Roasted Racks of Lamb *(page 118)*.

ISBN: 0-7853-3382-7

Library of Congress Catalog Card Number: 98-68240

Manufactured in U.S.A.

8 7 6 5 4 3 2 1

Microwave Cooking: Microwave ovens vary in wattage. Use the cooking times as guidelines and check for doneness before adding more time.

The HEALTHY CHOICE® recipes contained in this book have been tested by the manufacturers and have been carefully edited by the publisher. The publisher and the manufacturers cannot be held responsible for any ill effects caused by errors in the recipes, or by spoiled ingredients, unsanitary conditions, incorrect preparation procedures or any other cause.

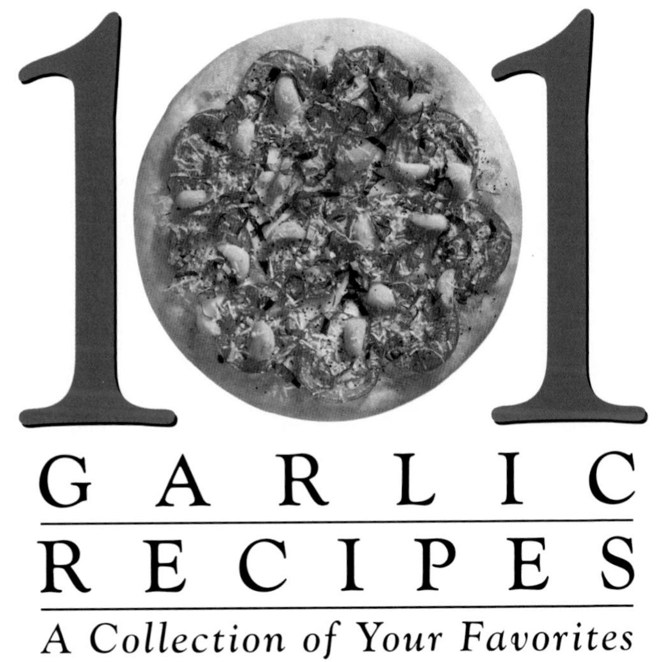

101 GARLIC RECIPES

A Collection of Your Favorites

Basic Garlic Facts

Throughout history, this wonderful little bulb has been hailed for its flavor, pungency and healing powers. Garlic was believed to give courage and strength, to cure diseases such as consumption and influenza and to ward off vampires.

But garlic has been popular for centuries for more than its medicinal qualities! It has found its way into the hearts of millions of people around the world because of its exceptional flavor and versatility. Garlic is a staple in Italian, Chinese, Mexican, Thai and Mediterranean cuisines, just to name a few. Garlic is the star ingredient in grilled London broil, buttery shrimp scampi, hearty bowls of chili and many savory dips and spreads.

A member of the lily family, garlic is a cousin to onions, leeks, chives and shallots. The edible bulb or head grows beneath the ground and, like the onion, is encased in a papery covering. But unlike its relatives, each garlic bulb is made up of 12 to 15 cloves, each in a closely fitting paper skin.

Although there are many varieties of garlic, most have the same characteristic pungent odor and bite and can be used interchangeably in recipes. The most common variety of garlic is American garlic, which has white skin and a strong flavor. The purple-skinned Mexican and Italian garlic tastes sweeter, and elephant garlic, with its large cloves, is very mild. Processed garlic is available in flakes (minced), powder, salt, juice and packed in oil (chopped or whole). While these may be convenient, they don't quite capture the true flavor of fresh garlic.

Garlic Know-How

When purchasing garlic, look for heads that are plump, firm to the touch and have no visible damp or brown spots. Avoid bulbs that are lightweight for their size, because they may be partially dried and shriveled. Store garlic heads, loosely covered, in a cool dark place with good air circulation.

Whole garlic heads will keep for up to two months if stored properly. Once broken from the head, individual unpeeled cloves will keep up to ten days. After peeling, they may be tightly wrapped in plastic and refrigerated for a day or two.

Peeling a clove of garlic is very simple—just trim off the ends and slightly crush the clove with the flat side of a large knife. The pressure of the knife separates the skin from the clove. To peel a whole head of garlic or many cloves at once, blanch them in boiling water for 5 to 10 seconds or microwave them for a few seconds. Then, plunge the garlic into cold water; separate the head into cloves and peel away the skins.

Garlic may be chopped, minced, pressed in a garlic press or crushed under the flat side of a knife blade to release its oils. These methods result in a stronger garlic flavor than coarsely chopping, slicing or leaving cloves whole. Keep this in mind when deciding how much garlic flavor you want in your dish.

Sprinkling a small amount of salt over the garlic while chopping or mincing it helps to keep it from sticking to the knife. Also, the salt helps retain more of the garlic flavor because it absorbs the juice. If using salt while chopping garlic, remember to adjust the amount of salt in the recipe accordingly.

There is no need to peel garlic if you are using a garlic press. The garlic passes through the press leaving the skin behind. Don't forget to thoroughly wash the garlic press after each use. The oils left behind in the press can quickly turn rancid and pass on an off flavor the next time the press is used.

When cooking garlic, generally, the slower the cooking process, the milder the flavor of the garlic. For example, roasting garlic produces a mild, sweet, nutty flavor. Because it is milder, roasted garlic can be used more liberally than raw or sautéed garlic. Garlic cooks quickly when it is sautéed or stir-fried. Because of this, you must be careful not to overcook it. Overcooked garlic has a harsh, bitter taste.

Garlic Clean-Up

Don't let fears of garlic odor stop you from enjoying one of the world's most popular flavors! Follow these easy steps to prevent it from lingering. Munching on fresh parsley, a coffee bean or fennel seeds after a garlic-heavy meal can help reduce garlic aftertaste and bad breath. To get rid of garlic odor from your hands, first rub them with fresh lemon juice and salt. Rinse, then wash your hands with soap and warm water. For cutting boards or utensils, rub them with a paste mixture of baking soda and water, then rinse.

Amazing Appetizers & Soups

Roasted Pepper & Tomato Salsa

3 yellow or red bell peppers
2 poblano peppers
1 large onion
4 cloves garlic, minced
2 tablespoons olive oil
1 teaspoon dried oregano
¾ teaspoon salt
½ teaspoon black pepper
2 cans (14½ ounces each) diced tomatoes
¾ cup tomato juice
¼ cup chopped fresh cilantro
1 tablespoon lime juice

1. Preheat oven to 350°F. Chop peppers and onion into ¾-inch pieces. Combine peppers, onion, garlic, olive oil, oregano, salt and black pepper in large bowl; toss to coat. Spread onto two 15×10×1-inch baking pans. Bake 20 minutes or until peppers and onion are lightly browned, stirring after 10 minutes.

2. Combine roasted vegetables and remaining ingredients in large bowl. Spoon into 4 labeled 1½-cup storage containers. Store in refrigerator up to 10 days or freeze up to 2 months.

Makes 4 (1½-cup) containers

Salsa Cruda

1 cup chopped tomato
2 tablespoons minced onion
2 tablespoons minced fresh cilantro
2 tablespoons lime juice
½ jalapeño pepper,* seeded and minced
3 cloves garlic, minced

*Jalapeño peppers can sting and irritate the skin; wear rubber gloves when handling peppers and do not touch eyes. Wash hands after handling.

Combine all ingredients in small bowl; mix well. Serve with tortilla chips. *Makes 4 servings*

Roasted Pepper & Tomato Salsa

ROASTED PEPPER
AND TOMATO SALSA

Chicken Satay with Peanut Sauce

½ cup lime juice
⅓ cup reduced-sodium soy sauce
¼ cup packed brown sugar
4 cloves garlic, minced
¼ teaspoon ground red pepper
3 boneless skinless chicken breast halves (about 1¼ pounds)
18 bamboo skewers (10 to 12 inches long)
¼ cup chunky or creamy peanut butter
¼ cup thick unsweetened coconut milk* or Thick Coconut Milk Substitute (recipe follows)
¼ cup finely chopped onion
1 teaspoon paprika
1 tablespoon finely chopped cilantro

*Coconut milk separates in the can, with thick cream (consistency may be soft like yogurt or firm like shortening) floating to the top over thin, watery milk. Spoon thick cream from top after opening can. If less than ¼ cup, make up difference with remaining coconut milk.

1. Stir lime juice, soy sauce, brown sugar, garlic and red pepper in medium bowl until sugar dissolves. Set ⅓ cup marinade aside in cup.

2. Slice chicken lengthwise into ⅓-inch-thick strips. Add to remaining marinade in bowl and stir to coat evenly.

3. Cover and set aside at room temperature 30 minutes or cover and refrigerate up to 12 hours.

4. Cover skewers with cold water. Soak 20 minutes to prevent them from burning; drain.

5. Place peanut butter in medium bowl. Stir in ⅓ cup reserved marinade, 1 tablespoon at a time, until smooth. Stir in coconut milk, onion and paprika. Transfer sauce to small serving bowl; set aside.

6. Drain chicken; discard marinade. Weave 1 or 2 slices chicken onto each skewer.

7. Grill chicken over hot coals or broil 2 to 3 minutes per side or until chicken is no longer pink in center. Transfer to serving platter.

8. Sprinkle sauce with cilantro; serve with skewers. Garnish as desired. *Makes 6 servings*

Thick Coconut Milk Substitute

⅓ cup milk
1 teaspoon cornstarch
½ teaspoon coconut extract

Combine milk and cornstarch in small saucepan. Stir constantly over high heat until mixture boils and thickens. Immediately pour into small bowl; stir in extract.

Chicken Satay with Peanut Sauce

Bruschetta

Nonstick cooking spray
1 cup thinly sliced onion
½ cup chopped seeded tomato
2 tablespoons capers
¼ teaspoon black pepper
3 cloves garlic, finely chopped
1 teaspoon olive oil
4 slices French bread
½ cup (2 ounces) shredded reduced-fat Monterey Jack cheese

1. Spray large skillet with cooking spray. Heat over medium heat until hot. Add onion. Cook and stir 5 minutes. Stir in tomato, capers and pepper. Cook 3 minutes.

2. Preheat broiler. Combine garlic and oil in small bowl; brush bread slices with mixture. Top with onion mixture; sprinkle with cheese. Place on baking sheet. Broil 3 minutes or until cheese melts. *Makes 4 servings*

Caponata

1 pound eggplant, cut into ½-inch cubes
3 large cloves garlic, minced
¼ cup olive oil
1 can (14½ ounces) DEL MONTE® Italian Recipe Stewed Tomatoes
1 medium green pepper, finely chopped
1 can (2¼ ounces) chopped ripe olives, drained
2 tablespoons lemon juice
1 teaspoon dried basil, crushed
1 baguette French bread, cut into ¼-inch slices

1. Cook eggplant and garlic in oil in large skillet over medium heat 5 minutes. Season with salt and pepper, if desired.

2. Stir in remaining ingredients except bread. Cook, uncovered, 10 minutes or until thickened.

3. Cover and chill. Serve with bread.
Makes approximately 4½ cups

Prep Time: 10 minutes
Cook Time: 15 minutes
Chill Time: 2 hours

Philly® Garlic & Herb Dip

1 package (8 ounces) PHILADELPHIA BRAND® Cream Cheese, softened
3 tablespoons milk
3 tablespoons finely chopped fresh basil
3 tablespoons finely chopped fresh parsley
2 tablespoons chopped fresh chives
1 clove garlic, minced

MIX cream cheese and milk with electric mixer on medium speed until smooth.

BLEND in remaining ingredients. Refrigerate. Serve with assorted cut-up vegetables, breadsticks or chips. *Makes 1 cup*

Prep Time: 10 minutes plus refrigerating

Bruschetta

Tortellini with Roasted Garlic Sauce

- 1 large bulb garlic
- 1 package (9 ounces) fresh tortellini pasta
- 2 to 3 tablespoons olive oil
- ½ cup reduced-fat mayonnaise
- ½ cup nonfat sour cream
- ⅓ cup grated Parmesan cheese
- 2 tablespoons FRANK'S® REDHOT® Hot Sauce

1. Preheat oven to 350°F. Cut ½-inch off top of garlic, discard. Remove papery outer skin, leaving cloves intact. Wrap garlic in foil; bake 1 hour or until tender when pierced with sharp knife. Let stand until cool enough to handle.

2. Cook tortellini according to package directions. Rinse under cold water; drain well on paper towels. Heat 2 tablespoons oil in large nonstick skillet over medium heat. Add tortellini in batches to oil, cook and stir 3 to 5 minutes or until lightly golden. Add more oil, if necessary. Drain on paper towels.

3. Separate garlic into cloves; pinch each clove so roasted flesh comes out. Place cloves in blender or food processor. Add mayonnaise, sour cream, Parmesan cheese and REDHOT sauce. Cover; process until very smooth. Spoon into small saucepan; cook and stir over low heat until hot and bubbly. Transfer to serving bowl.

4. To serve, arrange tortellini on serving platter. Dip into Roasted Garlic Sauce.

Makes 12 servings (about 1¼ cups sauce)

Prep Time: 35 minutes

Cook Time: about 1 hour

South-of-the-Border Nachos

- 4 ounces low-fat tortilla chips
- Nonstick cooking spray
- ¾ cup chopped onion
- 2 jalapeño peppers,* seeded and chopped
- 3 cloves garlic, finely chopped
- 2 teaspoons chili powder
- ½ teaspoon ground cumin
- 1 boneless skinless chicken breast (about 6 ounces), cooked and chopped
- 1 can (14½ ounces) Mexican-style diced tomatoes, drained
- 1 cup (4 ounces) shredded reduced-fat Monterey Jack cheese
- 2 tablespoons black olives, chopped

*Jalapeño peppers can sting and irritate the skin; wear rubber gloves when handling peppers and do not touch eyes. Wash hands after handling.

1. Preheat oven to 350°F. Place chips in 13×9-inch baking pan.

2. Spray large nonstick skillet with cooking spray. Heat over medium heat until hot. Add onion, peppers, garlic, chili powder and cumin. Cook 5 minutes or until vegetables are tender, stirring occasionally. Stir in chicken and tomatoes.

3. Spoon tomato mixture, cheese and olives over chips. Bake 5 minutes or until cheese melts. Serve immediately.

Makes 4 servings

Tortellini with Roasted Garlic Sauce

Three Mushroom Ratatouille

1 package (3½ ounces) fresh shiitake mushrooms*
1 tablespoon olive oil
1 large onion, chopped
4 cloves garlic, minced
1 package (8 ounces) button mushrooms, chopped
1 package (6 ounces) crimini mushrooms, chopped
1 cup chicken broth
1 small tomato, chopped
2 tablespoons chopped parsley
2 tablespoons grated Parmesan cheese
3 pita breads (6 inches each)

*Or, substitute 1 ounce dried black Chinese mushrooms. Place dried mushrooms in small bowl; cover with warm water. Soak 20 minutes to soften. Drain; squeeze out excess moisture.

Remove stems from shiitake mushrooms; discard stems. Chop caps. Preheat broiler. Heat oil in large skillet over medium heat until hot. Add onion and garlic. Cook 5 minutes, stirring occasionally. Add all 3 types of mushrooms. Cook 5 minutes more, stirring often. Add chicken broth. Bring to a boil. Cook about 10 minutes or until liquid is absorbed. Remove from heat. Stir in tomato, parsley and cheese. Spoon into bowl.

Meanwhile, split each pita bread horizontally in half. Stack halves; cut the stack into 6 wedges. Arrange wedges in single layer on baking sheet. Broil 4 inches from heat 1 to 3 minutes or until wedges are toasted. Arrange toasted pita bread triangles and warm dip in basket. Garnish, if desired.

Makes about 2¼ cups

Roasted Eggplant Spread

1 large eggplant
1 can (14½ ounces) diced tomatoes, drained
½ cup finely chopped green onions
½ cup chopped fresh parsley
2 tablespoons red wine vinegar
1 tablespoon olive oil
3 cloves garlic, finely chopped
½ teaspoon salt
½ teaspoon dried oregano leaves
2 pita breads

1. Preheat oven to 375°F.

2. Place eggplant on baking sheet. Bake 1 hour or until tender, turning occasionally. Remove eggplant from oven. Let stand 10 minutes or until cool enough to handle.

3. Cut eggplant lengthwise in half; remove pulp. Place pulp in medium bowl; mash with fork until smooth. Add tomatoes, onions, parsley, vinegar, oil, garlic, salt and oregano; blend well. Cover eggplant mixture; refrigerate 2 hours.

4. Preheat broiler. Split pita breads horizontally in half to form 4 rounds. Stack rounds; cut into sixths to form 24 wedges. Place wedges on baking sheet. Broil 3 minutes or until crisp.

5. Serve eggplant spread with warm pita bread wedges. Garnish with lemon and lime slices, if desired.

Makes 4 servings

Three Mushroom Ratatouille

Falafel with Garlic Tahini Sauce

- **¾ cup uncooked dried chick-peas, sorted and rinsed**
- **½ cup uncooked bulgur**
- **Garlic Tahini Sauce (recipe follows)**
- **1½ cups coarsely crumbled whole wheat bread**
- **½ cup water**
- **¼ cup fresh lemon juice**
- **3 tablespoons chopped fresh cilantro**
- **2 cloves garlic, minced**
- **1 teaspoon ground cumin**
- **½ teaspoon salt**
- **½ teaspoon red pepper flakes**
- **Vegetable oil**

To quick soak chick-peas, place in medium saucepan; cover with 4 inches water. Bring to a boil and cook 2 minutes. Remove from heat; cover. Let stand 1 hour; rinse and drain. Place in saucepan and cover with 4 cups water. Bring to a boil; reduce heat to low. Cover; simmer 2 hours or until tender. Rinse; drain and set aside. Meanwhile, prepare bulgur according to package directions; set aside. Prepare Garlic Tahini Sauce; set aside.

Place bread in small baking pan. Pour ½ cup water over bread and let stand 15 minutes or until water is absorbed. Squeeze water from bread.

Place chick-peas, lemon juice, cilantro, garlic, cumin, salt and red pepper in food processor; process until smooth. Add bread and bulgur to food processor; process until combined.

Shape chick-pea mixture into 1½-inch balls. Place on baking sheet lined with waxed paper. Dry at room temperature 1 hour.

Heat 2 to 3 inches oil in large heavy skillet over medium-high heat. Carefully add falafel to skillet; cook 3 to 3½ minutes until golden brown. Remove falafel with slotted spoon and place on paper towels to drain. Serve with Garlic Tahini Sauce.

Makes 8 to 10 servings

Garlic Tahini Sauce

- **½ cup plain yogurt**
- **¼ cup tahini***
- **3 tablespoons water**
- **2 tablespoons fresh lemon juice**
- **1 clove garlic, minced**
- **½ teaspoon cumin**
- **Salt and black pepper to taste**

*Tahini is a thick paste made from ground sesame seeds and is used in Middle Eastern cooking. It is available in many large supermarkets.

Combine all ingredients in small bowl. Stir with wire whisk until well blended. Cover; refrigerate 1 hour.

Makes about 1 cup

Falafel with Garlic Tahini Sauce

Pesto Cheese Wreath

Parsley-Basil Pesto* (recipe follows)
3 packages (8 ounces each) cream cheese, softened
½ cup mayonnaise
¼ cup whipping cream or half-and-half
1 teaspoon sugar
1 teaspoon onion salt
⅓ cup chopped roasted red peppers or pimiento, drained**
Pimiento strips and Italian flat leaf parsley leaves (optional)
Assorted crackers and cut-up vegetables

*One-half cup purchased pesto may be substituted for Parsley-Basil Pesto.

**Look for roasted red peppers packed in cans or jars in the Italian food section of the supermarket.

Prepare Parsley-Basil Pesto; set aside. Beat cream cheese and mayonnaise in medium bowl until smooth; beat in cream, sugar and onion salt.

Line 5-cup ring mold with plastic wrap. Spoon half the cheese mixture into prepared mold; spread evenly. Spread Parsley-Basil Pesto evenly over cheese mixture; top with chopped red peppers. Spoon remaining cheese mixture over peppers; spread evenly. Cover; refrigerate until cheese mixture is firm, 8 hours or overnight.

Uncover mold; invert onto serving plate. Carefully remove plastic wrap. Smooth top and sides of wreath with spatula. Garnish with pimiento strips and parsley leaves, if desired. Serve with assorted crackers and vegetables.

Makes 16 to 24 appetizer servings

Parsley-Basil Pesto

2 cups fresh parsley leaves
¼ cup pine nuts or slivered almonds
2 tablespoons grated Parmesan cheese
2 cloves garlic, peeled
1 tablespoon dried basil leaves, crushed
¼ teaspoon salt
2 tablespoons olive or vegetable oil

Process all ingredients except oil in food processor or blender until finely chopped. With machine running, add oil gradually, processing until mixture is smooth. *Makes about ½ cup*

Egg Rolls

Sweet and Sour Sauce (recipe follows)
Nonstick cooking spray
3 green onions, finely chopped
3 cloves garlic, finely chopped
½ teaspoon ground ginger
½ pound boneless skinless chicken breasts, cooked and finely chopped
2 cups bean sprouts, rinsed and drained
½ cup shredded carrots
2 tablespoons reduced-sodium soy sauce
¼ teaspoon black pepper
8 egg roll wrappers
2 teaspoons vegetable oil

1. Prepare Sweet and Sour Sauce.

2. Spray large nonstick skillet with cooking spray. Heat over medium-high heat. Add onions, garlic and ginger. Cook and stir 1 minute. Add chicken, bean sprouts and carrots. Cook and stir 2 minutes. Stir in soy sauce and pepper. Cook and stir 1 minute. Remove skillet from heat; cool.

3. Brush edges of egg roll wrappers with water. Spoon filling evenly down centers of wrappers. Fold ends over fillings; roll up jelly-roll fashion.

4. Heat oil in another large nonstick skillet over medium heat until hot. Add rolls. Cook 3 to 5 minutes or until golden brown, turning occasionally. Serve hot with Sweet and Sour Sauce.
Makes 4 servings

Sweet and Sour Sauce

4 teaspoons cornstarch
1 cup water
½ cup sugar
½ cup white vinegar
¼ cup tomato paste

Combine all ingredients in small saucepan. Bring to a boil over high heat, stirring constantly. Boil 1 minute, stirring constantly. Cool.
Makes about 1½ cups (4 servings)

Garlicky Chicken Wings

2 pounds chicken wings (about 15 wings)
2 heads garlic*
Boiling water
1 cup olive oil, divided
1 teaspoon hot pepper sauce, or to taste
1 cup grated Parmesan cheese
1 cup Italian-style bread crumbs
1 teaspoon black pepper
Carrot and celery slices for garnish

*The whole garlic bulb is called a head.

Preheat oven to 375°F.

Locate first and second joints in chicken wings. Cut through both joints for each wing using sharp knife on cutting board; remove and discard tips. Rinse wing sections; pat dry with paper towels.

To peel whole heads of garlic, drop garlic heads into enough boiling water in small saucepan to cover for 5 to 10 seconds. Immediately remove garlic with slotted spoon. Plunge garlic into cold water; drain. Peel away skins.

Place garlic, 1 cup oil and hot pepper sauce in food processor; cover and process until smooth.

Pour garlic mixture into small bowl. Combine cheese, bread crumbs and black pepper in shallow dish. Dip wing sections, one at a time, into garlic mixture, then roll in crumb mixture, coating evenly and shaking off excess.

Grease 13×9-inch nonstick baking pan; arrange wing sections in single layer in pan. Drizzle remaining garlic mixture over wing sections; sprinkle with remaining crumb mixture.

Bake 45 to 60 minutes or until chicken is brown and crisp. Garnish, if desired.
Makes about 6 servings

Herbed Blue Cheese Spread with Garlic Toasts

1⅓ cups 1% low-fat cottage cheese
1¼ cups (5 ounces) crumbled blue, feta or goat cheese
1 large clove garlic
2 teaspoons lemon juice
2 green onions with tops, sliced (about ¼ cup)
¼ cup chopped fresh basil or oregano *or* 1 teaspoon dried basil or oregano leaves
2 tablespoons toasted slivered almonds*
Garlic Toasts (recipe follows)

*To toast almonds, place almonds in shallow baking pan. Bake in preheated 350°F oven about 10 minutes or until lightly toasted, stirring occasionally. (Watch almonds carefully—they burn easily.)

1. Combine cottage cheese, blue cheese, garlic and lemon juice in food processor; process until smooth. Add green onions, basil and almonds; pulse until well blended but still chunky.

2. Spoon cheese spread into small serving bowl; cover. Refrigerate until ready to serve.

3. When ready to serve, prepare Garlic Toasts. Spread 1 tablespoon cheese spread onto each toast slice. Garnish, if desired.

Makes 16 servings

Garlic Toasts

32 French bread slices, ½ inch thick
Nonstick cooking spray
¼ teaspoon garlic powder
⅛ teaspoon salt

Place bread slices on nonstick baking sheet. Lightly coat both sides of bread slices with nonstick cooking spray. Combine garlic powder and salt in small bowl; sprinkle evenly onto bread slices. Broil, 6 to 8 inches from heat, 30 to 45 seconds on each side or until bread slices are lightly toasted on both sides. *Makes 32 pieces*

Roasted Garlic Spread with Three Cheeses

2 medium heads garlic
2 packages (8 ounces each) fat-free cream cheese, softened
1 package (3½ ounces) goat cheese
2 tablespoons (1 ounce) crumbled blue cheese
1 teaspoon dried thyme leaves

1. Preheat oven to 400°F. Cut tops off garlic heads to expose tops of cloves. Place garlic in small baking pan; bake 45 minutes or until garlic is very tender. Remove from pan; cool completely. Squeeze garlic into small bowl; mash with fork.

2. Beat cream cheese and goat cheese in small bowl until smooth; stir in blue cheese, garlic and thyme. Cover; refrigerate 3 hours or overnight. Spoon dip into serving bowl; serve with cucumbers, radishes, carrots, yellow bell peppers or crackers, if desired. Garnish with fresh thyme and red bell pepper strip, if desired.

Makes 21 (2-tablespoon) servings

Herbed Blue Cheese Spread with Garlic Toasts

Spicy Shrimp Gumbo

½ cup vegetable oil
½ cup all-purpose flour
1 large onion, chopped
½ cup chopped fresh parsley
½ cup chopped celery
½ cup sliced green onions
6 cloves garlic, minced
4 cups chicken broth or water*
1 package (10 ounces) frozen sliced okra, thawed (optional)
1 teaspoon salt
½ teaspoon ground red pepper
2 pounds raw medium shrimp, peeled and deveined
3 cups hot cooked rice
Fresh parsley sprigs for garnish

*Traditional gumbo's thickness is like stew. If you prefer it thinner, add 1 to 2 cups additional broth.

1. For roux, blend oil and flour in large heavy stockpot. Cook over medium heat 10 to 15 minutes or until roux is dark brown but not burned, stirring often.

2. Add chopped onion, chopped parsley, celery, green onions and garlic to roux. Cook over medium heat 5 to 10 minutes or until vegetables are tender. Add broth, okra, salt and red pepper. Cover; simmer 15 minutes.

3. Add shrimp; simmer 3 to 5 minutes or until shrimp turn pink and opaque.

4. Place about ⅓ cup rice into each wide-rimmed soup bowl; top with gumbo. Garnish, if desired.

Makes 8 servings

White Bean Soup

6 strips (about 6 ounces) bacon, cut into ½-inch pieces
3 cans (15 ounces each) white beans, drained and rinsed, divided
3 cans (about 14 ounces each) reduced-sodium chicken broth
1 medium onion, finely chopped
3 cloves garlic, minced
1½ teaspoons dried thyme leaves
1½ teaspoons dried rosemary leaves

1. Cook and stir bacon in Dutch oven over medium-high heat about 10 minutes or until crisp.

2. While bacon is cooking, blend 1½ cans beans and broth in blender or food processor until smooth.

3. Drain all but 1 tablespoon bacon fat from Dutch oven. Stir in onion, garlic, thyme and rosemary. Reduce heat to medium; cover and cook 3 minutes or until onion is transparent. Uncover and cook 3 minutes or until onion is tender, stirring frequently.

4. Add puréed bean mixture and remaining 1½ cans beans to bacon mixture. Cover and simmer 5 minutes or until heated through.

Makes 4 servings

Tip: For a special touch, sprinkle chopped fresh thyme over soup just before serving.

Prep and Cook Time: 28 minutes

Spicy Shrimp Gumbo

Mexican Tortilla Soup

- 1 tablespoon vegetable oil
- 1 rib celery, sliced
- ½ cup sliced carrots
- 3 green onions, sliced
- 4 cloves garlic, minced
- 2 cans (about 14 ounces each) chicken broth
- ⅓ to ½ cup lime juice
- Baked Tortilla Strips (recipe follows)
- ½ cup chopped tomato
- ½ small avocado, chopped
- ¼ cup chopped seeded cucumber
- 2 tablespoons finely chopped fresh cilantro

Heat oil in medium saucepan over medium heat. Add celery, carrots, green onions and garlic; cook and stir about 5 minutes or until tender. Add chicken broth and lime juice; bring to a boil over high heat. Reduce heat to low; simmer, covered, 15 minutes. Meanwhile, prepare Baked Tortilla Strips.

Ladle soup into 4 bowls; divide tomato, avocado and cucumber among bowls. Sprinkle with cilantro and tortilla strips. Serve immediately.

Makes 4 servings

Baked Tortilla Strips

- 2 (6-inch) flour tortillas
- Nonstick cooking spray
- Dash paprika

Preheat oven to 375°F. Cut tortillas into halves; cut halves into ¼-inch-wide strips. Arrange tortilla strips on cookie sheet. Spray lightly with cooking spray; toss to coat. Sprinkle with paprika.

Bake about 10 minutes or until browned, stirring occasionally. Let cool to room temperature.

Makes about 1½ cups

Pasta e Fagioli

- 1 teaspoon olive oil
- 3 cloves garlic, minced
- 1 (15-ounce) can cannellini or Great Northern beans, rinsed and drained
- 2 cans (about 14 ounces each) fat-free reduced-sodium chicken broth
- ½ cup white wine, divided
- 1 tablespoon dried basil leaves
- ½ teaspoon black pepper
- ¼ to ½ teaspoon red pepper flakes
- 6 ounces uncooked ditalini pasta or other small tube pasta
- 4 teaspoons grated Parmesan cheese

Heat oil in large saucepan over medium-low heat until hot. Add garlic and beans; cook and stir 3 minutes. Add chicken broth, ¼ cup wine, basil, pepper and red pepper flakes. Bring to a boil over medium-high heat. Add pasta; cook 10 to 12 minutes or until tender. Add remaining ¼ cup wine just prior to pasta being fully cooked. Sprinkle with grated cheese. Serve immediately.

Makes 4 (1-cup) servings

Note: This soup will be very thick.

Mexican Tortilla Soup

Grilled Summer Gazpacho

- **1 red bell pepper, stemmed, seeded and halved**
- **4 large (about 2 pounds) tomatoes, tops removed**
- **1 small onion, halved**
- **Nonstick cooking spray**
- **4 cloves garlic, divided**
- **6 (½-inch) slices French bread**
- **1 cup coarsely chopped peeled cucumber**
- **1 cup day-old French bread cubes, soaked in water and squeezed dry**
- **2 to 4 tablespoons chopped fresh cilantro**
- **2 tablespoons lemon juice**
- **1 tablespoon olive oil**
- **½ teaspoon salt**
- **2 cups ice water**
- **Additional cilantro leaves for garnish**

1. Prepare coals for grilling. Grill bell pepper halves skin-side down on covered grill over medium to hot coals 15 to 25 minutes or until skin is charred, without turning. Remove from grill and place in plastic bag until cool enough to handle, about 10 minutes. Remove skin; set peppers aside to cool.

2. Meanwhile, spray tomatoes and onion halves with cooking spray. Grill tomatoes and onion halves skin-side down on covered grill over medium coals 10 to 20 minutes or until grillmarked and tender, turning as needed. Thread 3 garlic cloves onto water-soaked wooden or bamboo skewer. Spray with cooking spray. Grill garlic on covered grill over medium coals about 8 minutes or until browned and tender. Remove vegetables from grill and let cool on cutting board.

3. While vegetables cool, cut remaining garlic clove in half. Spray both sides of French bread slices with cooking spray; rub with garlic clove halves. Grill bread slices on both sides until toasted and golden, watching carefully. Cool; cut into ½-inch croutons and set aside for garnish.

4. Gently squeeze cooled tomatoes to remove seeds and release skins. Scrape and discard any excess charring from onion. Coarsely chop bell pepper, tomatoes and onion; add with cucumber to food processor or blender. Cover and process until smooth. Transfer to large bowl.

5. Add soaked bread cubes, chopped cilantro, lemon juice, oil and salt to food processor; cover and process until smooth. Combine with grilled vegetable mixture; stir in ice water. Ladle soup into bowls; garnish with garlic croutons and additional cilantro leaves, if desired.

Makes 6 servings

Grilled Summer Gazpacho

Spicy Senegalese Soup

- 1 tablespoon unsalted butter
- 1 large white onion, chopped
- 4 cloves garlic, chopped
- 2 tablespoons all-purpose flour
- 4 teaspoons curry powder
- 2 cans (14½ ounces each) chicken broth
- ½ cup water
- 1 tart cooking apple, peeled, cored and sliced
- 1 cup thinly sliced carrots
- ¼ cup golden raisins
- ¼ cup FRANK'S® REDHOT® Hot Sauce
- 1 cup half 'n' half

1. Melt butter in large saucepan over medium heat. Add onion and garlic; cook 5 minutes or until tender, stirring occasionally. Add flour and curry powder; cook and stir 1 minute.

2. Gradually blend in broth and water. Add apple, carrots, raisins and REDHOT sauce. Bring to a boil. Reduce heat to low. Cook, covered, 25 minutes or until carrots are tender.

3. Place one-third of the soup in blender or food processor. Cover securely; process on low speed until mixture is puréed. Transfer to large bowl. Repeat with remaining soup. Return puréed mixture to saucepan. Stir in half 'n' half. Cook until heated through.

4. Serve hot or cold. Garnish with chopped apple and dollop of sour cream, if desired.

Makes 6 servings (about 6 cups)

Prep Time: 25 minutes

Cook Time: 30 minutes

Sweet Pepper Garlic Soup

- 2 teaspoons olive oil
- ½ cup chopped onion
- 6 cloves garlic, chopped
- 1 cup cubed unpeeled potato
- 1 cup chopped red bell pepper
- 3½ cups fat-free reduced-sodium chicken broth
- 1 cup low-fat cottage cheese
- 2 tablespoons plain nonfat yogurt
- ⅛ teaspoon black pepper
- Fresh parsley and bell pepper strips for garnish (optional)

1. Heat oil in medium saucepan over medium heat; add onion and garlic. Cook and stir 3 minutes or until onion is tender.

2. Add potato, bell pepper and chicken broth. Bring to a boil; reduce heat and simmer 10 to 15 minutes or until potato is easily pierced when tested with fork. Remove from heat; cool completely.

3. Place broth mixture in food processor or blender; process until smooth. Refrigerate until completely cool.

4. Place cottage cheese and yogurt in food processor or blender; process until smooth. Set aside ¼ cup cheese mixture. Stir remaining cheese mixture into chilled broth mixture until well blended. Add black pepper; mix well. Top with reserved cheese mixture. Garnish with parsley and bell pepper strips, if desired.

Makes 6 (¾-cup) servings

Spicy Senegalese Soup

Roasted Winter Vegetable Soup

- **1 small *or* ½ medium acorn squash, halved**
- **2 medium tomatoes**
- **1 medium onion, unpeeled**
- **1 green bell pepper, halved**
- **1 red bell pepper, halved**
- **2 small red potatoes**
- **3 cloves garlic, unpeeled**
- **1½ cups tomato juice**
- **½ cup water**
- **4 teaspoons vegetable oil**
- **1 tablespoon red wine vinegar**
- **¼ teaspoon black pepper**
- **¾ cup chopped fresh cilantro**
- **4 tablespoons nonfat sour cream**

1. Preheat oven to 400°F. Spray baking sheet with nonstick cooking spray.

2. Place acorn squash, tomatoes, onion, bell peppers, potatoes and garlic on prepared baking sheet. Bake 40 minutes, removing garlic and tomatoes after 10 minutes. Remove remaining vegetables from oven. Let stand 15 minutes or until cool enough to handle.

3. Peel vegetables and garlic; discard skins. Coarsely chop vegetables. Combine half of vegetables, tomato juice, water, oil and vinegar in food processor; process until smooth.

4. Combine vegetable mixture, remaining vegetables and black pepper in large saucepan. Bring to a simmer over medium-high heat. Simmer 5 minutes or until heated through, stirring constantly. Top individual servings with cilantro and sour cream. *Makes 4 servings*

Onion Soup with Pasta

- **Nonstick cooking spray**
- **3 cups sliced onions**
- **3 cloves garlic, minced**
- **½ teaspoon sugar**
- **2 cans (14½ ounces each) reduced-sodium beef broth**
- **½ cup uncooked small pasta stars**
- **2 tablespoons dry sherry**
- **¼ teaspoon salt**
- **⅛ teaspoon black pepper**
- **Grated Parmesan cheese**

1. Spray large saucepan with cooking spray; heat over medium heat until hot. Add onions and garlic. Cook, covered, 5 to 8 minutes or until onions are wilted. Stir in sugar; cook about 15 minutes or until onion mixture is very soft and browned.

2. Add broth to saucepan; bring to a boil. Add pasta and simmer, uncovered, 6 to 8 minutes or until tender. Stir in sherry, salt and pepper. Ladle soup into bowls; sprinkle lightly with Parmesan cheese. *Makes 4 first-course servings*

Onion Soup with Pasta

Beef and Pasta Soup

- 1 tablespoon vegetable oil
- ½ pound round steak, cut into ½-inch cubes
- 1 medium onion, chopped
- 3 cloves garlic, minced
- 4 cups beef broth
- 1 can (10¾ ounces) tomato purée
- 2 teaspoons dried Italian seasoning
- 2 bay leaves
- 1 package (9 ounces) frozen Italian green beans
- ½ cup uncooked orzo or rosamarina (rice-shaped pastas)
- Salt
- Lemon slices and fresh oregano for garnish
- Freshly grated Parmesan cheese (optional)
- French bread (optional)

1. Heat oil in 5-quart Dutch oven over medium-high heat; add beef, onion and garlic. Cook and stir until meat is crusty brown and onion is slightly tender.

2. Stir in broth, tomato purée, Italian seasoning and bay leaves. Bring to a boil over high heat. Reduce heat to medium-low; simmer, uncovered, 45 minutes.

3. Add beans and uncooked pasta. Bring to a boil over high heat. Simmer, uncovered, 8 minutes or until beans and pasta are tender, stirring frequently. Season with salt to taste.

4. Remove bay leaves. Ladle into bowls. Garnish, if desired. Serve with freshly grated Parmesan cheese and French bread if desired.

Makes 5 servings

Caribbean Callaloo Soup

- 6 tablespoons shredded sweetened coconut
- 1½ pound butternut squash
- 12 ounces boneless skinless chicken breasts
- 1 teaspoon olive oil
- 1 large onion, chopped
- 4 cloves garlic, minced
- 3 cans (about 14 ounces each) low-fat reduced-sodium chicken broth
- 2 jalapeño peppers,* stemmed, seeded and minced
- 2 teaspoons dried thyme leaves
- ½ package (10 ounces) spinach leaves, washed and torn

*Jalapeño peppers can sting and irritate the skin; wear rubber gloves when handling peppers and do not touch eyes. Wash hands after handling.

1. Preheat oven to 350°F. Place coconut in baking pan; bake 6 minutes, stirring every 2 minutes, until golden. Set aside. Peel squash; cut in half lengthwise and discard seeds. Cut into ½-inch cubes. Slice chicken crosswise into very thin strips.

2. Heat oil in large nonstick skillet over medium-low heat. Add onion and garlic; cook, covered, stirring often, 5 minutes or until onion is tender. Add squash, chicken broth, jalapeño peppers and thyme; bring to a boil over high heat. Reduce heat to low; simmer, covered, 15 to 20 minutes, until squash is very tender. Add chicken; cover and cook 2 minutes or until chicken is no longer pink in center. Remove skillet from heat; stir in spinach until wilted. Ladle into bowls; sprinkle with toasted coconut.

Makes 6 servings

Beef and Pasta Soup

Exceptional Pizzas & Pasta

Roasted Red Pepper, Eggplant, Goat Cheese and Olive Pizza

1 small eggplant, cut into ¼-inch-thick slices
1 tablespoon olive oil
¼ cup finely chopped onion
1 tablespoon minced fresh rosemary leaves *or* 2 teaspoons dried rosemary
3 large cloves garlic, minced
½ cup roasted red pepper strips
1 (12-inch) round prepared Italian bread shell
2 ounces goat cheese, crumbled
6 kalamata olives, pitted and halved
Coarse ground black pepper

1. Preheat oven to 500°F. Spray baking sheet with nonstick cooking spray. Place eggplant slices on pan; spray with cooking spray. Bake 8 to 10 minutes or until light golden. Turn slices over and bake 6 to 8 minutes more or until slices are golden and very tender. Set aside.

2. Meanwhile, in small skillet over medium heat combine oil, onion, rosemary and garlic. Cook and stir 3 to 4 minutes or until onion is translucent. Set aside.

3. Place red peppers in food processor or blender; process until smooth. Set aside.

4. Bake bread shell 3 to 4 minutes or until top is crisp and beginning to brown. Spread puréed red peppers evenly over pizza leaving 1-inch border. Arrange eggplant over top, slightly overlapping slices. Spoon or brush onion mixture over eggplant. Top with cheese, olives and black pepper. Bake 3 to 5 minutes more or until crust is deep golden. *Makes 4 servings*

Roasted Red Pepper, Eggplant, Goat Cheese and Olive Pizza

Sausage and Mushroom Pizza

New York-Style Pizza Crust (recipe follows)
1 large red bell pepper *or* ½ cup roasted red peppers, drained
3 cloves garlic, minced
1 teaspoon dried oregano leaves
2 teaspoons olive oil
4 to 6 ounces fat-free or reduced-fat sausage, cut into ⅛-inch-thick slices
5 medium mushrooms, thinly sliced
¼ cup chopped onion
½ cup (2 ounces) shredded part-skim mozzarella cheese
Red pepper flakes

1. Prepare New York-Style Pizza Crust.

2. Preheat broiler. Cut bell pepper in half lengthwise. Discard stem and seeds. Place bell pepper halves, cut side down, on baking sheet. Broil 1 to 2 inches from heat source 15 minutes or until skin turns black. Transfer bell pepper to plate and cover with plastic wrap. Let stand until cool enough to handle. Move oven rack to lowest position in oven and preheat to 500°F.

3. Peel skin from bell pepper and discard; coarsely chop meat. Combine bell pepper, garlic and oregano in food processor; process until smooth.

4. Brush crust with oil. Bake 3 to 4 minutes or until surface is dry and crisp. Spread bell pepper mixture over crust leaving 1-inch border. Top with sausage, mushrooms, onion and cheese. Bake 6 minutes or until crust is golden brown. Sprinkle with red pepper. *Makes 4 servings*

New York-Style Pizza Crust

1 teaspoon sugar
⅔ cup warm water (110° to 115°F)
½ (¼-ounce) package rapid-rise or active dry yeast
1¾ cups all-purpose or bread flour
½ teaspoon salt
1 tablespoon cornmeal (optional)

1. Stir sugar into water in small bowl. Add yeast; stir to combine. Let stand 5 to 10 minutes or until foamy.

2. Combine flour and salt in medium bowl. Stir in yeast mixture. Mix until mixture forms soft dough. Remove dough to lightly floured surface. Knead 5 minutes or until dough is smooth and elastic, adding additional flour as needed. Place dough in medium bowl coated with nonstick cooking spray. Turn dough so top is coated with cooking spray; cover with towel. Let rise in warm place 30 minutes or until doubled in bulk. Punch dough down; place on lightly floured surface. Knead about 2 minutes or until smooth. Pat dough into 7-inch disk. Let rest 2 to 3 minutes. Pat and gently stretch dough from edges until dough seems to not stretch anymore. Let rest 2 to 3 minutes. Continue patting and stretching until dough is 12 to 14 inches in diameter.

3. Spray 12- to 14-inch pizza pan with cooking spray; sprinkle with cornmeal. Press dough into pan. Preheat oven to 500°F. Follow directions for individual recipes, baking pizza on bottom rack of oven. *Makes 1 medium-thin 12-inch crust, 1 very thin 14-inch crust*

Sausage and Mushroom Pizza

Grilled Garlic & Herb Pizzas

Homemade Pizza Dough (recipe follows)
8 cloves Grilled Garlic (recipe follows)
1 medium yellow onion
Olive oil
1 medium red, yellow or orange bell pepper
1 cup crumbled goat cheese
¼ cup chopped fresh herb mixture (thyme, basil, oregano and parsley) *or* 4 teaspoons dry herb mixture
¼ cup grated Parmesan cheese

Prepare Homemade Pizza Dough. While dough is rising, light KINGSFORD® briquets in covered grill. Arrange medium-hot briquets on one side of the grill. Prepare Grilled Garlic. Lightly oil grid to prevent sticking. Cut onion into ½-inch-thick slices. Insert wooden picks into onion slices from edges to prevent separating into rings. (Soak wooden picks in hot water 15 minutes to prevent burning.) Brush onion lightly with oil. Place whole bell pepper and onion slices on grid around edge of briquets. Grill on covered grill 20 to 30 minutes until tender, turning once or twice. Remove picks from onion slices and separate into rings. Cut pepper in half and remove seeds; slice pepper halves into strips.

Roll or gently stretch each ball of dough into 7-inch round. Brush lightly with oil on both sides. Grill dough on grid directly above medium-hot KINGSFORD® briquets 1 to 3 minutes or until dough starts to bubble and bottom is lightly browned. Turn; grill 3 to 5 minutes or until second side is lightly browned and dough is cooked through. Remove from grill. Spread 2 cloves Grilled Garlic onto each crust; top with onion, pepper, goat cheese, herbs and Parmesan cheese, dividing equally. Place pizzas around edge of coals; grill covered 5 minutes until bottom crust is crisp, cheese melts and toppings are heated through.

Makes 4 individual pizzas

Note: A 1-pound loaf of frozen bread dough, thawed, can be substituted for Homemade Pizza Dough. Or, substitute 4 pre-baked individual Italian bread shells, add toppings and warm on the grill.

Homemade Pizza Dough

2¾ cups all-purpose flour, divided
1 package quick-rising yeast
¾ teaspoon salt
1 cup water
1½ tablespoons vegetable oil

Combine 1½ cups flour, yeast and salt in food processor. Heat water and oil in small saucepan until 120° to 130°F. With food processor running, add water and oil to flour mixture; process 30 seconds. Add 1 cup flour; process until dough comes together to form ball. Knead on floured board 3 to 4 minutes or until smooth and satiny, kneading in as much of the remaining ¼ cup flour as needed to prevent dough from sticking. Place dough in oiled bowl, turning once. Cover with towel; let rise in warm place 30 minutes until doubled in bulk. Divide dough into 4 equal balls.

Grilled Garlic

- 1 or 2 heads garlic
- Olive oil

Peel outermost papery skin from garlic heads. Brush heads with oil. Grill heads at edge of grid on covered grill over medium-hot KINGSFORD® Briquets 30 to 45 minutes or until cloves are soft and buttery. Remove from grill; cool slightly. Gently squeeze softened garlic head from root end so that cloves slip out of skins into small bowl. Use immediately or cover and refrigerate up to 1 week.

Roasted Garlic & Fresh Tomato Pizza

- New York-Style Pizza Crust (page 36)
- Roasted Garlic (recipe follows)
- 1 to 1¼ pounds ripe tomatoes, cored
- 1 tablespoon olive oil
- ½ cup (2 ounces) shredded Monterey Jack cheese or part-skim mozzarella cheese
- 2 tablespoons grated Parmesan cheese
- Cracked black pepper
- 10 to 12 fresh basil leaves

1. Prepare New York-Style Pizza Crust.

2. Prepare Roasted Garlic.

3. Slice tomatoes and place between double layers of paper towels. Press gently to remove juice.

4. Brush oil over entire surface of prepared crust. Pierce surface with fork 12 to 14 times. Sprinkle with Monterey Jack cheese leaving 1-inch border. Bake 3 to 4 minutes or until crust is light golden and cheese is melted.

5. Arrange tomato slices over cheese. Place garlic cloves on tomatoes. Sprinkle with Parmesan and pepper. Bake 4 to 6 minutes or until crust is dark golden. Top with whole or slivered basil leaves. Cut into 8 wedges. *Makes 4 servings*

Roasted Garlic: Cut off top third of garlic head (not the root end) to expose cloves; discard top. Place head of garlic, trimmed end up, on 10-inch square of foil. Rub garlic generously with olive oil and sprinkle with salt. Gather foil ends together and close tightly. Roast in preheated 350°F oven 45 minutes or until cloves are golden and soft. When cool enough to handle, squeeze roasted garlic cloves from skins; discard skins.

Greek Flat Breads

Basic Yeast Bread (recipe follows)
1 cup chopped kalamata olives
6 cloves garlic, minced
½ pound crumbled feta cheese
2 tablespoons olive oil
2 eggs
2 tablespoons water
Coarse salt (optional)

1. Prepare Basic Yeast Bread through Step 4. Grease 2 baking sheets; set aside. Turn out dough onto lightly oiled work surface; divide in half. Keep remaining half of dough covered. Divide dough into 16 equal pieces. Form each piece into ball. Cover with towel; let rest 5 minutes.

2. Combine olives, garlic, cheese and oil in medium bowl. Beat eggs with water in small bowl.

3. Flatten each ball of dough to ½ inch thick. Place 2 inches apart on prepared baking sheet. Brush dough with beaten egg. Divide half the olive mixture into 16 equal portions. Sprinkle each round of dough with 1 portion of olive mixture; press topping into dough slightly.

4. Cover with towel; let rise 45 minutes. Repeat with remaining half of dough.

5. Place heavy pan on lower rack of oven. Preheat oven to 400°F.

6. Sprinkle tops of dough with coarse salt, if desired. Place bread in oven. Carefully place 4 to 5 ice cubes in heavy pan; close door immediately. Bake 15 minutes or until lightly browned. Immediately remove bread from baking sheets; cool on wire rack. *Makes 32 flat breads*

Basic Yeast Bread

2 cups milk
¼ cup unsalted butter, softened
6½ to 7½ cups all-purpose flour, divided
2 packages active dry yeast
2 teaspoons salt
¼ cup sugar
2 eggs

1. Heat milk and butter in small saucepan over medium heat just until butter is melted. Remove from heat; cool to about 120° to 130°F.

2. Combine 4 cups flour, yeast, salt and sugar in large bowl. Add milk mixture and eggs. Beat vigorously 2 minutes. Add remaining flour, ¼ cup at a time, until dough begins to pull away from sides of bowl.

3. Turn out dough onto lightly floured work surface; flatten slightly. Knead 10 minutes or until smooth and elastic, adding flour if necessary to prevent sticking.

4. Shape dough into a ball. Place in large lightly oiled bowl; turn dough over once to oil surface. Cover with towel; let rise in warm place about 1 hour or until doubled in bulk.

5. Grease two 9×5-inch loaf pans; set aside. Turn out dough onto lightly oiled work surface; divide in half. Shape each half of dough into loaf; place in prepared pans. Cover with towel; let rise in warm place 45 minutes.

6. Preheat oven to 375°F. Bake 25 minutes or until loaves are golden and sound hollow when tapped. Immediately remove bread from pans and cool on wire rack. *Makes 2 loaves*

Greek Flat Breads

Pizza Puttanesca

New-York-Style Pizza Crust (page 36)
1½ teaspoons olive oil, divided
3 cloves garlic, minced
1 can (8 ounces) tomato sauce
1 teaspoon dried basil leaves
1 teaspoon dried rosemary leaves
½ teaspoon dried oregano leaves
¼ teaspoon fennel seed, crushed
⅛ teaspoon ground red pepper
1 small yellow bell pepper, cored, seeded and cut into strips
3 ounces cleaned squid tubes, cut into ½-inch-wide rings
3 ounces shrimp, peeled, deveined and halved
3 ounces scallops (1¼-inch diameter, about 8)
¾ cup (3 ounces) shredded part-skim mozzarella cheese, divided
2 tablespoons grated Romano cheese
2 teaspoons drained capers (optional)

1. Prepare New York-Style Pizza Crust.

2. Combine oil and garlic in 2- to 3-quart saucepan over medium-high heat. Cook and stir about 1 minute or until garlic is fragrant but not browned. Add tomato sauce, basil, rosemary, oregano, fennel and red pepper; bring to a boil. Reduce heat to medium and simmer, uncovered, about 5 minutes or until reduced by about ⅓. Stir in bell pepper; set aside.

3. Bring 1 quart water to a boil in 2- to 3-quart saucepan. Add squid and cook 30 seconds or until edges begin to curl. Transfer to colander. Add shrimp to saucepan; cook 1 minute or until pink and opaque. Transfer to colander with squid. Add scallops to saucepan. Remove from heat and let stand 2 to 3 minutes or until scallops are just slightly transparent in center. Drain.

4. Sprinkle half the mozzarella cheese over prepared crust leaving 1-inch border. Bake 4 to 5 minutes or until cheese is melted and crust is light golden brown. Spread tomato sauce over cheese. Top with squid, shrimp, scallops, remaining mozzarella cheese and Romano cheese. Bake 3 to 4 minutes or until crust is deep golden brown. Sprinkle with capers, if desired. Cut into 8 wedges. *Makes 4 servings*

Pizza Puttanesca

Mu Shu Pork Calzones

New York-Style Pizza Crust (page 36)
4 dry shiitake mushrooms (optional)
Nonstick cooking spray
¼ cup fat-free egg substitute
1 boneless pork chop (5 to 6 ounces), fat trimmed and cut into thin slices
½ to 1 jalapeño pepper,* seeded and minced (optional)
1 tablespoon minced ginger
3 cloves garlic, minced
2 cups very thinly sliced Napa cabbage
⅓ cup thinly sliced green onions
2 tablespoons hoisin sauce
1 tablespoon dark sesame oil
1 teaspoon canola oil

*Jalapeño peppers can sting and irritate the skin; wear rubber gloves when handling peppers and do not touch eyes. Wash hands after handling.

1. Prepare New York-Style Pizza Crust as directed through step 2.

2. Cover mushrooms with hot water in small bowl; let stand 15 minutes or until caps are tender. Drain; squeeze water from mushrooms. Cut out and discard tough stems. Thinly slice caps; set aside.

3. Spray large skillet generously with cooking spray. Heat over medium-high heat until hot. Add egg substitute; cover and cook 2 minutes or until set on top. Loosen egg from skillet and transfer to plate. When egg mixture is cool enough to handle, roll up and slice into ¼-inch-wide strips; set aside.

4. Spray same large skillet with nonstick cooking spray. Heat over medium-high heat until hot. Add pork, jalapeño pepper, ginger and garlic. Cook and stir about 2 minutes or until pork is no longer pink. Add cabbage and green onions; cook and stir 1½ to 2 minutes or until cabbage is wilted. Spoon mixture into medium bowl and gently stir in mushroom and egg strips; set aside.

5. Combine hoisin and sesame oil in small bowl.

6. Divide dough in half. On lightly floured surface, roll each half into 9- to 10-inch round. Cut each round in half. Brush half of each dough piece with about 1 teaspoon hoisin mixture leaving ½-inch border. Spoon pork mixture over top. Drizzle remaining hoisin mixture evenly over pork mixture (about 1 teaspoon each). Brush edges with water. Fold dough over filling and press edges together. Seal with tines of fork. Place on lightly oiled baking sheet. Brush calzones with canola oil. Bake 6 to 7 minutes or until light golden brown. *Makes 4 servings*

Mu Shu Pork Calzone

Tempting Tuna Parmesano

- 2 large cloves garlic
- 1 package (9 ounces) refrigerated fresh angel hair pasta
- ¼ cup butter or margarine
- 1 cup whipping cream
- 1 cup frozen peas
- ¼ teaspoon salt
- 1 can (6 ounces) white tuna in water, drained
- ¼ cup grated Parmesan cheese, plus additional cheese for serving
- Black pepper

1. Fill large deep skillet ¾ full with water. Cover and bring to a boil over high heat. Meanwhile, peel and mince garlic.

2. Add pasta to skillet; boil 1 to 2 minutes or until pasta is al dente. Do not overcook. Drain; set aside.

3. Add butter and garlic to skillet; cook over medium-high heat until butter is melted and sizzling. Stir in cream, peas and salt; bring to a boil.

4. Break tuna into chunks and stir into skillet with ¼ cup cheese. Return pasta to skillet; cook until heated through; toss gently. Serve with additional cheese and pepper to taste.

Makes 2 to 3 servings

Serving Suggestion: Serve with a tossed romaine and tomato salad with Italian dressing.

Prep and Cook Time: 16 minutes

Penne with Arrabiatta Sauce

- ½ pound uncooked penne
- 2 tablespoons olive oil or oil from sun-dried tomatoes
- 8 cloves garlic
- 1 can (28 ounces) crushed tomatoes in purée
- ¼ cup chopped sun-dried tomatoes packed in oil
- 3 tablespoons FRANK'S® REDHOT® Hot Sauce
- 8 kalamata olives, pitted and chopped
- 6 fresh basil leaves *or* 1½ teaspoons dried basil leaves
- 1 tablespoon capers

1. Cook pasta according to package directions; drain.

2. Heat oil in large nonstick skillet over medium heat. Add garlic; cook until golden, stirring frequently. Add remaining ingredients. Bring to a boil. Simmer, partially covered, 10 minutes. Stir occasionally.

3. Toss pasta with half of the sauce mixture. Spoon into serving bowl. Pour remaining sauce mixture over pasta.

Makes 4 servings (3 cups sauce)

Prep Time: 15 minutes

Cook Time: 20 minutes

Tempting Tuna Parmesano

Easy Cheesy Lasagna

- **2 tablespoons olive oil**
- **3 small zucchini, quartered and thinly sliced**
- **1 package (8 ounces) mushrooms, thinly sliced**
- **1 medium onion, chopped**
- **5 cloves garlic, minced**
- **2 containers (15 ounces each) reduced-fat ricotta cheese**
- **¼ cup grated Parmesan cheese**
- **2 eggs**
- **½ teaspoon dried Italian seasoning**
- **¼ teaspoon garlic salt**
- **⅛ teaspoon black pepper**
- **1 can (28 ounces) crushed tomatoes in purée, undrained**
- **1 jar (26 ounces) spaghetti sauce**
- **1 package (16 ounces) lasagna noodles, uncooked**
- **4 cups (16 ounces) shredded mozzarella cheese, divided**

Preheat oven to 375°F. Spray 13×9-inch baking dish or lasagna pan with nonstick cooking spray.

Heat oil in large skillet over medium heat until hot. Add zucchini, mushrooms, onion and garlic. Cook and stir 5 minutes or until vegetables are tender. Set aside.

Combine ricotta, Parmesan, eggs, Italian seasoning, garlic salt and pepper in medium bowl. Combine tomatoes and spaghetti sauce in another medium bowl.

Spread about ¾ cup tomato mixture in prepared dish. Place layer of noodles over tomato mixture, overlapping noodles. Spread half of vegetable mixture over noodles; top with half of ricotta mixture. Sprinkle 1 cup mozzarella over ricotta mixture. Place second layer of noodles over mozzarella. Spread about 1 cup tomato mixture over noodles. Top with remaining vegetable and ricotta cheese mixtures. Sprinkle 1 cup mozzarella over ricotta mixture. Place third layer of noodles over mozzarella. Spread remaining tomato mixture over noodles. Sprinkle remaining 2 cups mozzarella evenly over top.

Cover tightly with foil and bake 1 hour or until noodles in center are soft. Uncover; bake 5 minutes or until cheese is melted and lightly browned. Remove from oven; cover and let stand 15 minutes before serving. *Makes 6 servings*

Spaghetti with Garlic

- **12 ounces uncooked spaghetti**
- **4½ teaspoons FILIPPO BERIO® Olive Oil**
- **1 clove garlic, sliced**
- **Salt and freshly ground black pepper**
- **Grated Parmesan cheese**

Cook pasta according to package directions until al dente (tender but still firm). Drain; transfer to large bowl. In small skillet, heat olive oil over medium heat until hot. Add garlic; cook and stir 2 to 3 minutes or until golden. Discard garlic. Pour oil over hot pasta; toss until lightly coated. Season to taste with salt and pepper. Top with cheese. *Makes 4 servings*

Easy Cheesy Lasagna

Fusilli Pizzaiolo

- 1 package (16 ounces) uncooked fusilli pasta
- ¼ cup olive oil
- 8 ounces mushrooms, sliced
- 1 large red bell pepper, chopped
- 1 large green bell pepper, chopped
- 1 large yellow bell pepper, chopped
- 3 large shallots, chopped
- 10 green onions, chopped
- 1 large onion, diced
- 8 cloves garlic, coarsely chopped
- ½ cup chopped fresh basil *or* 2 teaspoons dried basil leaves, crushed
- 2 tablespoons chopped fresh oregano *or* 1 teaspoon dried oregano, crushed
- Dash red pepper flakes
- 4 cups canned or fresh tomatoes, undrained and chopped
- Salt and black pepper to taste
- Fresh basil sprigs and miniature plum tomatoes for garnish

1. Cook fusilli according to package directions. Drain in colander.

2. Heat oil in large skillet over medium-high heat. Cook and stir mushrooms, bell peppers, shallots, onions, garlic, chopped basil, oregano and red pepper flakes in hot oil until lightly browned.

3. Add tomatoes with juice; bring to a boil. Reduce heat to low; simmer, uncovered, 20 minutes. Season with salt and black pepper.

4. Place fusilli on plates. Spoon sauce over fusilli. Garnish, if desired. *Makes 6 to 8 servings*

Spinach Chicken Manicotti

- 8 uncooked manicotti
- ¼ teaspoon salt
- ½ teaspoon black pepper, divided
- 12 ounces boneless skinless chicken breasts
- 1 package (10 ounces) frozen chopped spinach, thawed and squeezed dry
- 1 container (16 ounces) nonfat cottage cheese
- ½ cup (2 ounces) crumbled blue cheese
- 4 cloves garlic, minced
- 1 can (14½ ounces) no-salt-added spaghetti sauce, divided

1. Cook pasta according to package directions, omitting salt. Drain; set aside.

2. Meanwhile, fill medium saucepan with water. Add salt and ¼ teaspoon pepper. Bring to a boil over high heat; add chicken. Reduce heat to medium; simmer, covered, about 30 minutes or until chicken is tender and no longer pink in center. Remove chicken from saucepan; cool slightly and shred.

3. Preheat oven to 350°F. Spray 11×7-inch baking pan with nonstick cooking spray; set aside. Combine spinach, cottage cheese, blue cheese, garlic, remaining ¼ teaspoon pepper and chicken in large bowl. Fill manicotti with spinach-chicken mixture. Pour half the spaghetti sauce into bottom of prepared pan. Place filled manicotti on top; top with remaining spaghetti sauce. Bake, covered, 20 minutes or until heated through. *Makes 4 servings*

Fusilli Pizzaiolo

Creamy Chicken and Red Pepper Pasta

- **3 tablespoons vegetable oil, divided**
- **¼ cup pine nuts or coarsely chopped walnuts**
- **1½ pounds boneless skinless chicken thighs**
- **Salt and black pepper**
- **1 pound fettuccine**
- **¼ cup butter or margarine**
- **3 cloves garlic, minced**
- **2 tablespoons all-purpose flour**
- **1½ cups half-and-half**
- **½ cup chicken broth**
- **½ cup prepared roasted red peppers, drained and sliced**
- **¼ cup sliced pitted black olives**
- **⅓ cup grated Romano cheese**

1. Heat 1 tablespoon oil in small skillet over medium-low heat. Add pine nuts; cook and stir 30 to 45 seconds until light brown, shaking pan constantly. Drain on paper towels.

2. Sprinkle chicken with salt and black pepper. Heat remaining 2 tablespoons oil in large skillet over medium-high heat. Add chicken and cook 12 to 15 minutes until browned on both sides and no longer pink in center. Remove chicken from skillet. Refrigerate until cool enough to handle. Cut into bite-size pieces.

3. Cook fettuccine according to package directions. Rinse under warm water; drain.

4. Melt butter in medium saucepan over medium heat. Add garlic; cook and stir until golden. Stir in flour until smooth. Cook 1 minute. Gradually stir in half-and-half and chicken broth. Bring to a boil over medium heat; continue boiling 3 to 4 minutes or until slightly thickened and reduced.

5. Place fettuccine in large bowl. Add chicken, pine nuts, peppers and olives. Toss gently to coat. Pour sauce over fettuccine; toss gently. Add cheese and salt and black pepper to taste; toss. Garnish as desired. *Makes 4 main-dish servings*

Spinach Pesto Pasta

- **10 ounces uncooked linguine**
- **1 package (10 ounces) frozen chopped spinach, thawed and squeezed dry**
- **1 cup water**
- **1 teaspoon chicken bouillon granules**
- **4 cloves garlic, peeled**
- **2 tablespoons extra virgin olive oil***
- **2 tablespoons fresh lemon juice**
- **2 tablespoons dried basil leaves**
- **¼ to ½ teaspoon black pepper**
- **¼ cup grated Parmesan cheese**
- **½ teaspoon salt, divided**
- **4 plum tomatoes, seeded and chopped**

*Use extra virgin olive oil only for best flavor.

1. Cook pasta according to package directions, omitting salt. Drain; set aside.

2. Meanwhile, place spinach, water, bouillon granules, garlic, olive oil, lemon juice, basil and black pepper in food processor or blender; process until smooth.

3. Place pasta in large bowl. Add spinach mixture, Parmesan cheese and ¼ teaspoon salt; toss to coat. Top with tomatoes and remaining ¼ teaspoon salt. *Makes 4 servings*

Creamy Chicken and Red Pepper Pasta

Triple Pepper Tomato Provolone Lasagna

1 red bell pepper, chopped
1 yellow bell pepper, chopped
1 green bell pepper, chopped
1 package (8 ounces) sliced fresh mushrooms
½ cup chopped onion
1 cup thinly sliced zucchini
4 cloves garlic, minced
1½ cups vegetable juice cocktail
1 can (16 ounces) diced tomatoes, undrained
1½ to 1¾ teaspoons Italian seasoning
1 tablespoon olive oil
9 uncooked lasagna noodles
1 cup nonfat cottage cheese
⅓ cup grated Parmesan cheese
4 ounces sliced reduced-fat provolone cheese

1. Preheat oven to 350°F. Combine peppers, mushrooms, onion, zucchini, garlic, vegetable juice cocktail, tomatoes and Italian seasoning in Dutch oven. Bring to a boil over high heat. Reduce heat to low; simmer, uncovered, 15 minutes. Remove from heat; stir in oil.

2. Spray 12×8-inch baking pan with nonstick cooking spray. Place 3 lasagna noodles on bottom of pan. Spread ⅓ of the sauce over noodles. Spread ½ cup cottage cheese evenly over sauce; sprinkle with 2 tablespoons Parmesan cheese. Repeat layers, ending with sauce.

3. Bake, uncovered, 1 hour or until bubbly. Tear provolone cheese in small pieces; place on top of lasagna. Sprinkle with remaining Parmesan cheese. Bake 5 minutes longer or until cheese is melted. Let stand 15 minutes before serving.

Makes 6 servings

Tip: For extra convenience, purchase 3 cups chopped red, green and yellow bell pepper mixture from the grocery store salad bar.

Spinach-Stuffed Shells

1 package (10 ounces) chopped frozen spinach, thawed and drained
1½ cups nonfat ricotta cheese
½ cup grated Parmesan cheese
½ cup cholesterol-free egg substitute
3 cloves garlic, finely chopped
1 teaspoon dried oregano leaves
½ teaspoon salt
½ teaspoon dried basil leaves
½ teaspoon dried marjoram leaves
¼ teaspoon ground black pepper
24 cooked large pasta shells
2 cans (14½ ounces each) crushed tomatoes, undrained
1 cup (4 ounces) shredded reduced-fat mozzarella cheese

1. Preheat oven to 350°F. Spray 13×9-inch baking pan with nonstick cooking spray.

2. Combine spinach, ricotta and Parmesan cheeses, egg substitute and seasonings in large bowl. Spoon into shells. Place shells in prepared pan. Top with tomatoes with liquid and mozzarella cheese. Bake 20 minutes or until cheese melts.

Makes 4 servings

Spinach-Stuffed Shells

Spinach-Garlic Pasta with Garlic-Onion Sauce

½ pound fresh spinach, trimmed
1½ cups all-purpose flour, divided
2 whole eggs
4 egg yolks
1 tablespoon olive oil
6 large cloves garlic, minced
½ teaspoon salt
Garlic-Onion Sauce (recipe follows)
Grated Parmesan cheese (optional)

1. To blanch spinach, heat 1 quart of lightly salted water in a 2-quart saucepan over high heat to a boil. Add spinach; return to a boil. Boil 2 to 3 minutes until crisp-tender; drain and immediately plunge into cold water to stop cooking. Drain in colander. Cool. Squeeze moisture from spinach; finely chop.

2. Place 1 cup flour on cutting board. Make a well in center. Whisk whole eggs, yolks and olive oil in small bowl until well blended. Gradually pour into well in flour mixture while mixing with fingertips or fork to form ball of dough.

3. Add spinach, garlic and salt. Mix, working in more flour as needed.

4. Place dough on lightly floured surface; flatten slightly. Knead dough about 5 minutes or until smooth and elastic, adding more flour to prevent sticking if necessary. Cover with plastic wrap. Let dough stand 15 minutes.

5. Unwrap dough and knead briefly. Roll out dough to ⅛-inch-thick circle using lightly floured rolling pin. Let rest until dough is slightly dry but can be handled without breaking.

6. Lightly flour dough circle; roll loosely onto rolling pin. Slide rolling pin out; press dough roll gently with hand and cut into ¼-inch-wide strips. Carefully unfold strips.*

7. Prepare Garlic-Onion Sauce.

8. Cook pasta in boiling salted water 1 to 2 minutes just until tender. Drain; place in large bowl. Toss sauce over pasta. Serve with cheese.

Makes 2 to 4 servings

*Fettuccine can be dried and stored at this point. Hang fettuccine strips over pasta rack or clean broom handle covered with plastic wrap and propped between two chairs. Dry for at least 3 hours; store in airtight container at room temperature up to 4 days. To serve, cook fettuccine in large pot of boiling salted water 3 to 4 minutes just until tender. Drain in colander.

Garlic-Onion Sauce

12 large cloves fresh garlic
½ cup butter
1 tablespoon olive oil
1 pound Vidalia or other sweet onions, sliced
1 tablespoon honey (optional)
¼ cup Marsala wine

1. To quickly peel garlic cloves, trim off ends. Drop cloves into boiling water. Boil 5 to 10 seconds. Remove with slotted spoon and plunge into cold water. Drain. Peel garlic and chop enough to equal ⅓ cup.

2. Heat butter and oil in large skillet over medium heat. Add onions and garlic; cover and cook until soft. Add honey, if desired; reduce heat to low. Cook, uncovered, 30 minutes, stirring occasionally. Add wine; cook 5 to 10 minutes more. *Makes about 2¼ cups*

Spinach Tortellini with Roasted Red Peppers

- 2 packages (9 ounces each) fresh spinach tortellini
- 1 jar (7 ounces) roasted red peppers or pimientos, drained
- 2 tablespoons butter or olive oil
- 4 cloves garlic, minced
- ¼ cup chopped fresh basil *or* 2 teaspoons dried basil leaves
- ½ cup chopped walnuts, toasted
- 1 cup prepared HIDDEN VALLEY® Original Ranch Salad Dressing

Cook tortellini according to package directions; drain and set aside. Slice red peppers into strips; set aside. In large saucepan, melt butter; add garlic. Cook and stir about 2 minutes. Add red pepper strips, ¼ cup chopped basil and tortellini. Stir to coat; add walnuts. Stir in enough salad dressing so mixture is creamy and tortellini are coated.

Makes 4 to 6 servings

Orzo Pasta with Shrimp

- 8 ounces uncooked orzo pasta
- 3 tablespoons plus ½ teaspoon FILIPPO BERIO® Olive Oil, divided
- 3 cloves garlic, minced
- 1¼ pounds small shrimp, shelled
- 1½ medium tomatoes, chopped
- 2 tablespoons chopped fresh cilantro
- 2 tablespoons chopped fresh Italian parsley
- Juice of 1 lemon
- 2 ounces feta cheese, crumbled
- Salt and freshly ground black pepper

Cook pasta according to package directions until al dente (tender but still firm). Drain. Toss with ½ teaspoon olive oil; set aside. Heat remaining 3 tablespoons olive oil in large skillet over medium heat until hot. Add garlic; cook and stir 2 to 3 minutes or until golden. Add shrimp; cook and stir 3 to 5 minutes or until shrimp are opaque *(do not overcook)*. Stir in pasta. Add tomatoes, cilantro, parsley and lemon juice. Sprinkle with feta cheese. Season to taste with salt and pepper.

Makes 4 servings

Pasta Twists with Spinach Pesto

- 1 bunch spinach, washed, stemmed and torn
- 1 cup fresh parsley sprigs
- ⅔ cup grated Parmesan cheese
- ½ cup walnut pieces
- 6 cloves garlic, minced
- 2 anchovy filets
- 1 teaspoon dried basil leaves
- 1 teaspoon salt
- 1 teaspoon black pepper
- 1 cup olive oil
- Pasta twists, cooked according to package directions and drained

Place spinach, parsley, cheese, walnuts, garlic, anchovies, basil, salt and pepper in food processor. Process until smooth.

With processor running, add oil in thin stream. Adjust seasonings, if desired. Pour desired amount of pesto over pasta; toss gently to coat.

Makes 4 servings

Egg Noodles and Vegetables with Pesto

- 1 package (16 ounces) enriched fine egg noodles
- 5 tablespoons olive oil, divided
- 10 cloves garlic
- 3 cups fresh basil leaves, lightly packed
- 3 cups fresh spinach, lightly packed
- ½ cup fat-free Italian salad dressing
- 4 cups broccoli florets
- 4 cups cauliflower florets
- 2 large sweet onions, cut into strips
- 2 cups sliced mushrooms
- ½ teaspoon red pepper flakes
- 2 pints cherry tomatoes, cut into halves
- ½ cup shredded Asiago cheese

1. Cook noodles according to package directions, taking care not to overcook. Drain; place in large bowl. Toss with 1 tablespoon oil.

2. To make pesto, place garlic in food processor; process briefly until chopped. Add basil; process using on/off pulsing action until finely chopped. Transfer to medium bowl. Process spinach until chopped. Add 3 tablespoons oil and salad dressing; process briefly to blend. Add to basil in bowl.

3. Heat remaining 1 tablespoon oil in large nonstick skillet or wok over medium heat until hot. Add broccoli, cauliflower and onions. Cover and cook 5 minutes, stirring occasionally. Add mushrooms and red pepper; cook 5 minutes or until vegetables are crisp-tender. Add vegetable mixture, tomatoes and pesto to noodles; toss until well blended. Serve with cheese.

Makes 8 servings

Bow Tie Pasta with Chicken and Roasted Garlic

- 1 head garlic
- 3 tablespoons plus 1 teaspoon olive oil, divided
- 1½ pounds assorted wild mushrooms (such as shiitake, portobello or cremini), sliced
- 1 can (14½ ounces) diced tomatoes, undrained
- ¾ cup chopped green onions
- 1½ cups chicken broth
- 1½ pounds cooked skinless boneless chicken breasts, diced
- ¼ cup chopped fresh cilantro
- 2 teaspoons salt
- 1 teaspoon black pepper
- 1 pound bow tie pasta, cooked and drained

1. Preheat oven to 325°F. Cut off ¼-inch of garlic top. Rub 1 teaspoon olive oil on garlic head. Wrap garlic in aluminum foil, cook 45 minutes; let cool. Squeeze garlic pulp into small bowl, set aside.

2. Heat remaining 3 tablespoons olive oil in large skillet over high heat until hot. Add mushrooms; cook and stir 3 minutes. Add tomatoes and green onions; cook and stir 2 minutes. Add broth, scraping bottom of skillet clean. Simmer 5 minutes or until broth reduces to 1 cup. Add garlic, chicken, cilantro, salt and pepper; cook 2 minutes.

3. Combine sauce with pasta in large bowl; stir gently.

Makes 6 servings

Egg Noodles and Vegetables with Pesto

Mediterranean Linguine

- **8 ounces uncooked linguine**
- **½ package (1½ ounces) sun-dried tomatoes, drained**
- **Nonstick cooking spray**
- **8 ounces sliced fresh mushrooms**
- **4 cloves garlic, minced**
- **¾ cup finely chopped onion**
- **½ medium green bell pepper, thinly sliced**
- **1½ teaspoons dried Italian seasoning**
- **½ teaspoon red pepper flakes**
- **2 tablespoons dry red wine**
- **12 ounces medium shrimp, peeled**
- **12 kalamata olives, pitted and sliced *or* 20 medium pitted black olives, halved**
- **¼ cup chopped fresh parsley**
- **½ teaspoon salt**
- **3 tablespoons grated Parmesan cheese**
- **2 teaspoons extra virgin olive oil**

1. Cook pasta according to package directions, omitting salt. Drain; set aside.

2. Meanwhile, bring 2 cups water to a boil over high heat; add tomatoes. Reduce heat to low; simmer, uncovered, 4 minutes. Drain well; cool slightly. Cut into thin strips; set aside.

3. Spray large nonstick skillet with cooking spray. Heat over medium-high heat until hot. Add mushrooms and garlic; cook 4 minutes. Add onion, bell pepper, Italian seasoning and red pepper flakes; cook 4 minutes. Add wine, tomatoes and shrimp; cook 6 to 8 minutes or until shrimp are opaque.

4. Add olives, parsley, salt, pasta and Parmesan cheese; toss to blend. Remove from heat; drizzle with olive oil. *Makes 4 servings*

Red Pepper & White Bean Pasta Sauce

- **12 ounces uncooked penne or ziti pasta**
- **1 teaspoon olive oil**
- **3 cloves garlic, chopped**
- **1 jar (11.5 ounces) GUILTLESS GOURMET® Roasted Red Pepper Salsa**
- **¾ cup canned cannellini beans (white kidney beans), rinsed well**
- **½ cup low sodium chicken or vegetable broth, defatted**
- **⅓ cup chopped fresh cilantro**
- **¼ cup crumbled feta cheese**
- **Fresh thyme sprigs (optional)**

Cook pasta according to package directions. Drain and keep warm.

Meanwhile, heat oil in medium nonstick skillet over medium-high heat until hot. Add garlic; cook and stir 30 seconds or until softened. Do not brown. Add salsa, beans, broth and cilantro; bring just to a boil, stirring occasionally. (If mixture appears too thick, add water, 1 tablespoon at a time, to desired consistency.) To serve, place pasta in large serving bowl. Add salsa mixture; toss to coat well. Sprinkle with feta cheese. Garnish with thyme, if desired. *Makes 4 servings*

Red Pepper & White Bean Pasta Sauce

Fettuccine Alfredo

- 2 teaspoons margarine
- 3 cloves garlic, finely chopped
- 4½ teaspoons all-purpose flour
- 1½ cups fat-free (skim) milk
- ½ cup grated Parmesan cheese
- 3½ teaspoons Neufchâtel cheese
- ¼ teaspoon white pepper
- 4 ounces hot cooked fettuccine
- ¼ cup chopped fresh parsley

Melt margarine in medium saucepan. Add garlic. Cook and stir 1 minute. Stir in flour. Gradually stir in milk. Cook and stir until thickened. Add cheeses and pepper; cook until melted. Serve on pasta; top with parsley. *Makes 4 servings*

Shrimp Ravioli with Curry Sauce

- Nonstick cooking spray
- ½ cup finely chopped mushrooms
- 4 green onions, including tops, thinly sliced
- 2 tablespoons minced fresh ginger
- 3 cloves garlic, minced
- 8 ounces shrimp, finely chopped
- Salt and black pepper to taste
- 32 wonton wrappers
- Curry Sauce (recipe follows)
- 2 tablespoons finely chopped fresh cilantro

1. Spray medium skillet with cooking spray; heat over medium heat. Add mushrooms, onions, ginger and garlic; cook and stir 2 to 3 minutes or until tender. Add shrimp; cook 3 to 5 minutes or until shrimp turn pink and opaque. Season with salt and pepper.

2. Place slightly rounded tablespoonful shrimp mixture in center of 1 wonton wrapper; brush edges of wrapper lightly with water. Top with additional wonton wrapper; press edges together to seal. Repeat with remaining shrimp mixture and wonton wrappers.

3. Bring about 2 quarts water to a boil in large saucepan; add 4 to 6 ravioli. Simmer, uncovered, 3 to 4 minutes or until ravioli float to surface and are tender. Remove ravioli with slotted spoon; repeat with remaining ravioli. Spoon warm Curry Sauce over top and sprinkle with cilantro.
Makes 4 servings

Curry Sauce

- Nonstick cooking spray
- ¼ cup finely chopped onion
- 1 clove garlic, minced
- 4½ teaspoons all-purpose flour
- 1½ teaspoons curry powder
- ⅛ teaspoon ground cumin
- 1 cup canned fat-free reduced-sodium chicken broth
- Salt and black pepper to taste

1. Coat small saucepan with cooking spray; heat over medium heat until hot. Add onion and garlic; cook and stir 2 to 3 minutes or until tender. Stir in flour, curry powder and cumin; cook and stir 1 to 2 minutes.

2. Stir chicken broth into saucepan; bring to a boil. Boil, stirring constantly, about 1 minute or until thickened. Season with salt and pepper.
Makes about 1 cup

Shrimp Ravioli with Curry Sauce

Pasta Salad in Artichoke Cups

5 cloves garlic, peeled
½ cup white wine
6 medium artichokes
1 lemon, cut into halves
6 cups chicken broth
1 tablespoon plus 1 teaspoon olive oil, divided
1 package (2 ounces) artichoke hearts
8 ounces corkscrew pasta or pasta twists
½ teaspoon dried basil leaves
Basil Vinaigrette Dressing (recipe follows)

1. Place garlic and wine in small saucepan. Bring to a boil over high heat; reduce heat to low. Simmer 10 minutes.

2. Meanwhile, cut bottoms off artichokes; remove outer leaves. Cut 1 inch off tops of artichokes. Snip tips from remaining leaves with scissors. Rub ends with lemon.

3. Bring chicken broth to a boil in Dutch oven over high heat. Add artichokes, wine mixture and 1 tablespoon oil. Reduce heat to low. Cover; simmer 25 to 30 minutes or until leaves pull easily from base. Drain.

4. Cook artichoke hearts according to package directions. Drain well. Cut into slices to make 2 cups. Set aside.

5. Cook pasta according to package directions, drain. Place pasta in large bowl. Sprinkle with remaining 1 teaspoon oil and basil.

6. Prepare Basil Vinaigrette Dressing. Add artichoke hearts and 1 cup dressing to pasta; toss gently to coat.

7. Carefully spread outer leaves of whole artichokes. Remove small heart leaves by grasping with fingers, then pulling and twisting. Scoop out fuzzy choke with spoon.

8. Fill artichokes with pasta mixture. Cover; refrigerate until serving time. Serve with remaining dressing. Garnish as desired.

Makes 6 servings

Basil Vinaigrette Dressing

⅓ cup white wine vinegar
2 tablespoons Dijon mustard
3 cloves garlic, peeled
¾ cup coarsely chopped fresh basil leaves
1 cup olive oil
Salt and black pepper to taste

1. Place vinegar, mustard and garlic in blender or food processor. Cover; process using on/off pulses until well mixed. Add basil; continue to pulse until mixture is blended.

2. With motor running, slowly pour in olive oil. Season to taste with salt and pepper.

Makes about 1½ cups

Pasta Salad in Artichoke Cup

Sweet Garlic with Chicken Pasta

- 1¼ pounds boneless skinless chicken breast halves
- 1 package (16 ounces) bow tie pasta
- 5 tablespoons olive oil
- 8 ounces garlic, chopped
- 1½ pounds shiitake mushrooms, sliced
- 2 cups chopped seeded fresh plum tomatoes
- 1 cup chopped green onions
- 1 teaspoon red pepper flakes
- 2 cups chicken broth
- 4 ounces cilantro, chopped and divided

1. Prepare grill for direct cooking. Lightly oil hot grid. Grill chicken, on covered grill, 6 to 8 minutes until chicken is no longer pink in center, turning chicken over halfway through cooking.

2. Refrigerate grilled chicken until cool enough to handle. Cut chicken into ½-inch cubes. Set aside.

3. Cook pasta according to package directions. Drain in colander.

4. Heat oil in large skillet over medium-high heat. Cook and stir garlic until lightly browned. Add mushrooms, tomatoes, green onions and red pepper flakes. Cook and stir 2 minutes.

5. Add broth; simmer mixture to reduce slightly. Add chicken, pasta and half of cilantro; heat through. Garnish with remaining cilantro.

Makes 6 to 8 servings

Spaghetti with Marinara Sauce

- 1 teaspoon olive oil
- ¾ cup chopped onion
- 3 cloves garlic, finely chopped
- 2 cups water
- 1 can (16 ounces) no-salt-added tomato sauce
- 1 can (6 ounces) tomato paste
- 2 bay leaves
- 1 teaspoon dried oregano leaves
- 1 teaspoon dried basil leaves
- ½ teaspoon dried marjoram leaves
- ½ teaspoon honey
- ¼ teaspoon black pepper
- 8 ounces uncooked spaghetti, cooked, drained and kept hot

1. Heat oil in large saucepan. Add onion and garlic. Cook and stir 5 minutes or until onion is tender. Add water, tomato sauce, tomato paste, bay leaves, oregano, basil, marjoram, honey and pepper. Bring to a boil, stirring occasionally. Reduce heat; simmer 1 hour, stirring occasionally.

2. Remove and discard bay leaves. Measure 2 cups sauce; reserve remaining sauce for another use. Serve sauce on pasta. *Makes 4 servings*

Sweet Garlic with Chicken Pasta

Hearty White Bean and Green Pepper Pasta

- 4 ounces uncooked yolk-free egg noodles
- Nonstick cooking spray
- 8 ounces boneless skinless chicken breast, cut into ½-inch pieces
- 2 cups chopped green bell peppers
- 2 cups chopped onions
- 6 cloves garlic, minced
- 1 cup chicken broth
- 2 teaspoons all-purpose flour
- 1 teaspoon dried oregano leaves
- 1 can (16 ounces) Great Northern beans, rinsed and drained
- ¼ cup ketchup
- 1 can (14½ ounces) tomatoes, drained and cut up
- Black pepper to taste

1. Cook noodles according to package directions, omitting salt. Drain; set aside.

2. Meanwhile, spray Dutch oven with cooking spray. Heat over medium-high heat until hot. Add chicken, bell peppers, onions and garlic. Cook and stir 5 to 7 minutes or until onions are tender.

3. Whisk broth into flour in bowl until smooth. Add to chicken mixture. Bring to a boil over high heat. Add oregano and beans. Return to a boil. Reduce heat to low; simmer, uncovered, 20 minutes or until peppers are tender.

4. Remove from heat. Stir in ketchup and tomatoes until well blended. Add noodles; stir. Let stand, uncovered, 5 to 8 minutes. Season with black pepper. *Makes 4 servings*

Pasta with Fresh Vegetables in Garlic Sauce

- 3 medium carrots
- 2 small zucchini
- ¼ cup butter or margarine
- 1 large onion, chopped
- 4 cloves garlic, minced
- ½ cup chicken broth
- ½ cup heavy cream
- ½ teaspoon salt
- ½ teaspoon dried tarragon leaves
- ¼ teaspoon black pepper
- 2 cups hot cooked pasta (fettuccine, ziti or shells)

Cut carrots and zucchini lengthwise into thin slices with vegetable peeler. Bring 1 inch water to a boil in medium saucepan; add carrots and zucchini. Cook until crisp-tender. Remove from saucepan and drain; set aside. Melt butter in same saucepan over medium heat. Add onion and garlic; cook until tender. Gradually stir in broth, cream, salt, tarragon and pepper; simmer 5 minutes or until sauce is slightly thickened. Add vegetables; heat thoroughly, stirring occasionally. Add vegetables and sauce to hot cooked pasta; toss lightly. *Makes 4 servings*

Pasta with Fresh Vegetables in Garlic Sauce

Spectacular Vegetarian & Side Dishes

Southwest Hopping John

- **1½ cups dried black-eyed peas**
- **2 tablespoons olive oil**
- **1 medium onion, chopped**
- **4 cloves garlic, minced**
- **2 medium red or green bell peppers, chopped**
- **1 jalapeño pepper,* minced**
- **1 teaspoon ground cumin**
- **2½ cups canned chicken broth**
- **1 cup uncooked brown basmati rice**
- **¼ pound smoked ham, diced**
- **4 medium tomatoes, seeded and chopped**
- **½ cup minced fresh cilantro**

*Jalapeño peppers can sting and irritate the skin; wear rubber gloves when handling peppers and do not touch eyes. Wash hands after handling.

1. Rinse peas thoroughly in colander under cold running water. Place in large bowl; cover with 4 inches of water. Let stand at least 8 hours, then rinse and drain.

2. Transfer peas to medium saucepan; cover with water. Bring to a boil over high heat. Reduce heat to low; simmer, covered, 1 hour or until tender. Drain in colander; set aside.

3. Heat oil in Dutch oven over medium-high heat. Add onion and garlic; cook and stir 2 minutes. Add bell and jalapeño peppers; cook and stir 2 minutes. Stir in cumin; cook and stir 1 minute.

4. Stir in chicken broth, rice and ham. Bring to a boil over high heat. Reduce heat to low; simmer, covered, 35 minutes.

5. Add peas; simmer 10 minutes or until liquid is absorbed. Stir tomatoes and cilantro into rice mixture just before serving. *Makes 6 servings*

Southwest Hopping John

Green Beans and Shiitake Mushrooms

10 to 12 dried shiitake mushrooms (about 1 ounce)
¾ cup water, divided
3 tablespoons oyster sauce
1 tablespoon cornstarch
4 cloves garlic, minced
⅛ teaspoon red pepper flakes
1 tablespoon vegetable oil
¾ to 1 pound fresh green beans, ends trimmed
⅓ cup slivered fresh basil leaves or chopped cilantro
2 green onions, sliced diagonally
⅓ cup roasted peanuts (optional)

1. Place mushrooms in bowl; cover with hot water. Let stand 30 minutes or until caps are soft.

2. Drain mushrooms; squeeze out excess water. Remove and discard stems. Slice caps into thin strips.

3. Combine ¼ cup water, oyster sauce, cornstarch, garlic and red pepper in small bowl; mix well. Set aside.

4. Heat wok or medium skillet over medium-high heat. Add oil and swirl to coat surface. Add mushrooms, beans and remaining ½ cup water; cook and stir until water boils.

5. Reduce heat to medium-low; cover and cook 8 to 10 minutes or until beans are crisp-tender, stirring occasionally.

6. Stir cornstarch mixture; add to wok. Cook and stir until sauce thickens and coats beans. (If cooking water has evaporated, add enough water to form thick sauce.)

7. Stir in basil, green onions and peanuts, if desired; mix well. Transfer to serving platter. Garnish as desired. *Makes 4 to 6 servings*

Tomato Ginger Chutney

1 tablespoon minced gingerroot *or* ½ teaspoon ground ginger
2 cloves garlic, minced
½ teaspoon ground cinnamon
Dash cayenne pepper
1 teaspoon vegetable oil
1 can (14½ ounces) DEL MONTE® Cajun Recipe Stewed Tomatoes
¼ cup firmly packed brown sugar
¼ cup cider vinegar

1. Cook ginger, garlic, cinnamon and cayenne in small saucepan in oil. Add tomatoes, sugar and vinegar.

2. Cook, uncovered, over medium-high heat 15 minutes, stirring occasionally.

3. Reduce heat; cook 5 minutes or until thickened. Serve with poultry, beef or lamb. *Makes approximately ¾ cup*

Prep Time: 5 minutes
Cook Time: 20 minutes

Green Beans and Shiitake Mushrooms

Green Bean & Bell Pepper Frittata

1¾ cups chicken broth
1 tablespoon plus ¼ teaspoon dried Italian seasoning, divided
½ pound fresh green beans, cut into 1-inch pieces
3 tablespoons olive oil, divided
¾ cup chopped onion
1½ cups chopped seeded red bell peppers
4 cloves garlic, minced
½ teaspoon salt
¼ teaspoon black pepper
3 tablespoons dry sherry
8 eggs
¼ cup plus 3 tablespoons grated Romano cheese, divided
¼ cup heavy cream
Dash ground red pepper

1. Combine chicken broth and ¼ teaspoon Italian seasoning in 2-quart saucepan. Bring to a boil over medium-high heat. Add beans. Reduce heat to low; simmer, covered, 17 to 20 minutes until beans are tender. Drain.

2. Preheat oven to 325°F. Heat 2 tablespoons oil in 10-inch nonstick ovenproof skillet over medium-high heat. Add onion and remaining 1 tablespoon Italian seasoning; cook 4 to 5 minutes until onion is golden brown.

3. Add remaining 1 tablespoon oil, bell peppers and garlic to skillet; cook 3 to 5 minutes until peppers are tender. Stir in green beans, salt and black pepper; mix well. Reduce heat to medium. Add sherry; stir 2 to 3 minutes.

4. Place eggs, ¼ cup cheese, cream and ground red pepper in blender. Blend at medium speed 1 minute or until just blended. Pour egg mixture over filling in skillet. Reduce heat to low; cook 6 to 7 minutes until frittata starts to set.

5. Transfer skillet to oven. Bake 6 to 7 minutes until center is just set.

6. Top frittata with remaining 3 tablespoons cheese. Bake 5 to 7 minutes until cheese melts. Let stand 5 minutes before serving. Garnish with fresh parsley, if desired. *Makes 4 to 6 servings*

Guiltless Zucchini

Nonstick cooking spray
4 medium zucchini, sliced
⅓ cup chopped onion
4 cloves garlic, minced
¼ teaspoon dried oregano leaves
½ cup GUILTLESS GOURMET® Salsa
¼ cup (1 ounce) shredded low-fat mozzarella cheese

Coat large nonstick skillet with cooking spray; heat over medium heat until hot. Add zucchini; cook and stir 5 minutes. Add onion, garlic and oregano; cook 5 minutes more or until zucchini and onion are lightly browned. Stir in salsa. Bring just to a boil. Reduce heat to low; simmer 5 minutes more or until zucchini is crisp-tender. Sprinkle cheese on top; cover and cook 1 to 2 minutes or until cheese melts. Serve hot.
Makes 4 servings

Green Bean & Bell Pepper Frittata

Bay

Spring Vegetable Curry

- Curry Powder (recipe follows)
- 2½ cups canned chicken broth
- ¾ teaspoon salt, divided
- 1 cup uncooked dried split green peas, rinsed and sorted
- 1 tablespoon olive oil
- 2 cups chopped onions
- 2 medium carrots, peeled and diagonally sliced
- 4 cloves garlic, minced
- 2 cups frozen cauliflower florets
- 1 medium zucchini, cut in half lengthwise and diagonally sliced
- 1½ cups canned unsweetened coconut milk
- ¼ teaspoon red pepper flakes
- 1½ cups chopped seeded tomatoes
- ½ cup fresh or frozen green peas
- Hot cooked white rice

1. Prepare Curry Powder; set aside. Combine chicken broth, 1 tablespoon Curry Powder and ½ teaspoon salt in medium saucepan. Bring to a boil over high heat. Stir in split peas. Reduce heat to low; simmer, covered, 15 minutes.

2. Heat oil in large skillet over medium-high heat. Add onions; cook and stir 3 minutes or until tender. Add carrots and garlic; cook and stir 5 to 7 minutes until carrots are crisp-tender. Add to split peas in saucepan.

3. Stir in cauliflower, zucchini, coconut milk, red pepper and remaining ¼ teaspoon salt; simmer, covered, 20 to 25 minutes until split peas are tender. Stir in tomatoes and green peas just before serving. Serve over hot rice.

Makes 6 to 8 servings

Curry Powder

- 2 teaspoons ground cumin
- 1 teaspoon ground ginger
- 1 teaspoon turmeric
- ½ teaspoon ground cinnamon
- ¼ teaspoon ground mace
- ¼ teaspoon ground cardamom
- ¼ teaspoon dry mustard
- ¼ teaspoon black pepper

Combine all ingredients in small bowl; mix well.

Lemon Garlic Greens

- 1½ pounds beet greens
- 2 teaspoons olive oil
- ¼ cup finely chopped onion
- 4 cloves garlic, minced
- 2 tablespoons lemon juice
- ¼ teaspoon salt
- ¼ teaspoon black pepper

Wash beet greens. Drain but do not pat dry; leave some water clinging to leaves. Remove stems; coarsely chop.

Heat oil in large saucepan over medium heat. Add beet greens, onion and garlic; cook and stir 5 minutes. Stir in lemon juice, salt and pepper; continue cooking about 5 minutes or until greens are wilted and onion is tender. Serve warm.

Makes 4 servings

Spring Vegetable Curry

Braised Eggplant in Garlic Sauce

1 medium eggplant (1¼ pounds), cut into chunks
1 teaspoon salt
2 tablespoons light soy sauce
1 tablespoon dark sesame oil
1 tablespoon rice wine or dry sherry
1 tablespoon rice vinegar or white vinegar
2 teaspoons cornstarch
2 teaspoons sugar
2 tablespoons vegetable oil
2 cloves garlic, minced
¼ cup chicken broth
1 small red bell pepper, cut into strips
1 green onion with tops, cut into 1-inch lengths
Lemon balm for garnish

1. Place eggplant in large colander over bowl; sprinkle with salt. Let stand 30 minutes to extract moisture.

2. Combine soy sauce, sesame oil, rice wine, vinegar, cornstarch and sugar in cup; mix well. Set aside.

3. Rinse eggplant with cold water; pat dry with paper towels. Heat wok over high heat about 1 minute or until hot. Drizzle vegetable oil into wok; heat 15 seconds. Add eggplant and stir-fry about 5 minutes or until lightly browned. Add garlic; stir-fry 15 seconds.

4. Add chicken broth to wok; cover and reduce heat to medium. Cook eggplant 3 minutes.

5. Uncover wok. Increase heat to medium-high. Add bell pepper and onion; stir-fry 2 minutes. Stir cornstarch mixture; add to wok. Cook and stir until liquid boils and thickens. Transfer to warm serving dish. Garnish, if desired. Serve immediately. *Makes 6 servings*

Braised Eggplant in Garlic Sauce

Savory Lentil Casserole

- 1¼ cups uncooked dried brown or green lentils, rinsed and sorted
- 2 tablespoons olive oil
- 1 large onion, chopped
- 3 cloves garlic, minced
- 8 ounces fresh shiitake or button mushrooms, sliced
- 2 tablespoons all-purpose flour
- 1½ cups canned beef broth
- 1 tablespoon Worcestershire sauce
- 1 tablespoon balsamic vinegar
- 4 ounces Canadian bacon, minced
- ½ teaspoon salt
- ½ teaspoon black pepper
- ½ cup grated Parmesan cheese
- 2 to 3 plum tomatoes, seeded and chopped

1. Preheat oven to 400°F. Place lentils in medium saucepan; cover with 1 inch water. Bring to a boil over high heat. Reduce heat to low. Simmer, covered, 20 to 25 minutes until lentils are barely tender; drain.

2. Meanwhile, heat oil in large skillet over medium heat. Add onion and garlic; cook and stir 10 minutes. Add mushrooms; cook and stir 10 minutes or until liquid is evaporated. Sprinkle flour over mushroom mixture. Cook and stir 1 minute. Stir in beef broth, Worcestershire, vinegar, bacon, salt and pepper. Cook and stir until mixture is thick and bubbly.

3. Grease 1½-quart casserole. Stir lentils into mushroom mixture. Spread evenly into prepared casserole. Sprinkle with cheese. Bake 20 minutes.

4. Sprinkle tomatoes over casserole just before serving. *Makes 4 servings*

Bean and Vegetable Burritos

- 2 tablespoons chili powder
- 2 teaspoons dried oregano leaves
- 1½ teaspoons ground cumin
- 1 large sweet potato, peeled and diced
- 1 can black beans or pinto beans, drained, rinsed
- 4 cloves garlic, minced
- 1 medium onion, halved and thinly sliced
- 1 jalapeño pepper, seeded and minced
- 1 green bell pepper, chopped
- 1 cup frozen corn, thawed and drained
- 3 tablespoons lime juice
- 1 tablespoon chopped cilantro
- ¾ cup (3 ounces) shredded Monterey Jack cheese
- 4 (10-inch) flour tortillas
- Sour cream (optional)

Combine chili powder, oregano and cumin in small bowl. Set aside.

Layer ingredients in slow cooker in the following order: sweet potato, beans, half of chili powder mix, garlic, onion, jalapeño pepper, bell pepper, remaining half of chili powder mix and corn. Cover and cook on LOW 5 hours or until sweet potato is tender. Stir in lime juice and cilantro.

Preheat oven to 350°F. Spoon 2 tablespoons cheese in center of each tortilla. Top with 1 cup filling. Fold all 4 sides to enclose filling. Place burritos seam side down on baking sheet. Cover with foil and bake 20 to 30 minutes or until heated through. Serve with sour cream, if desired. *Makes 4 servings*

Bean and Vegetable Burrito

Grilled Balsamic-Herb Ratatouille

- 2 tablespoons balsamic vinegar
- 1 tablespoon olive oil
- Balsamic-Herb Vinaigrette (recipe follows)
- 2 yellow or red bell peppers, seeded and halved
- 1 medium eggplant (about 1 pound)
- 1 small onion, peeled and quartered
- 12 mushrooms
- 2 small yellow squash, halved lengthwise
- ½ pint cherry tomatoes
- ⅓ cup slivered fresh basil

1. Prepare coals for grilling. Spray medium casserole with nonstick cooking spray; set aside. To make basting mixture, combine vinegar and oil in small bowl; set aside. Prepare Balsamic-Herb Vinaigrette.

2. Grill bell pepper halves skin side down on covered grill over hot coals 15 to 25 minutes or until skin is charred. Place in plastic bag 10 minutes. Remove skin and discard. Dice bell peppers; place in casserole and keep warm.

3. Slice eggplant into ½-inch-thick rounds. Thread onion quarters onto metal skewers. Baste eggplant and onion; grill on covered grill over medium coals 20 to 30 minutes or until tender, basting and turning every 10 minutes. Cut eggplant into ½-inch strips. Add onion and eggplant to casserole.

4. Thread mushrooms onto metal skewers. Baste mushrooms and cut sides of squash. Grill mushrooms and squash on covered grill over medium coals 10 to 15 minutes or until tender, basting and turning once. Cut squash into ½-inch slices. Add mushrooms and squash to casserole. Thread tomatoes onto skewers. Grill on covered grill over medium coals 5 minutes or until blistered, basting and turning once. Add to casserole. Stir in Balsamic-Herb Vinaigrette and basil.

Makes 6 servings

Balsamic-Herb Vinaigrette

- 4 cloves garlic, minced
- 3 tablespoons balsamic vinegar
- 1 tablespoon minced fresh oregano
- 1 tablespoon minced fresh thyme
- 1 teaspoon Dijon mustard
- ½ teaspoon black pepper

Whisk together all ingredients in small bowl.

Makes about ¼ cup

Taos Tossed Salad

- Baked Tortilla Strips (recipe follows)
- ¼ cup orange juice
- 1 tablespoon white wine vinegar
- 1 teaspoon olive oil
- 4 cloves garlic, minced
- ¼ teaspoon ground cumin
- ¼ teaspoon black pepper
- 3 cups washed and torn romaine leaves
- 1 cup washed and torn Boston lettuce leaves
- 1 cup julienned jicama
- 2 medium oranges, cut into segments
- 1 medium tomato, cut into wedges
- ¼ cup thinly sliced red onion

Prepare Baked Tortilla Strips; set aside.

For dressing, combine orange juice, vinegar, oil, garlic, cumin and pepper in small jar with tight-fitting lid; shake well. Refrigerate until ready to use.

Combine lettuces, jicama, oranges, tomato and onion in large bowl. Shake dressing; pour over salad and toss gently to coat. Sprinkle with Baked Tortilla Strips. Serve immediately.

Makes 6 servings

Baked Tortilla Strips

2 (6-inch) flour tortillas
Nonstick cooking spray
Dash paprika

Preheat oven to 375°F. Cut tortillas into halves; cut halves into ¼-inch-wide strips. Arrange tortilla strips on cookie sheet. Spray lightly with cooking spray; toss to coat. Sprinkle with paprika.

Bake about 10 minutes or until browned, stirring occasionally. Let cool to room temperature.

Makes about 1½ cups

Parmesan Polenta

4 cups chicken broth
1¼ cups yellow cornmeal
1 small onion, minced
4 cloves garlic, minced
1 tablespoon minced fresh rosemary *or* 1 teaspoon dried rosemary
½ teaspoon salt
6 tablespoons grated Parmesan cheese
1 tablespoon olive oil, divided

1. Spray 11×7-inch baking pan with nonstick cooking spray; set aside. Spray one side of 7-inch-long sheet of waxed paper with cooking spray; set aside. Combine chicken broth, cornmeal, onion, garlic, rosemary and salt in medium saucepan. Cover and bring to a boil over high heat. Reduce heat to medium and simmer 10 to 15 minutes or until mixture has consistency of thick mashed potatoes. Remove from heat and stir in cheese.

2. Spread polenta evenly in prepared pan; place waxed paper, sprayed-side down, on polenta and smooth. (If surface is bumpy, it is more likely to stick to grill.) Cool on wire rack 15 minutes or until firm. Remove waxed paper; cut into 6 squares. Remove squares from pan.

3. To prevent sticking, spray grid with cooking spray. Prepare coals for grilling. Brush tops of squares with half the oil. Grill oil-side down on covered grill over medium to low coals for 6 to 8 minutes or until golden. Brush with remaining oil and gently turn over. Grill 6 to 8 minutes more or until golden. Serve warm.

Makes 6 servings

Bean and Roasted Garlic Ragout

1 tablespoon Roasted Garlic Purée (recipe follows)
¾ cup uncooked navy beans, rinsed and sorted
¾ cup uncooked brown lentils, rinsed and sorted
1 medium onion, chopped
½ cup chopped carrot
¼ teaspoon dried sage leaves
⅛ teaspoon dried rosemary
⅓ cup canned diced tomatoes, drained
1 teaspoon salt
¼ teaspoon black pepper
½ cup chopped honey-baked ham (about 4 ounces)

1. Prepare Roasted Garlic Purée; set aside. Place navy beans in large saucepan; cover with 4 inches water. Bring to a boil, covered, over high heat. Uncover; boil 2 minutes. Remove from heat; cover. Let stand 1 hour; rinse and drain.

2. Place lentils in 1-quart saucepan; cover with 2 inches cold water.

3. Bring lentils to a boil over high heat. Reduce heat to low; simmer, partially covered, 30 minutes or until just barely tender.

4. Cover navy beans with 2 inches cold water. Return navy beans to a boil over high heat. Reduce heat to low; simmer, partially covered, 35 to 40 minutes until tender. Drain; reserve ¾ cup liquid.

5. Heat 4½ teaspoons reserved oil from Roasted Garlic Purée in 4-quart saucepan over medium-high heat. Stir in onion; cook 3 to 4 minutes or until tender. Add carrot, sage and rosemary; cook 2 to 3 minutes. Stir in tomatoes; mix well.

6. Add navy beans, lentils, reserved navy bean liquid, 1 tablespoon Roasted Garlic Purée, salt and pepper; simmer, covered, 7 minutes. Stir in ham; cook 1 to 2 minutes. Serve immediately. Garnish as desired. *Makes 4 to 6 servings*

Roasted Garlic Purée

1 medium head garlic
½ teaspoon dried rosemary
¼ teaspoon dried sage leaves
¼ cup olive oil

1. Preheat oven to 400°F. Cut top third of garlic head (not the root end) to expose cloves; discard top.

2. Place head, cut-side up, in small shallow baking dish. Sprinkle rosemary and sage over cloves. Drizzle oil over cloves. Cover with foil.

3. Bake 45 minutes or until tender. Remove foil; bake 15 minutes or until garlic skin is golden brown and papery.

4. Cool in baking dish. Reserve oil from dish.

5. Squeeze head from stem end to remove pulp from all cloves. Squeeze individual cloves if pulp remains. Purée garlic in small bowl with fork.

Bean and Roasted Garlic Ragout

Grilled Ratatouille Sandwich

⅓ cup olive oil
⅓ cup FRENCH'S® Deli Brown Mustard
1 tablespoon chopped fresh rosemary *or* 1 teaspoon dried rosemary
3 cloves garlic, minced
½ cup kalamata olives, pitted and chopped
½ of a small eggplant (about ¾ pound)
1 medium zucchini
1 large red onion
2 large ripe plum tomatoes
1 large red bell pepper, seeded
1 (12-inch) sourdough baguette, cut lengthwise in half (about 12 ounces)

1. Combine oil, mustard, rosemary and garlic in bowl. Place olives and 2 tablespoons mustard mixture in food processor. Process until smooth; set aside. Reserve remaining mustard mixture.

2. Cut eggplant and zucchini lengthwise into ¼-inch-thick slices. Cut onion and tomatoes into ½-inch-thick slices. Cut bell pepper into 2-inch-wide pieces. Baste vegetables with reserved mustard mixture.

3. Place vegetables on oiled grid. Grill over medium-high heat 3 to 5 minutes or until tender, basting and turning once.

4. To serve, remove and discard excess bread from bread halves. Spread olive mixture on cut surfaces of bread. Layer vegetables on bottom half of bread; cover with top half. Cut crosswise into 4 portions. *Makes 4 servings*

Prep Time: 25 minutes
Cook Time: 5 minutes

OLIVE TAPENADE DIP: Combine 1½ cups (10 ounces) kalamata olives, pitted; 3 tablespoons *each* olive oil and FRENCH'S® Deli Brown Mustard; 1 teaspoon minced dried rosemary and 1 clove garlic in food processor. Process until puréed. Serve with vegetable crudités. *Makes about 1 cup dip*

Dragon Tofu

¼ cup soy sauce
1 tablespoon creamy peanut butter
1 package (12 ounces) firm tofu, drained
2 teaspoons peanut or vegetable oil
½ teaspoon hot chili oil
2 cloves garlic, minced
1 medium zucchini, cut into strips
1 medium yellow squash, cut into strips
2 cups (packed) torn fresh spinach leaves
¼ cup coarsely chopped cashews or peanuts

Whisk soy sauce into peanut butter in small bowl. Press tofu between paper towels; cut into ¾-inch cubes. In shallow dish, pour soy sauce mixture over tofu to coat all surfaces. Let stand 20 minutes. Heat oils in nonstick skillet over medium-high heat. Add garlic, zucchini and squash; stir-fry 3 minutes. Add tofu mixture; cook 2 minutes or until hot and sauce is thickened, stirring occasionally. Stir in spinach. Sprinkle with cashews. *Makes 2 servings*

Grilled Ratatouille Sandwich and Olive Tapenade Dip

Greek White Bean Risotto

- 3 teaspoons low-sodium chicken flavor bouillon granules
- Nonstick cooking spray
- 3 cloves garlic, minced
- 1½ cups uncooked arborio rice
- 2 teaspoons dried oregano leaves
- ⅓ cup finely chopped dry-pack sun-dried tomatoes
- 1 cup rinsed drained canned cannellini beans (white kidney beans)
- ¾ cup (3 ounces) crumbled feta cheese
- ⅓ cup grated Parmesan cheese
- 1 teaspoon lemon juice
- ½ teaspoon black pepper

1. Combine 5½ cups water and bouillon granules in large saucepan; cover. Bring to a simmer over medium-low heat. Keep hot.

2. Spray large saucepan with cooking spray; heat over medium heat until hot. Add garlic; cook and stir 1 minute. Add rice and oregano; reduce heat to medium-low.

3. Stir 1 cup broth into rice mixture; cook until broth is absorbed, stirring constantly. Stir ½ cup broth into rice mixture, stirring constantly until broth is absorbed. Add tomatoes.

4. Stir remaining broth into rice mixture, ½ cup at a time, stirring constantly until all broth is absorbed before adding more. (Total cooking time for broth absorption is about 35 to 40 minutes or until rice is just tender but still firm.)

5. Stir beans into rice mixture; cook and stir 1 minute. Remove from heat. Stir in cheeses, lemon juice and pepper. Cover; let stand 5 minutes. Stir before serving. *Makes 5 servings*

Lemon-Garlic Broccoli over Spaghetti Squash

- 1 spaghetti squash (2 pounds)
- 1 can (about 14 ounces) chicken broth
- 10 large cloves garlic, peeled and halved
- 2 tablespoons lemon juice
- 3 fresh sage leaves
- 2 cups broccoli florets

1. Place spaghetti squash in large saucepan. Pierce skin with fork. Add enough water to cover. Bring to a boil over high heat. Reduce heat to low; simmer, covered, 20 to 30 minutes or until squash is soft. Cut squash in half lengthwise; remove seeds. Set aside.

2. Meanwhile, combine broth and garlic in small saucepan. Bring to a boil over high heat. Reduce heat to low; simmer 15 minutes or until tender. Remove from heat; cool slightly.

3. Place broth, garlic, lemon juice and sage in food processor; process until smooth. Return mixture to saucepan; keep warm.

4. Combine broccoli and ¼ cup water in large nonstick skillet with tight-fitting lid. Bring to a boil over high heat. Reduce heat to medium. Cover and steam 5 minutes or until broccoli is crisp-tender.

5. Scoop out inside of squash. Place squash and broccoli in medium bowl; pour lemon-garlic mixture over squash mixture. Mix well. Garnish as desired. Serve immediately.

Makes 6 servings

Lemon-Garlic Broccoli over Spaghetti Squash

Rosemary-Garlic Mashed Potatoes

- 2½ pounds Yukon Gold potatoes (5 medium), peeled and cut into 1-inch pieces
- 1½ teaspoons salt, divided
- ½ cup heavy cream
- ½ cup milk
- 2 tablespoons butter
- 1 tablespoon minced fresh rosemary *or* 1 teaspoon dried rosemary
- Roasted Garlic (recipe follows), mashed
- ⅛ teaspoon white pepper

Place potatoes in medium saucepan; add water to cover and 1 teaspoon salt. Bring to a boil. Reduce heat to medium-low; simmer, uncovered, about 12 to 15 minutes until tender. Do not overcook. Drain water from pan; cover.

Place cream, milk, butter and rosemary in small saucepan; heat over medium-high heat about 3 minutes or until butter melts and mixture simmers, stirring often. Mash potatoes. Add roasted garlic and milk mixture; beat with electric mixer until smooth. Beat in remaining ½ teaspoon salt and pepper.

Makes 4 to 6 servings

Roasted Garlic: Cut off top third of 1 large garlic head (not the root end) to expose cloves; discard top. Place head of garlic, trimmed end up, on 10-inch square of foil. Rub garlic generously with olive oil and sprinkle with salt. Gather foil ends together and close tightly. Roast in preheated 350°F oven 45 minutes or until cloves are golden and soft. Let cool. Squeeze garlic cloves from skins; discard skins.

South-of-the-Border Vegetable Kabobs

- 5 cloves garlic, peeled
- ½ cup A.1.® Bold & Spicy Steak Sauce
- ¼ cup PARKAY® 70% Vegetable Oil Spread, melted
- 1 tablespoon finely chopped cilantro
- ¾ teaspoon ground cumin
- ¼ teaspoon coarsely ground black pepper
- ⅛ teaspoon ground red pepper
- 3 ears corn, cut crosswise into 1½-inch slices and blanched
- 3 medium plum tomatoes, cut into ½-inch slices
- 1 small zucchini, cut lengthwise into thin slices
- 1 cup baby carrots, blanched

Mince 1 garlic clove; halve remaining garlic cloves and set aside. In small bowl, combine steak sauce, spread, cilantro, minced garlic, cumin and peppers; set aside.

Alternately thread vegetables and halved garlic cloves onto 6 (10-inch) metal skewers. Grill kabobs over medium heat for 7 to 9 minutes or until done, turning and basting often with steak sauce mixture. Remove from skewers; serve immediately. *Makes 6 servings*

South-of-the-Border Vegetable Kabobs

Szechuan Vegetable Stir-Fry

8 ounces firm tofu, drained and cut into cubes
1 cup canned vegetable broth, divided
½ cup orange juice
⅓ cup soy sauce
1 to 2 teaspoons hot chili oil
½ teaspoon fennel seeds
½ teaspoon black pepper
2 tablespoons cornstarch
3 tablespoons vegetable oil
1 cup sliced green onions and tops
3 medium carrots, sliced
3 cloves garlic, minced
2 teaspoons minced fresh ginger
¼ pound button mushrooms, sliced
1 medium red bell pepper, seeded and cut into 1-inch squares
¼ pound fresh snow peas, cut diagonally in half
8 ounces broccoli florets, steamed
½ cup peanuts
4 to 6 cups hot cooked rice

1. Place tofu in 8-inch round or square glass baking dish. Combine ½ cup broth, orange juice, soy sauce, chili oil, fennel seeds and black pepper in 2-cup measure; pour over tofu. Let stand 15 to 60 minutes. Drain, reserving marinade.

2. Combine cornstarch and remaining ½ cup broth in medium bowl. Add reserved marinade; set aside.

3. Heat vegetable oil in wok or large skillet over high heat until hot. Add onions, carrots, garlic and ginger; stir-fry 3 minutes. Add tofu, mushrooms, bell pepper and snow peas; stir-fry 2 to 3 minutes or until vegetables are crisp-tender. Add broccoli; stir-fry 1 minute or until heated through.

4. Stir cornstarch mixture. Add to wok; cook 1 to 2 minutes or until bubbly. Stir in peanuts. Serve over rice. *Makes 4 to 6 servings*

Vegetables in Garlic Cream Sauce

1 cup water
4 cups cut-up vegetables such as DOLE® Asparagus, Bell Peppers, Broccoli, Carrots, Cauliflower or Sugar Peas
1 teaspoon olive or vegetable oil
4 cloves garlic, finely chopped
⅓ cup fat free or reduced fat mayonnaise
⅓ cup nonfat or low fat milk
2 tablespoons chopped fresh parsley

• Place water in large saucepan; bring to a boil. Add vegetables; reduce heat to low. Cook, uncovered, 9 to 12 minutes or until vegetables are tender-crisp; meanwhile, prepare sauce.

• Heat oil in small saucepan over medium heat. Add garlic; cook and stir garlic until golden brown. Remove from heat; stir in mayonnaise and milk.

• Drain vegetables; place in serving bowl. Pour in garlic sauce; toss to evenly coat. Sprinkle with parsley. *Makes 4 servings*

Prep Time: 10 minutes

Cook Time: 15 minutes

Vegetables in Garlic Cream Sauce

Vegetable Tart

Pastry Dough (recipe follows)
Olive oil flavored nonstick cooking spray
1 small sweet potato
1 tablespoon olive or vegetable oil
1 cup sliced mushrooms
½ cup thinly sliced leeks
1 medium zucchini, sliced
1 parsnip, sliced
1 medium red bell pepper, cut into 1-inch pieces
8 to 10 cloves garlic, minced
1 teaspoon dried basil leaves
½ teaspoon dried rosemary
½ teaspoon salt
Black pepper (optional)
2 to 4 tablespoons grated Parmesan cheese
1 egg white, beaten

1. Preheat oven to 400°F. Prepare Pastry Dough. While dough is resting, begin preparing vegetables for tart.

2. Spray nonstick baking sheet with cooking spray. Slice sweet potato into ¼-inch-thick slices. Place on prepared baking sheet; spray tops of slices with cooking spray. Bake 15 to 20 minutes or until potatoes are tender, turning slices once.

3. Heat oil in large skillet over medium heat until hot. Add mushrooms, leeks, zucchini, parsnip, bell pepper, garlic, basil and rosemary; cook and stir 8 to 10 minutes or until vegetables are tender. Season to taste with salt and black pepper, if desired.

4. Roll out Pastry Dough on lightly floured surface to a 14-inch round; place on cookie sheet or large pizza pan. Place sweet potato slices evenly over crust, leaving a 2½-inch border around side. Spoon vegetable mixture evenly over potatoes; sprinkle with cheese. Fold edge of dough over edge of vegetable mixture, pleating dough as necessary to fit. Brush edge of dough with egg white.

5. Bake 25 minutes or until pastry is golden brown. Garnish with fresh basil and rosemary, if desired. Cut into wedges; serve warm.

Makes 16 servings

Pastry Dough

1 teaspoon active dry yeast
⅓ cup warm water (115°F)
1 egg, beaten
3 tablespoons nonfat sour cream
1¼ cups all-purpose flour
¼ cup whole wheat flour
¼ teaspoon salt

To proof yeast, sprinkle over warm water in medium bowl; stir until yeast is dissolved. Let stand 5 minutes or until mixture is bubbly. Add egg and sour cream, mixing until smooth. Stir in flours and salt, making soft dough. Knead dough on lightly floured surface 1 to 2 minutes or until smooth. Shape dough into ball; place in large bowl sprayed with olive oil flavored nonstick cooking spray. Turn dough over to grease top. Cover bowl with towel; let rest in warm place 20 minutes. *Makes pastry for 1 tart*

Vegetable Tart

Sensational BEEF, PORK & LAMB

Roasted Herb & Garlic Tenderloin

1 well-trimmed beef tenderloin roast (3 to 4 pounds)
1 tablespoon black peppercorns
2 tablespoons chopped fresh basil *or* 2 teaspoons dried basil leaves, crushed
4½ teaspoons chopped fresh thyme *or* 1½ teaspoons dried thyme leaves, crushed
1 tablespoon chopped fresh rosemary *or* 1 teaspoon dried rosemary, crushed
1 tablespoon minced garlic
Salt and black pepper (optional)

1. Preheat oven to 425°F.

2. To hold shape of roast, tie roast with cotton string in 1½-inch intervals.

3. Place peppercorns in small heavy resealable plastic food storage bag. Squeeze out excess air; seal bag tightly. Pound peppercorns with flat side of meat mallet or rolling pin until cracked.

4. Place roast on meat rack in shallow roasting pan. Combine cracked peppercorns, basil, thyme, rosemary and garlic in small bowl; rub over top surface of roast.

5. Insert meat thermometer into thickest part of roast. Roast in oven 40 to 50 minutes or until thermometer registers 125° to 130°F for rare or 135° to 145°F for medium-rare, depending on thickness of roast.

6. Transfer roast to carving board; tent with foil. Let stand 10 minutes before carving. Remove string; discard.

7. To serve, carve crosswise into ½-inch-thick slices with large carving knife. Season with salt and pepper. *Makes 10 to 12 servings*

Roasted Herb & Garlic Tenderloin

Texas-Style Chili

- Nonstick cooking spray
- 1 pound lean boneless beef chuck, cut into ½-inch pieces
- 2 cups chopped onions
- 5 cloves garlic, minced
- 2 tablespoons chili powder
- 1 tablespoon ground cumin
- 1 teaspoon ground coriander
- 1 teaspoon dried oregano leaves
- 2½ cups fat-free reduced-sodium beef broth
- 1 cup prepared salsa or picante sauce
- 2 cans (16 ounces each) pinto or red beans (or one of each), rinsed and drained
- ½ cup chopped fresh cilantro
- ½ cup nonfat sour cream
- 1 cup chopped ripe tomatoes

1. Spray Dutch oven or large saucepan with cooking spray; heat over medium-high heat until hot. Add beef, onions and garlic; cook and stir until beef is no longer pink, about 5 minutes. Sprinkle mixture with chili powder, cumin, coriander and oregano; mix well. Add beef broth and salsa; bring to a boil. Cover; simmer 45 minutes.

2. Stir in beans; continue to simmer uncovered 30 minutes or until beef is tender and chili has thickened, stirring occasionally.

3. Stir in cilantro. Ladle into bowls; top with sour cream and tomatoes. Garnish with pickled jalapeño peppers, if desired. *Makes 8 servings*

South-of-the-Border Kabobs

- 5 cloves garlic
- ½ cup A.1.® Original or A.1.® Bold & Spicy Steak Sauce
- ¼ cup PARKAY® 70% Vegetable Oil Spread, melted
- 1 tablespoon finely chopped fresh cilantro
- ¾ teaspoon ground cumin
- ⅛ teaspoon ground red pepper
- 1 (1½-pound) beef flank steak, thinly sliced across grain
- 2 small zucchini, cut lengthwise into thin slices
- 3 medium plum tomatoes, cut into ½-inch slices
- ¾ cup baby carrots, blanched
- Hot cooked rice or noodles

Soak 8 (10-inch) wooden skewers in water at least 30 minutes.

Mince 1 clove garlic; halve remaining cloves and set aside. In small bowl, combine steak sauce, PARKAY® 70% Vegetable Oil Spread, cilantro, minced garlic, cumin and red pepper; set aside.

Alternately thread steak strips and zucchini (accordion style), reserved garlic, tomatoes and carrots onto skewers. Grill kabobs over medium heat or broil 6 inches from heat source 10 to 12 minutes or until steak is desired doneness, turning and basting often with reserved steak sauce mixture. (Discard any remaining steak sauce mixture.) Serve immediately with rice.

Makes 4 servings

Texas-Style Chili

Pepper Stuffed Flank Steak with Chef's Signature Steak Sauce

1 flank steak (about 1½ pounds)
Salt
Ground black pepper
2 cups thinly sliced bell peppers (green, red and/or yellow)
1 small onion, thinly sliced
Chef's® Signature Steak Sauce (recipe follows)

Lay steak flat on baking sheet lined with plastic wrap. Cover and freeze about 2 hours or until nearly firm. Place steak on cutting board. Hold large sharp knife parallel to steak. Carefully cut steak in half lengthwise. Thaw in refrigerator until steak can be rolled up easily. Sprinkle inside of each piece of meat with salt and black pepper. Arrange bell peppers and onion on meat, leaving ½-inch edge around meat. Tightly roll up jelly-roll style; tie with kitchen string or secure with toothpicks.*

Prepare Chef's Signature Steak Sauce; set aside. Place steak on oiled grid. Grill over medium-hot coals 25 minutes for medium doneness, turning often. Baste with some of Chef's Signature Steak Sauce during last 10 minutes of cooking. Remove string or toothpicks. Let steak stand 5 minutes. Slice steak diagonally. Serve with remaining sauce. *Makes 6 servings*

*Soak toothpicks in water 20 minutes to prevent burning.

Chef's Signature Steak Sauce

½ cup ketchup
¼ cup FRENCH'S® Worcestershire Sauce
1 to 2 tablespoons FRANK'S® REDHOT® Hot Sauce or to taste
2 cloves garlic, minced

Combine ingredients in small bowl; stir until smooth. *Makes ¾ cup*

Sizzle Steak Marinade: Combine ¼ cup *each* French's® Worcestershire Sauce and red wine vinegar, 2 tablespoons *each* olive oil and French's® Dijon Mustard, and 1 teaspoon garlic powder. Use to marinate 2 pounds steak in refrigerator. (Drain and discard marinade before grilling.)

Prep Time: 30 minutes

Freeze Time: 2 hours

Cook Time: 25 minutes

Pepper Stuffed Flank Steak with Chef's Signature Steak Sauce

Beef Burgundy and Mushrooms

8 ounces uncooked yolk-free egg noodles
¼ cup water
2 tablespoons all-purpose flour
1 can (10 ounces) beef broth
2 tablespoons dry red wine
½ teaspoon Worcestershire sauce
¾ teaspoon granulated sugar
1 bay leaf
Nonstick cooking spray
1½ teaspoons extra virgin olive oil
1 package (16 ounces) sliced fresh mushrooms
4 cloves garlic, minced
1 pound beef sirloin, cut into thin strips
½ cup chopped green onions with tops
¼ cup chopped fresh parsley
Black pepper

1. Cook noodles according to package directions, omitting salt. Drain; set aside.

2. Meanwhile, combine water and flour in small bowl; whisk until smooth. Slowly whisk in beef broth, wine, Worcestershire sauce, sugar and bay leaf; set aside.

3. Spray large nonstick skillet with cooking spray; add oil. Heat over high heat until hot. Add mushrooms and garlic; cook 2 minutes. Reduce heat to medium-high; cook 3 to 4 minutes or until tender. Place in separate bowl.

4. Recoat skillet with nonstick cooking spray. Brown sirloin strips over high heat 2 to 3 minutes. Add green onions, mushrooms and broth mixture. Bring to a boil. Reduce heat to medium-low; simmer, uncovered, 30 minutes or until meat is tender. Remove from heat; add parsley. Sprinkle with pepper to taste. Let stand 10 minutes before serving. Spoon over egg noodles.

Makes 4 servings

London Broil Dijon

2 tablespoons olive or vegetable oil
2 large heads garlic, separated into cloves and peeled
1 can (14½ ounces) reduced-sodium beef broth
½ cup water
1 sprig fresh oregano or parsley
4½ teaspoons Dijon mustard
2 pounds beef top round steak or London broil (about 1½ inches thick)
Salt and black pepper

Heat oil in medium saucepan; add garlic and sauté over medium-low heat, stirring frequently, until garlic just starts to brown in spots. Add broth, water and oregano. Simmer until mixture is reduced by about one third. Process broth mixture, in batches, in blender or food processor until smooth. Return to saucepan; whisk in mustard. Set aside. Season meat with salt and pepper.

Oil hot grid to help prevent sticking. Grill beef, on a covered grill, over medium-low KINGSFORD® briquets, 10 to 14 minutes for medium-rare doneness; 12 to 16 minutes for medium doneness, turning once or twice. Let stand 5 minutes before slicing. Cut across grain into thin, diagonal slices. Rewarm sauce and serve as accompaniment.

Makes 6 servings

Beef Burgundy and Mushrooms

Thai Meatballs and Noodles

Thai Meatballs (recipe follows)
12 ounces uncooked egg noodles
2 cans (about 14 ounces each) reduced-sodium chicken broth
2 tablespoons packed brown sugar
2 tablespoons fish sauce or reduced-sodium soy sauce
1 small piece fresh ginger (about 1×½ inch), cut into thin strips
1 medium carrot, cut into matchstick-size strips
1 pound bok choy, cut into ½-inch-wide strips
½ cup slivered fresh mint or basil leaves or chopped cilantro

Prepare Thai Meatballs. While meatballs are cooking, cook noodles according to package directions; drain. Transfer noodles to large serving bowl; keep warm.

Heat chicken broth in large saucepan or wok over high heat. Add brown sugar, fish sauce and ginger; stir until sugar is dissolved. Add meatballs and carrot to saucepan; bring to a boil. Reduce heat to medium-low; cover and simmer 15 minutes or until meatballs are heated through.

Add bok choy; simmer 4 to 5 minutes or until stalks are crisp-tender. Stir in mint; spoon mixture over noodles in serving bowl. Garnish as desired. *Makes 6 servings*

Thai Meatballs

1½ pounds ground beef or pork
¼ cup chopped fresh basil leaves
¼ cup chopped fresh mint leaves
2 tablespoons finely chopped fresh ginger
4 teaspoons fish sauce
6 cloves garlic, minced
1 teaspoon ground cinnamon
½ teaspoon fennel seeds, crushed
½ teaspoon black pepper
2 tablespoons peanut oil, divided

Combine beef, basil, mint, ginger, fish sauce, garlic, cinnamon, fennel and pepper in large bowl; mix until well blended. Rub cutting board with 1 tablespoon oil. Pat meat mixture into 12×8-inch rectangle on board. Cut into 32 squares. Shape each square into a ball.

Heat remaining 1 tablespoon oil in large skillet or wok over medium-high heat. Add meatballs in single layer; cook 8 to 10 minutes or until no longer pink in center, turning to brown all sides. (Cook in several batches.) Remove meatballs with slotted spoon to paper towels; drain. *Makes 32 meatballs*

Thai Meatballs and Noodles

Exotic Pork & Vegetables

- 1 large carrot, peeled
- ¼ cup water
- 2 teaspoons cornstarch
- 4 tablespoons peanut oil, divided
- 6 whole dried hot red chili peppers
- 4 cloves garlic, peeled and sliced
- 1 pork tenderloin (about ¾ pound), sliced thinly
- 2 ounces fresh oyster, shiitake or button mushrooms*, cut into halves
- 1 baby eggplant
- 5 ounces fresh snow peas, ends trimmed
- 3 tablespoons brown sugar
- 2 tablespoons fish sauce
- 1 tablespoon dark sesame oil
- Hot cooked rice

*Or, substitute ½ ounce dried Oriental mushrooms, soaked according to package directions.

1. To make scalloped edges on carrot, use citrus stripper or grapefruit spoon to cut groove into carrot, cutting lengthwise from stem end to tip. Continue to cut grooves around carrot about ¼ inch apart. Cut carrot crosswise into ¼-inch-thick slices.

2. Combine water and cornstarch in cup; set aside.

3. Heat wok or large skillet over high heat 1 minute or until hot. Drizzle 2 tablespoons peanut oil into wok and heat 30 seconds. Add peppers and garlic; stir-fry about 1 minute. Add pork; stir-fry 3 to 4 minutes or until no longer pink in center. Remove pork mixture to bowl and set aside.

4. Add remaining 2 tablespoons peanut oil to wok. Add carrot, mushrooms, and eggplant; stir-fry 2 minutes. Add snow peas and pork mixture; stir-fry 1 minute.

5. Stir cornstarch mixture; add to wok. Cook 1 minute or until thickened. Stir in brown sugar, fish sauce and sesame oil; cook until heated through. Serve over rice. *Makes 4 servings*

Peanut Pork Tenderloin

- ⅓ cup chunky unsweetened peanut butter
- ⅓ cup regular or light canned coconut milk
- ¼ cup lemon juice or dry white wine
- 3 tablespoons soy sauce
- 3 cloves garlic, minced
- 2 tablespoons sugar
- 1 piece (1-inch cube) fresh ginger, minced
- ½ teaspoon salt
- ¼ to ½ teaspoon cayenne pepper
- ¼ teaspoon ground cinnamon
- 1½ pounds pork tenderloin

Combine peanut butter, coconut milk, lemon juice, soy sauce, garlic, sugar, ginger, salt, cayenne pepper and cinnamon in 2-quart glass dish until blended. Add pork; turn to coat. Cover and refrigerate at least 30 minutes or overnight. Remove pork from marinade; discard marinade. Grill pork on covered grill over medium KINGSFORD® briquets about 20 minutes until just barely pink in center, turning 4 times. Cut crosswise into ½-inch slices. Serve immediately. *Makes 4 to 6 servings*

Exotic Pork & Vegetables

Pork Tenderloin with Grilled Apple Cream Sauce

- 1 can (6 ounces) frozen apple juice concentrate, thawed and divided
- ½ cup Calvados or brandy, divided
- 2 tablespoons Dijon mustard
- 1 tablespoon olive oil
- 3 cloves garlic, minced
- 1¼ teaspoons salt, divided
- ¼ teaspoon black pepper
- 1½ pounds pork tenderloin
- 2 green or red apples, cored
- 1 tablespoon butter
- ½ large red onion, cut into thin slivers
- ½ cup heavy cream
- Fresh thyme sprigs

Reserve 2 tablespoons juice concentrate. Combine remaining juice concentrate, ¼ cup Calvados, mustard, oil, garlic, 1 teaspoon salt and pepper in glass dish. Add pork; turn to coat. Cover and refrigerate 2 hours, turning pork occasionally. Cut apples crosswise into ⅜-inch rings. Remove pork from marinade; discard marinade. Grill pork on covered grill over medium KINGSFORD® briquets about 20 minutes, turning 3 times, until meat thermometer inserted in thickest part registers 155°F. Grill apples about 4 minutes per side until tender; cut rings into quarters. Melt butter in large skillet over medium heat. Add onion; cook and stir until soft. Stir in apples, remaining ¼ cup Calvados, ¼ teaspoon salt and reserved 2 tablespoons juice concentrate. Add cream; heat through. Cut pork crosswise into ½-inch slices; spoon sauce over pork. Garnish with fresh thyme.

Makes 4 servings

Carnival Pork Stew

- 3 pounds lean boneless pork loin, cut into 2-inch pieces
- Salt and fresh ground pepper
- 2 tablespoons oil
- 8 ounces smoked ham, cut into ½-inch chunks
- 2 medium onions, chopped
- 2 stalks celery, chopped
- 2 green bell peppers, chopped
- 6 cloves garlic, minced
- ½ teaspoon dried thyme
- 1 (28-ounce) can whole tomatoes, undrained, cut up
- ¾ cup SMUCKER'S® Peach Preserves
- 1 cup water
- 1 tablespoon hot pepper sauce
- 1 cup uncooked long-grain rice
- ½ cup chopped fresh parsley
- ½ cup chopped green onions

Sprinkle pork with salt and pepper. Heat oil in large Dutch oven. Add pork; cook 5 to 8 minutes or until well browned. Remove pork with slotted spoon; set aside.

Add ham, onions, celery, green peppers, garlic and thyme. Cook over medium-high heat until vegetables are wilted, about 6 minutes. Add browned pork, tomatoes, preserves, water and hot pepper sauce. Cover and simmer for 45 minutes.

Add rice, parsley and green onions; stir to blend well. Cover and simmer 20 to 25 minutes or until rice is tender. Season to taste with salt and pepper.

Makes 8 servings

Pork Tenderloin with Grilled Apple Cream Sauce

Italian Sausage and Vegetable Stew

1 pound hot or mild Italian sausage, cut into 1-inch pieces
1 package (16 ounces) frozen mixed vegetables (onions and bell peppers)
1 can (14½ ounces) diced Italian-style tomatoes, undrained
2 medium zucchini, sliced
1 jar (4½ ounces) sliced mushrooms, drained
4 cloves garlic, minced
2 tablespoons Italian-style tomato paste

Heat large skillet over high heat until hot. Add sausage, cook about 5 minutes, or until browned. Pour off any drippings.

Combine sausage, frozen vegetables, tomatoes, zucchini, mushrooms and garlic in slow cooker. Cover and cook on LOW 4 to 4½ hours or until zucchini is tender. Stir in tomato paste. Cover and cook 30 mintues or until juices have thickened. *Makes 6 (1-cup) servings*

Greek-Style Loin Roast

1 boneless pork loin roast (3 pounds)
¼ cup olive oil
¼ cup lemon juice
1 teaspoon dried oregano leaves, crushed
1 teaspoon salt
1 teaspoon black pepper
6 cloves garlic, minced
Spicy Yogurt Sauce (recipe follows)

Place pork loin in large resealable plastic food storage bag. Combine all remaining ingredients except Spicy Yogurt Sauce in small bowl; pour over pork. Seal bag and marinate in refrigerator overnight, turning bag occasionally. Meanwhile, prepare Spicy Yogurt Sauce.

Prepare grill with rectangular foil drip pan. Bank briquets on either side of drip pan for indirect cooking. Remove pork, discarding marinade. Place pork on grid over drip pan. Grill, on covered grill, over low coals 1½ hours or to an internal temperature of 155°F. Let rest 10 minutes. (Internal temperature will rise slightly upon standing.) To serve, thinly slice roast and serve with Spicy Yogurt Sauce.

Makes 8 servings

Spicy Yogurt Sauce: Combine 1 cup plain yogurt, 1 peeled and chopped cucumber, ¼ cup minced red onion, ½ teaspoon crushed garlic, ½ teaspoon crushed coriander seeds and ¼ teaspoon crushed red pepper in small bowl; blend well. Cover and refrigerate until ready to serve.

Favorite recipe from **National Pork Producers Council**

Spanish Roasted Pork Loin and Eggplant Purée

1 (2½-pound) boneless pork loin roast
2 tablespoons FILIPPO BERIO® Olive Oil
2 cloves garlic, minced
1 tablespoon paprika
1½ teaspoons dried oregano leaves
½ teaspoon salt
¼ teaspoon freshly ground black pepper
Eggplant Purée (recipe follows)

Place pork in large shallow glass dish. In small bowl, combine olive oil, garlic, paprika, oregano, salt and pepper. Spread over all sides of pork. Cover; marinate in refrigerator at least 2 hours or overnight.

Preheat oven to 350°F. Remove pork from refrigerator 1 hour before roasting. Place in large shallow roasting pan; insert meat thermometer into center of thickest part of pork. Roast, uncovered, 1 hour and 15 minutes or until meat thermometer registers 160°F. Transfer pork to carving board; tent with foil. Let stand 5 to 10 minutes before carving. Cut into thin slices. Serve on bed of Eggplant Purée.

Makes 8 servings

Eggplant Purée

2 small eggplants (about 1 pound each)
11 tablespoons FILIPPO BERIO® Olive Oil, divided
8 cloves garlic, unpeeled
1 egg yolk
1 tablespoon salt
2 tablespoons lemon juice

Preheat oven to 350°F. Cut eggplants in half lengthwise. Brush cut sides with 2 tablespoons olive oil. Place, cut side down, on baking sheet. In small bowl, toss garlic with 1 tablespoon olive oil. Place on same baking sheet. Bake 30 minutes; remove garlic. Bake eggplant an additional 45 minutes or until tender; cool.

Scrape flesh from eggplant into blender container or food processor. Slip off skins from garlic. Add garlic, egg yolk and salt to blender; process until smooth. While machine is running, slowly drizzle in remaining 8 tablespoons olive oil. Add lemon juice. Transfer mixture to medium saucepan. Cook over low heat 10 minutes, stirring often, until hot. *Do not boil.*

Makes about 3 cups

Stuffed Pork Loin Genoa Style

4 to 5 pound boneless pork loin roast
1¼ cups fresh parsley, chopped and divided
½ cup fresh basil leaves, chopped
½ cup pine nuts
½ cup grated Parmesan cheese
6 cloves garlic, peeled and chopped
½ pound ground pork
½ pound Italian sausage
1 cup dry bread crumbs
¼ cup milk
1 egg
1 teaspoon ground black pepper

In food processor or blender, blend 1 cup parsley, basil, pinenuts, Parmesan cheese and garlic. Set aside.

Mix ground pork, Italian sausage, bread crumbs, milk, egg, remaining ¼ cup parsley and pepper.

Place roast fat-side down on cutting board. Spread with the herb-cheese mixture; place ground pork mixture along center of loin. Fold in half; tie with kitchen string. Roast on rack in shallow baking pan at 350°F for 1½ hours. Slice to serve.

Makes 10 servings

Prep Time: 15 minutes

Cook Time: 90 minutes

Favorite recipe from **National Pork Producers Council**

Two-Onion Pork Shreds

½ teaspoon Szechuan peppercorns*
1 teaspoon cornstarch
4 teaspoons soy sauce, divided
4 teaspoons dry sherry, divided
7½ teaspoons vegetable oil, divided
8 ounces boneless lean pork
2 teaspoons red wine vinegar
½ teaspoon sugar
2 cloves garlic, minced
½ small yellow onion, cut into ¼-inch slices
8 green onions with tops, cut into 2-inch pieces
½ teaspoon dark sesame oil

*Szechuan peppercorns are deceptively potent. Wear rubber or plastic gloves when crushing peppercorns and do not touch eyes or lips when handling.

1. For marinade, place peppercorns in small skillet. Cook over medium-low heat, shaking skillet frequently, until fragrant, about 2 minutes. Let cool. Crush peppercorns with mortar and pestle (or place between paper towels and crush with hammer).

2. Transfer peppercorns to medium bowl. Add cornstarch, 2 teaspoons soy sauce, 2 teaspoons sherry and 1½ teaspoons vegetable oil; mix well.

3. Slice meat ⅛-inch thick; cut into 2×½-inch pieces. Add to marinade; stir to coat well. Let stand 30 minutes.

4. Combine remaining 2 teaspoons soy sauce, 2 teaspoons sherry, vinegar and sugar in small bowl; mix well.

5. Heat remaining 6 teaspoons vegetable oil in wok or large skillet over high heat. Stir in garlic. Add meat; stir-fry until no longer pink in center, about 2 minutes. Add yellow onion; stir-fry 1 minute. Add green onion; stir-fry 30 seconds. Add soy-vinegar mixture; cook and stir 30 seconds. Stir in sesame oil.

Makes 2 to 3 servings

Grilled Spiced Pork Tenderloin

1 whole pork tenderloin (1¼ pounds)
2 tablespoons lemon juice
1 tablespoon FILIPPO BERIO® Olive Oil
2 cloves garlic, minced
½ teaspoon ground coriander
½ teaspoon ground cumin
½ teaspoon chili powder

Place tenderloin in shallow glass dish. In small bowl, combine lemon juice, olive oil, garlic, coriander, cumin and chili powder. Spread olive oil mixture over all sides of tenderloin. Cover; marinate in refrigerator at least 2 hours or overnight, turning once. Remove tenderloin, reserving marinade.

Brush barbecue grid with olive oil. Grill tenderloin, on covered grill, over hot coals 25 to 30 minutes, or until tenderloin is juicy and barely pink in center, turning and brushing with reserved marinade halfway through grilling time.

Makes 3 to 4 servings

Two-Onion Pork Shreds

Apricot-Glazed Spareribs

- 6 pounds pork spareribs, cut into 2-rib portions
- 4 cloves garlic, crushed
- 1 cup (12-ounce jar) SMUCKER'S® Apricot Preserves
- ¼ cup chopped onion
- ¼ cup ketchup
- 2 tablespoons firmly packed brown sugar
- 1 tablespoon oil
- 1 teaspoon ginger
- 1 teaspoon soy sauce
- ½ teaspoon salt

Early in day or day ahead—in very large saucepot or Dutch oven, combine pork spareribs and garlic; cover with water. Over high heat, heat to boiling. Reduce heat to low; cover and simmer 1 hour or until spareribs are fork-tender. Remove ribs to platter; cover and refrigerate.

Meanwhile, prepare apricot glaze—combine preserves, onion, ketchup, brown sugar, oil, ginger, soy sauce and salt in small saucepan; mix well. Heat to boiling; boil 1 minute. Cover and refrigerate apricot glaze.

About 1 hour before serving—heat grill. When ready to barbecue, place cooked spareribs on grill over medium heat. Cook 12 to 15 minutes or until heated through, turning spareribs often. Brush occasionally with apricot glaze during last 10 minutes of cooking. *Makes 6 servings*

Note: The precooked spareribs can be broiled in the oven. Place spareribs on broiler pan; brush with some apricot glaze. Broil about 7 to 9 inches from heat for 7 to 8 minutes, brushing with apricot glaze halfway through cooking time. Turn ribs, brush with apricot glaze and broil for 5 to 6 minutes, brushing with apricot glaze halfway through cooking time.

Pork with Couscous & Root Vegetables

- 1 teaspoon vegetable oil
- ½ pound pork tenderloin, thinly sliced
- 2 sweet potatoes, peeled and chopped
- 2 medium turnips, peeled and chopped
- 1 carrot, sliced
- 3 cloves garlic, finely chopped
- 1 can (about 15 ounces) chick-peas, rinsed and drained
- 1 cup reduced-sodium vegetable broth
- ½ cup pitted prunes, cut into thirds
- 1 teaspoon ground cumin
- ½ teaspoon ground cinnamon
- ¼ teaspoon ground allspice
- ¼ teaspoon ground nutmeg
- ¼ teaspoon ground black pepper
- 1 cup quick-cooking couscous, cooked
- 2 tablespoons dried currants

1. Heat oil in large nonstick skillet over medium-high heat until hot. Add pork, sweet potatoes, turnips, carrot and garlic. Cook and stir 5 minutes. Stir in chickpeas, vegetable broth, prunes, cumin, cinnamon, allspice, nutmeg and pepper. Cover; bring to a boil over high heat. Reduce heat to medium-low. Simmer 30 minutes.

2. Serve pork and vegetables on couscous. Top servings evenly with currants. Garnish with thyme, if desired. *Makes 4 servings*

Pork with Couscous & Root Vegetables

Hot and Spicy Spareribs

1 rack pork spareribs (3 pounds)
2 tablespoons butter or margarine
1 medium onion, finely chopped
2 cloves garlic, minced
1 can (15 ounces) tomato sauce
⅔ cup packed brown sugar
⅔ cup cider vinegar
2 tablespoons chili powder
1 tablespoon prepared mustard
½ teaspoon black pepper

Melt butter in large skillet over low heat. Add onion and garlic; cook and stir until tender. Add remaining ingredients, except ribs, and bring to a boil. Reduce heat and simmer 20 minutes, stirring occasionally.

Place large piece of aluminum foil over coals to catch drippings. Baste meaty side of ribs with sauce. Place ribs on grill, meaty side down, about 6 inches above low coals; baste top side. Cover. Cook about 20 minutes; turn ribs and baste. Cook 45 minutes more or until done, basting every 10 to 15 minutes with sauce.

Makes 3 servings

Favorite recipe from **National Pork Producers Council**

Chili Verde

½ to ¾ pound boneless lean pork, cut into 1-inch cubes
1 large onion, halved and thinly sliced
6 cloves garlic, chopped or sliced
½ cup water
1 pound fresh tomatillos
1 can (about 14 ounces) chicken broth
1 can (4 ounces) diced mild green chilies
1 teaspoon ground cumin
1½ cups cooked navy or Great Northern beans *or* 1 can (15 ounces) Great Northern beans, rinsed and drained
½ cup lightly packed fresh cilantro, chopped
Sour cream

1. Place pork, onion, garlic and water in large saucepan. Cover; simmer over medium-low heat 30 minutes, stirring occasionally (add more water if necessary). Uncover; boil over medium-high heat until liquid evaporates and meat browns.

2. Stir in tomatillos and broth. Cover; simmer over medium heat 20 minutes or until tomatillos are tender. Tear tomatillos apart with 2 forks. Add chilies and cumin.

3. Cover; simmer over medium-low heat 45 minutes or until meat is tender and tears apart easily. (Add more water or broth, if necessary, to keep liquid level the same.) Add beans; simmer 10 minutes or until heated through. Stir in cilantro. Serve with sour cream.

Makes 4 servings

Hot and Spicy Spareribs

Sun-Dried Tomato and Pepper Stuffed Leg of Lamb with Garlic Chèvre Sauce

1 (6- to 7-pound) leg of lamb, boned and butterflied
Salt and black pepper
4½ ounces sun-dried tomatoes in oil, drained (about ¾ cup)
2 red or green bell peppers, roasted, peeled and seeded
1½ cups olive oil
2 tablespoons minced fresh rosemary
2 tablespoons minced fresh thyme
3 cloves garlic, minced
1 teaspoon TABASCO® brand Pepper Sauce
Garlic Chèvre Sauce (recipe follows)

Set lamb, skin side down, on work surface. Pat dry. Sprinkle with salt and black pepper. Arrange tomatoes and bell peppers down center of lamb. Roll up lamb; secure with kitchen string. Set in roasting pan. Whisk oil, herbs, garlic and TABASCO® Sauce in small bowl. Pour over lamb, turning to coat. Cover and refrigerate 24 hours. Preheat oven to 450°F. Place lamb, uncovered, in oven and reduce temperature to 325°F. Cook about 2 hours or 20 minutes per pound. Let stand 15 minutes before slicing. Serve with Garlic Chèvre Sauce. *Makes 8 servings*

Garlic Chèvre Sauce

1 package (4 ounces) goat cheese
½ cup light cream
3 cloves garlic, minced
¼ teaspoon TABASCO® brand Pepper Sauce
1 sprig fresh rosemary

Combine goat cheese, cream, garlic and TABASCO® Sauce in microwavable dish; stir to combine. Microwave, uncovered, at MEDIUM (50% power) 45 seconds. Let stand 5 minutes and refrigerate. Garnish with rosemary sprig.

Herb-Roasted Racks of Lamb

½ cup mango chutney, chopped
2 to 3 cloves garlic, minced
2 whole racks (6 ribs each) lamb loin chops (2½ to 3 pounds)
1 cup fresh French or Italian bread crumbs
1 tablespoon chopped fresh thyme *or* 1 teaspoon dried thyme leaves, crushed
1 tablespoon chopped fresh rosemary *or* 1 teaspoon dried rosemary, crushed
1 tablespoon chopped fresh oregano *or* 1 teaspoon dried oregano

1. Preheat oven to 400°F. Combine chutney and garlic; spread evenly over meaty side of lamb. Combine remaining ingredients in separate bowl; pat crumb mixture evenly over chutney mixture.

2. Place lamb racks, crumb sides up, on rack in shallow roasting pan. Roast in oven about 30 minutes or until instant-read thermometer inserted into lamb, but not touching bone, registers 135°F for rare or to desired doneness.

3. Place lamb on carving board. Slice between ribs into individual chops with large carving knife. Garnish with additional fresh herbs and mango slices, if desired. *Makes 4 servings*

Herb-Roasted Racks of Lamb

Greek Lamb Burgers

- ¼ cup pine nuts
- 1 pound lean ground lamb
- ¼ cup finely chopped onion
- 3 cloves garlic, minced and divided
- ¾ teaspoon salt
- ¼ teaspoon black pepper
- ¼ cup plain yogurt
- ¼ teaspoon sugar
- 4 slices red onion (¼ inch thick)
- 1 tablespoon olive oil
- 8 pumpernickel bread slices
- 12 thin cucumber slices
- 4 tomato slices

Prepare grill for direct cooking. Meanwhile, heat small skillet over medium heat until hot. Add pine nuts; cook 30 to 45 seconds until light brown, shaking pan occasionally.

Combine lamb, pine nuts, chopped onion, 2 cloves garlic, salt and pepper in large bowl; mix well. Shape mixture into 4 patties, about ½ inch thick and 4 inches in diameter. Combine yogurt, sugar and remaining 1 clove garlic in small bowl; set aside.

Brush 1 side of each patty and onion slice with oil; place on grid, oiled sides down. Brush tops with oil. Grill, on covered grill, over medium-hot coals 8 to 10 minutes for medium or to desired doneness, turning halfway through grilling time. Place bread on grid to toast during last few minutes of grilling time; grill 1 to 2 minutes per side.

Top 4 bread slices with patties and red onion slices; top each with 3 cucumber slices and 1 tomato slice. Dollop evenly with yogurt mixture. Top sandwiches with remaining 4 bread slices. Serve immediately. *Makes 4 servings*

Garlic-Dijon Butterflied Lamb

- ½ cup red wine vinegar
- ¼ cup coarse-grained mustard
- 8 cloves garlic, minced
- 2 tablespoons minced fresh rosemary
- 1 tablespoon olive oil
- ½ teaspoon salt
- ½ teaspoon black pepper
- 4 pounds butterflied boneless leg of lamb

Combine vinegar, mustard, garlic, rosemary, oil, salt and pepper in large glass dish. Add lamb; turn to coat. Cover and refrigerate at least 8 hours or up to 2 days, turning occasionally. Remove lamb from marinade; discard marinade. Grill lamb on covered grill over medium KINGSFORD® briquets about 25 to 30 minutes until thickest portion is medium-rare or to desired doneness, turning 4 times.

Makes 8 to 10 servings

Greek Lamb Burger

Marinated Grilled Lamb Chops

8 well-trimmed lamb loin chops, 1 inch thick (about 2¼ pounds)
3 cloves garlic, minced
2 tablespoons chopped fresh rosemary *or* 2 teaspoons dried rosemary, crushed
2 tablespoons chopped fresh mint leaves *or* 2 teaspoons dried mint leaves, crushed
¾ cup dry red wine
⅓ cup butter or margarine, softened
¼ teaspoon salt
¼ teaspoon black pepper
Fresh mint leaves for garnish

1. To marinate, place chops in large resealable plastic food storage bag. Combine garlic, rosemary and chopped mint in small bowl. Combine ½ of garlic mixture and wine in glass measuring cup. Pour wine mixture over chops in bag. Close bag securely; turn to coat. Marinate chops in refrigerator at least 2 hours or up to 4 hours, turning occasionally.

2. Add butter, salt and pepper to remaining garlic mixture; mix well. Spoon onto center of sheet of plastic wrap. Using plastic wrap as a guide, shape butter mixture into 4×1½-inch log. Wrap securely in plastic wrap; refrigerate until ready to serve.

3. Prepare grill for direct cooking. Drain chops, discarding marinade. Place chops on grid. Grill, on covered grill, over medium coals about 9 minutes or until instant-read thermometer inserted into chops registers 160°F for medium or to desired doneness, turning once.

4. Cut butter log crosswise into 8 (½-inch) slices. To serve, top each chop with slice of seasoned butter. Garnish, if desired. *Makes 4 servings*

Leg of Lamb with Wine Marinade

1½ cups red wine
1 onion, chopped
1 carrot, chopped
1 rib celery, chopped
2 tablespoons chopped fresh parsley
2 tablespoons olive oil
3 cloves garlic, minced
1 tablespoon dried thyme leaves
1 teaspoon salt
1 teaspoon black pepper
1½ pounds boneless leg of lamb, trimmed

Combine all ingredients, except lamb, in medium bowl. Place lamb in large resealable plastic food storage bag. Add wine mixture to bag. Close bag securely, turning to coat. Marinate in refrigerator 2 hours or overnight.

Prepare grill for indirect cooking. Drain lamb; reserve marinade.

Place lamb on grid directly over drip pan. Grill, covered, over medium heat 45 minutes or until meat thermometer inserted into thickest part of lamb registers 160°F for medium or until desired doneness is reached, turning occasionally. Brush occasionally with reserved marinade. (Do not brush with marinade during last 5 minutes of grilling.) *Makes 4 servings*

Leg of Lamb with Wine Marinade

Tantalizing CHICKEN & TURKEY

Thai Barbecued Chicken

1 cup coarsely chopped cilantro
2 jalapeño peppers,* coarsely chopped
8 cloves garlic, peeled and coarsely chopped
2 tablespoons fish sauce
1 tablespoon packed brown sugar
1 teaspoon curry powder
Grated peel of 1 lemon
1 cut-up frying chicken (about 3 pounds)

*Jalapeño peppers can sting and irritate the skin; wear rubber gloves when handling peppers and do not touch eyes. Wash hands after handling.

Place cilantro, jalepeño peppers, garlic, fish sauce, brown sugar, curry powder and lemon peel in blender or food processor; blend to form coarse paste.

Rinse chicken pieces; pat dry with paper towels. Work fingers between skin and meat on breast and thigh pieces. Rub about 1 teaspoon seasoning paste under skin on each piece. Rub chicken pieces on all sides with remaining paste. Place chicken in large resealable plastic food storage bag or covered container; marinate in refrigerator 3 to 4 hours or overnight.

Prepare coals for grill.** Brush grid lightly with oil. Grill chicken over medium coals, skin side down, about 10 minutes or until well browned. Turn chicken and grill 20 to 30 minutes more or until breast meat is no longer pink in center and thigh meat at bone is no longer pink. (Thighs and legs may require 10 to 15 minutes more cooking time than breasts.) If chicken is browned on both sides but still needs additional cooking, move to edge of grill, away from direct heat, to finish cooking. Garnish as desired.

Makes 4 servings

**To cook in oven, place chicken skin side up in lightly oiled baking pan. Bake in preheated 375°F oven 30 to 45 minutes or until no longer pink in center.

Thai Barbecued Chicken

Chicken Fajitas with Cowpoke Barbecue Sauce

SAUCE

½ teaspoon vegetable oil
⅓ cup chopped green onions
2 cloves garlic, finely chopped
1 can (8 ounces) tomato sauce
¼ cup ketchup
2 tablespoons water
2 tablespoons orange juice
1 tablespoon cider vinegar
1 tablespoon chili sauce
Dash Worcestershire sauce

FAJITAS

Nonstick cooking spray
10 ounces boneless skinless chicken breasts, cut lengthwise into 1×½-inch pieces
2 green or red bell peppers, thinly sliced
1 cup sliced onion
2 cups tomato wedges
4 (6-inch) warm flour tortillas

Combine all Cowpoke Barbecue Sauce ingredients in slow cooker. Cover and cook on HIGH 1½ hours.

Spray large nonstick skillet with cooking spray. Add chicken and cook over medium heat until browned. Reduce slow cooker heat to LOW. Add cooked chicken, bell peppers and onion to slow cooker. Stir until well coated. Cover and cook 3 to 4 hours or until chicken is no longer pink and vegetables are tender.

Add tomatoes; cover and cook 30 to 45 minutes or until heated through. Serve with warm tortillas. *Makes 4 servings*

Tandoori-Style Chicken

½ cup plain regular or lowfat yogurt
¼ cup chopped fresh mint
¼ cup A.1.® Steak Sauce
1 teaspoon paprika
3 cloves garlic, crushed
½ teaspoon ground red pepper
1 (2½- to 3-pound) chicken, cut into 4 pieces
Raita (recipe follows)

In small bowl, combine yogurt, mint, steak sauce, paprika, garlic and red pepper. Place chicken pieces in glass dish; coat with yogurt mixture. Cover; chill 1 hour, turning occasionally.

Remove chicken from marinade. Grill chicken over medium heat for 30 to 35 minutes or until done, turning occasionally. Serve with Raita. *Makes 4 servings*

Raita: In small bowl, combine ½ cup plain regular or lowfat yogurt; ½ cup diced seeded peeled cucumber; 1 tablespoon A.1. Steak Sauce; 1 tablespoon finely chopped fresh mint and 2 teaspoons honey. Cover; chill until serving time.

Chicken Fajitas with Cowpoke Barbecue Sauce

Chicken with White Beans and Spinach

¾ pound boneless skinless chicken breasts, cut in ¾-inch pieces
¼ teaspoon salt
¼ teaspoon black pepper
1 tablespoon olive oil
3 cups thinly sliced onion
4 cloves garlic, minced
2 cans (19 ounces each) white beans, such as Great Northern or cannellini, rinsed and drained
1 small dried hot pepper, crumbled *or* ¼ teaspoon red pepper flakes
¾ cup water
1 package (10 ounces) fresh spinach, washed and torn

1. Preheat oven to 425°F. Spray 2-quart casserole with nonstick cooking spray; set aside.

2. Sprinkle chicken with salt and pepper. Heat olive oil in nonstick skillet over medium heat. Add chicken; cook without stirring 2 minutes or until golden. Turn chicken; cook 2 minutes. Add onion; cook and stir until onion is crisp-tender, about 5 minutes. Add garlic and cook 1 minute.

3. Stir in beans, hot pepper and water. Cook and stir about 3 minutes. Place in prepared casserole. Cover; bake 10 minutes.

3. Meanwhile, drop spinach into pot of boiling water; cook 30 seconds or until spinach turns bright green. Remove from water with slotted spoon; drain.

4. Add spinach to bean mixture; stir gently. Cover; bake 15 minutes. *Makes 6 servings*

Olympic Seoul Chicken

2 tablespoons peanut oil
8 chicken thighs, skinned
¼ cup white vinegar
3 tablespoons soy sauce
2 tablespoons honey
¼ teaspoon ground ginger
10 cloves garlic, coarsely chopped
½ to 1 teaspoon red pepper flakes
2 ounces Chinese rice stick noodles
Snow peas, steamed
Diagonally sliced yellow squash, steamed

1. Heat oil in large skillet over medium-high heat. Add chicken to skillet in single layer. Cook 10 minutes or until chicken is evenly browned and no longer pink in center, turning once.

2. Combine vinegar, soy sauce, honey and ginger in small bowl; set aside.

3. When chicken is browned, add garlic and red pepper flakes to skillet; cook and stir 2 to 3 minutes.

4. Spoon off excess fat from skillet. Add vinegar mixture. Cover; reduce heat and simmer 15 minutes or until chicken is tender and juices run clear.

5. Meanwhile, prepare rice stick noodles according to package directions; keep warm.

6. Uncover skillet; cook 2 minutes or until sauce is reduced and thickened. Place chicken on individual serving plates; spoon sauce over chicken. Serve with rice stick noodles, snow peas and squash. Garnish as desired.

Makes 4 servings

Olympic Seoul Chicken

Forty-Clove Chicken

- 1 frying chicken (3 pounds), cut into serving pieces
- Salt and black pepper
- 1 to 2 tablespoons olive oil
- ¼ cup dry white wine
- ⅛ cup dry vermouth
- 2 tablespoons chopped fresh parsley *or* 2 teaspoons dried parsley leaves
- 2 teaspoons dried basil leaves
- 1 teaspoon dried oregano leaves
- Pinch of red pepper flakes
- 40 cloves garlic (about 2 heads*), peeled
- 4 ribs celery, sliced
- Juice and peel of 1 lemon
- Fresh herbs (optional)

*The whole garlic bulb is called a head.

SLOW COOKER DIRECTIONS

Remove skin from chicken, if desired. Sprinkle with salt and pepper. Heat oil in large skillet over medium heat. Add chicken; cook 10 minutes or until browned on all sides. Remove to platter.

Combine wine, vermouth, parsley, basil, oregano and red pepper flakes in large bowl. Add garlic and celery; coat well. Transfer garlic and celery to slow cooker with slotted spoon. Add chicken to remaining herb mixture; coat well. Place chicken on top of celery in slow cooker. Sprinkle lemon juice and peel in slow cooker; add remaining herb mixture. Cover and cook on LOW 6 hours or until chicken is no longer pink in center. Garnish with fresh herbs, if desired.

Makes 4 to 6 servings

Middle East Baked Chicken Thighs with Couscous

- 6 boneless skinless chicken thighs (about 1½ pounds)
- ¼ cup lemon juice
- 6 cloves garlic, minced
- 2 teaspoons ground cumin
- 2 teaspoons paprika
- 1 teaspoon dried thyme leaves
- ½ teaspoon ground cinnamon
- ¼ teaspoon ground red pepper
- 1⅓ cups quick-cooking couscous
- 2 medium zucchini
- ½ cup (4 ounces) crumbled feta cheese

1. Preheat oven to 425°F. Place chicken thighs in large ovenproof casserole. Combine lemon juice, garlic, cumin, paprika, thyme, cinnamon and ground red pepper in small bowl. Pour over chicken; turn to coat completely. Cover and bake 25 minutes.

2. Meanwhile, cook couscous according to package directions. Trim ends from zucchini. Slice in half lengthwise then slice thinly crosswise. Place in microwavable container; cover, vent and microwave on HIGH power 4 minutes, stirring halfway through cooking, or until crisp-tender.

3. Uncover chicken and stir. Bake, uncovered, 15 to 20 minutes or until chicken is tender and no longer pink in center. Tear chicken into pieces and mix with pan juices. Place couscous in large bowl. Spoon chicken and pan juices over couscous. Arrange zucchini around side. Sprinkle with feta cheese.

Makes 6 servings

Forty-Clove Chicken

Grilled Chicken and Vegetable Kabobs

- ⅓ cup olive oil
- ¼ cup lemon juice
- 4 cloves garlic, coarsely chopped
- ½ teaspoon salt
- ½ teaspoon lemon pepper
- ½ teaspoon dried tarragon leaves
- 1 pound chicken tenders
- 6 ounces mushrooms
- 1 cup sliced zucchini
- ½ cup cubed green bell pepper
- ½ cup cubed red bell pepper
- 1 red onion, quartered
- 6 cherry tomatoes
- 3 cups hot cooked rice

Combine oil, lemon juice, garlic, salt, lemon pepper and tarragon in large resealable plastic food storage bag. Add chicken, mushrooms, zucchini, bell peppers, onion and tomatoes. Seal and shake until well coated. Refrigerate at least 8 hours, turning occasionally.

Soak 6 (10-inch) wooden skewers in water 30 minutes; set aside.

Remove chicken and vegetables from marinade; discard marinade. Thread chicken and vegetables onto skewers.

Coat grill grid with nonstick cooking spray; place skewers on grid. Grill covered over medium-hot coals 3 to 4 minutes on each side or until chicken is no longer pink in center.

Remove chicken and vegetables from skewers and serve over rice. *Makes 6 servings*

Microwave Chicken Pot-au-Feu

- 2 boneless skinless chicken breasts, cut into 1-inch cubes (about 1¼ pounds)
- 1½ cups chicken broth
- 1 large onion, coarsely chopped
- 3 medium carrots, trimmed, peeled and cut into 2×¼-inch sticks
- ½ cup dry white wine
- 1 rib celery, sliced ½ inch thick
- 3 cloves garlic, minced
- ½ teaspoon TABASCO® brand Pepper Sauce
- 1 tablespoon cornstarch
- 1 cup peas (fresh, canned or frozen)
- ½ cup finely chopped fresh parsley *or* 2 teaspoons parsley flakes
- 1½ tablespoons fresh rosemary leaves *or* 1 teaspoon dried rosemary leaves
- ¼ teaspoon salt
- ¼ teaspoon black pepper

MICROWAVE DIRECTIONS

In 2-quart microwave-safe casserole, place chicken, broth, onion, carrots, wine, celery, garlic, and TABASCO® Sauce. Cover; microwave at HIGH 15 minutes or until chicken is no longer pink in center and vegetables are tender, stirring once. Uncover. Dissolve cornstarch in ¼ cup cooking liquid. Add to chicken mixture; stir thoroughly until blended. Add peas, parsley and rosemary. Cover; microwave at HIGH 3 minutes or until sauce has thickened. Season with salt, pepper and additional TABASCO® Sauce.

Makes 4 servings

Grilled Chicken and Vegetable Kabob

Moroccan Stir-Fry

- 4 to 6 cloves garlic, minced
- 2 teaspoons ground ginger
- 1 teaspoon ground cumin
- ½ teaspoon ground cinnamon
- Nonstick cooking spray
- 1 medium onion, chopped
- 12 ounces boneless skinless chicken thighs, cut into 1-inch pieces
- 1¼ pounds butternut squash, peeled and cut into 1-inch pieces
- 1 can (about 14 ounces) fat-free reduced-sodium chicken broth
- ½ cup raisins
- 1 medium zucchini, cut in half lengthwise and sliced crosswise
- 2 tablespoons chopped fresh cilantro
- 1 cup water
- ⅔ cup quick-cooking couscous

1. Combine garlic, ginger, cumin and cinnamon in small bowl; set aside.

2. Spray large nonstick skillet with cooking spray; heat over high heat. Add onion; cook and stir until crisp-tender and golden. Add chicken; cook without stirring 1 minute or until golden. Turn chicken; cook 1 minute more. Add spice mixture; stir 30 seconds or until fragrant. Stir in butternut squash, chicken broth and raisins; bring to a boil. Reduce heat to low; simmer, covered, 15 to 20 minutes, or until butternut squash is tender when pierced. Add zucchini. Simmer uncovered 5 to 7 minutes, until zucchini is tender. Stir in cilantro.

3. Meanwhile, place water in small saucepan over high heat; bring to a boil. Stir in couscous; cover and remove from heat. Let stand 5 minutes. Fluff couscous with fork; spoon onto serving platter. Arrange chicken mixture over couscous.

Makes 4 servings

Chicken Ribbons Satay

- ½ cup creamy peanut butter
- ½ cup water
- ¼ cup soy sauce
- 4 cloves garlic, sliced
- 3 tablespoons lemon juice
- 2 tablespoons firmly packed brown sugar
- ¾ teaspoon ground ginger
- ½ teaspoon crushed red pepper flakes
- 4 boneless skinless chicken breast halves
- Sliced green onion tops for garnish

Combine peanut butter, water, soy sauce, garlic, lemon juice, brown sugar, ginger and red pepper flakes in a small saucepan. Cook over medium heat 1 minute or until smooth; cool. Remove garlic from sauce; discard. Reserve half of sauce for dipping. Cut chicken lengthwise into 1-inch-wide strips. Thread onto 8 metal or bamboo skewers. (Soak bamboo skewers in water at least 20 minutes to keep them from burning.)

Oil hot grid to help prevent sticking. Grill chicken, on a covered grill, over medium-hot KINGSFORD® Briquets, 6 to 8 minutes until chicken is no longer pink in center, turning once. Baste with sauce once or twice during cooking. Serve with reserved sauce garnished with sliced green onion.

Makes 4 servings

Chicken Ribbons Satay

Tarragon Lemon Chicken

¼ cup all-purpose flour
Salt and freshly ground black pepper
4 boneless skinless chicken breast halves
4 tablespoons FILIPPO BERIO® Olive Oil, divided
1 large onion, chopped
1 red bell pepper, seeded and cut into strips
2 ribs celery, thinly sliced
1 cup chicken broth
1 cup dry white wine
1 tablespoon chopped fresh tarragon *or* 1 teaspoon dried tarragon leaves
3 cloves garlic, crushed
Finely grated peel and juice of 1 lemon
Lemon slices and fresh tarragon sprigs (optional)

Preheat oven to 375°F. In small shallow bowl, combine flour with salt and black pepper to taste. Coat each chicken piece in flour mixture; reserve any remaining flour mixture. In large skillet, heat 2 tablespoons olive oil over medium heat until hot. Add onion, bell pepper and celery; cook and stir 5 minutes or until onion is softened. Remove onion mixture from skillet.

Add remaining 2 tablespoons olive oil to skillet; heat over medium heat until hot. Add chicken; cook 5 minutes or until brown, turning occasionally. Add reserved flour mixture to skillet; mix well. Add chicken broth, wine, tarragon, garlic, lemon peel and lemon juice; bring to a boil. Return onion mixture to skillet; mix well. Transfer mixture to large casserole. Cover with foil. Bake 40 minutes or until chicken is no longer pink in center and juices run clear. Garnish, if desired. *Makes 4 servings*

Jamaican Grilled Chicken

1 whole chicken (4 pounds), cut into pieces *or* 6 whole chicken legs
1 cup coarsely chopped fresh cilantro leaves and stems
½ cup FRANK'S® REDHOT® Hot Sauce
⅓ cup vegetable oil
6 cloves garlic, coarsely chopped
¼ cup fresh lime juice (juice of 2 limes)
1 teaspoon grated lime peel
1 teaspoon ground turmeric
1 teaspoon ground allspice

1. Loosen and pull back skin from chicken pieces. Do not remove skin. Place chicken pieces in large resealable plastic food storage bag or large glass bowl.

2. Place remaining ingredients in blender or food processor. Cover; process until smooth. Reserve ⅓ cup marinade. Pour remaining marinade over chicken pieces, turning to coat evenly. Seal bags or cover bowl; refrigerate 1 hour.

3. Prepare grill. Reposition skin on chicken pieces. Place chicken on oiled grid. Grill, over medium to medium-low coals, 45 minutes or until chicken is no longer pink near bone and juices run clear, turning and basting often with reserved marinade. *Makes 6 servings*

Prep Time: 15 minutes

Marinate Time: 1 hour

Cook Time: 45 minutes

Jamaican Grilled Chicken

Caponata Stir-Fry

- 1 can (about 14 ounces) fat-free reduced-sodium chicken broth plus 1 can water
- 1 cup polenta or whole grain cornmeal
- 2 tablespoons minced garlic, divided
- ½ teaspoon black pepper
- ¼ cup shredded Parmesan cheese
- 1 medium eggplant, cut into 1½-inch cubes
- 8 ounces boneless skinless chicken breasts
- Nonstick cooking spray
- 1 medium onion, chopped
- 1 tablespoon olive oil
- 1 can (15 ounces) no-salt-added stewed tomatoes
- 1 small green bell pepper, diced
- 1 small red bell pepper, diced
- 2 tablespoons drained capers
- 1½ teaspoons dried Italian herbs
- 2 tablespoons balsamic vinegar

1. Spray 8×8×2-inch baking pan with nonstick cooking spray; set aside. Place broth, water, polenta, 1 tablespoon garlic and black pepper in large saucepan. Bring to a boil over high heat. Reduce to a simmer; stir 5 minutes, until polenta thickens and pulls away from side of saucepan. Fold in Parmesan cheese. Spread into prepared pan; cool.

2. Place eggplant in large microwavable bowl; cover. Microwave at HIGH 10 to 12 minutes, stirring every 3 minutes, until tender. Set aside.

3. Preheat broiler. Cut chicken into thin strips. Spray large nonstick skillet with cooking spray; heat over high heat. Add chicken; stir-fry 3 minutes or until no longer pink. Remove chicken; set aside. Add onion to same skillet; stir-fry 4 minutes or until golden. Remove onion.

4. Heat oil in same skillet. Add eggplant and remaining 1 tablespoon garlic; stir-fry 2 to 3 minutes, until golden. Add chicken, onion, tomatoes, bell peppers, capers and Italian herbs. Reduce heat to medium; simmer 4 to 6 minutes, until liquid evaporates. Remove from heat. Stir in vinegar.

5. Meanwhile, spray top of polenta with cooking spray. Broil 2 to 3 inches from heat 3 to 4 minutes or until top is golden. Cut into 4 pieces. Transfer to plates; spoon caponata mixture over top. *Makes 4 servings*

Herb Garlic Grilled Chicken

- ¼ cup chopped parsley
- 1½ tablespoons minced garlic
- 4 teaspoons grated lemon peel
- 1 tablespoon chopped fresh mint
- 1 chicken (2½ to 3 pounds), quartered

Combine parsley, garlic, lemon peel and mint. Loosen skin from breast and thigh portions of chicken quarters by running fingers between skin and meat. Rub some of seasoning mixture evenly over meat under skin, then replace skin and rub remaining seasonings over outside of chicken to cover evenly. Arrange medium-hot KINGSFORD® briquets on one side of covered grill. Place chicken on grid opposite coals. Cover grill and cook chicken 45 to 55 minutes, turning once or twice. Chicken is done when juices run clear. *Makes 4 servings*

Herb Garlic Grilled Chicken

Moroccan Spiced Chicken Bisteeyas

Nonstick cooking spray
1 pound boneless skinless chicken breasts
2 tablespoons (10 to 12 cloves) garlic, minced
2 teaspoons ground cumin
1 teaspoon ground cinnamon
½ teaspoon ground ginger
½ teaspoon black pepper
¼ teaspoon turmeric (optional)
1 medium onion, chopped
1 cup fat-free reduced-sodium chicken broth
1 cup cholesterol-free egg substitute
2 tablespoons powdered sugar
¼ cup chopped fresh cilantro
2 tablespoons lemon juice
1 teaspoon grated lemon peel
8 sheets phyllo dough
2 tablespoons margarine, melted

1. Spray medium nonstick skillet with cooking spray; heat over high heat. Add chicken; cook 3 minutes or until golden. Turn; cook 3 minutes. Remove chicken; set aside. Combine garlic, cumin, cinnamon, ginger, pepper and turmeric in small bowl; set aside.

2. Add onion to skillet; cook and stir 4 minutes or until crisp-tender and golden. Add spice mixture; stir 30 seconds or until fragrant. Add chicken broth; bring to a boil. Return chicken breasts and accumulated juices to skillet. Reduce heat to low; simmer, covered, 10 to 12 minutes or until chicken is no longer pink in center. Remove chicken; cool slightly. Simmer onion mixture, uncovered, 4 to 6 minutes, until thick but not dry. Add egg substitute; cook, stirring gently, 2 to 3 minutes, until softly set. Remove from heat. Stir in powdered sugar and cilantro. Shred chicken into large bite-size pieces with fork. Combine chicken, lemon juice and lemon peel in medium bowl.

3. Preheat oven to 375°F. Spray baking sheet with cooking spray. Unroll phyllo dough. Cover with plastic wrap or damp kitchen towel to prevent dough from drying out.

4. Lay 1 phyllo sheet on work surface. Brush with ½ teaspoon margarine; fold in half crosswise and set aside. Lay another sheet on work surface and brush with ½ teaspoon margarine. Lay folded sheets in center of work surface, long edges parallel. Place ¼ chicken in center forming 4-inch circle. Mound ¼ egg mixture on top of chicken.

5. Lift 1 corner and fold over filling. Working around circle, fold dough over filling every 2 inches or so until filling is completely encased. Move phyllo packet to prepared baking sheet. Brush surface with margarine. Repeat with remaining phyllo sheets, margarine, chicken and egg mixture to make 4 bisteeyas. Bake 20 to 25 minutes, until golden. To garnish, sift powdered sugar over tops of bisteeyas and sprinkle with cinnamon. *Makes 4 servings*

Lemon-Garlic Roasted Chicken

- 1 chicken (3½ to 4 pounds)
- Salt and black pepper
- 2 tablespoons butter or margarine, softened
- 2 lemons, cut into halves
- 4 to 6 cloves garlic, peeled and left whole
- 5 to 6 sprigs fresh rosemary
- Garlic Sauce (recipe follows)
- Additional rosemary sprigs and lemon wedges

Rinse chicken; pat dry with paper towels. Season with salt and pepper, then rub skin with butter. Place lemons, garlic and rosemary in cavity of chicken. Tuck wings under back and tie legs together with cotton string.

Arrange medium-low KINGSFORD® Briquets on each side of rectangular metal or foil drip pan. Pour in hot tap water to fill pan half full. Place chicken, breast side up, on grid, directly above drip pan. Grill chicken, on covered grill, about 1 hour or until meat thermometer inserted in thigh registers 175° to 180°F or until joints move easily and juices run clear when chicken is pierced. Add a few briquets to both sides of fire, if necessary, to maintain constant temperature.

While chicken is cooking, prepare Garlic Sauce. When chicken is done, carefully lift from grill to wide shallow bowl so that juices from the cavity run into bowl. Transfer juices to small saucepan; bring to a boil. Boil juices 2 minutes; transfer to small bowl or gravy boat. Carve chicken; serve with Garlic Sauce and cooking juices. Garnish with rosemary sprigs and lemon wedges.

Makes 4 servings

Garlic Sauce

- 2 tablespoons olive oil
- 1 large head of garlic, cloves separated and peeled
- 2 (1-inch-wide) strips lemon peel
- 1 can (14½ ounces) low-salt chicken broth
- ½ cup water
- 1 sprig each sage and oregano *or* 2 to 3 sprigs parsley
- ¼ cup butter, softened

Heat oil in a saucepan; add garlic cloves and lemon peel. Sauté over medium-low heat, stirring frequently, until garlic just starts to brown in a few spots. Add broth, water and herbs; simmer to reduce mixture by about half. Discard herb sprigs and lemon peel. Transfer broth mixture to a blender or food processor; process until smooth. Return garlic purée to the saucepan and whisk in butter over very low heat until smooth. Sauce can be rewarmed before serving.

Makes about 1 cup

Tip: The chicken is delicious served simply with its own juices, but the Garlic Sauce is so good you may want to double the recipe.

Baked Chicken and Garlic Orzo

- 4 chicken breast halves, skinned
- ¼ cup dry white wine
- 10 ounces uncooked orzo pasta
- 1 cup chopped onions
- 4 cloves garlic, minced
- 2 tablespoons chopped fresh parsley
- 1 teaspoon dried oregano leaves
- 1 can (about 14 ounces) fat-free reduced-sodium chicken broth
- ¼ cup water
- Paprika
- 1 teaspoon lemon pepper
- ¼ teaspoon salt
- 2 teaspoons olive oil
- 1 lemon, cut into 8 wedges

1. Preheat oven to 350°F. Spray large nonstick skillet with cooking spray. Heat over high heat until hot. Add chicken breast halves. Brown, meat side down, 1 to 2 minutes or until lightly browned. Remove chicken from skillet; set aside.

2. Reduce heat to medium-high; add wine. Stir with flat spatula, scraping brown bits from bottom of pan. Cook 30 seconds or until slightly reduced; set aside.

3. Spray 9-inch square baking pan with nonstick cooking spray. Add pasta, onions, garlic, parsley, oregano, chicken broth, water and wine mixture; stir. Place chicken breasts on top. Sprinkle lightly with paprika and lemon pepper. Bake, uncovered, 1 hour and 10 minutes. Remove chicken. Add salt and olive oil to baking pan; mix well. Place chicken on top. Serve with fresh lemon wedges. *Makes 4 servings*

Garlic Chicken and Corn Stir-Fry

- 4 boneless skinless chicken thighs, cut into 1-inch cubes
- 1 tablespoon soy sauce
- 4 cloves garlic, minced
- ¼ teaspoon black pepper
- ½ cup chicken broth
- ¾ teaspoon onion powder
- 1½ teaspoons cornstarch
- 2 teaspoons vegetable oil
- 1 large red bell pepper, cut into 1-inch squares
- 2 large ribs celery, cut into 1-inch slices
- 1 package (10 ounces) frozen corn, thawed and drained
- 2 cups hot cooked rice

Place chicken in small bowl. Add soy sauce, garlic and black pepper; stir to coat. Marinate 15 minutes at room temperature.

Meanwhile, stir chicken broth and onion powder into cornstarch in small bowl until smooth; set aside. Heat oil in wok over high heat. Reduce heat to medium-high. Add chicken; stir-fry 2 minutes. Add bell pepper and celery; stir-fry 2 minutes. Add corn; cook and stir 3 minutes. Stir in cornstarch mixture; cook and stir over high heat until mixture boils and slightly thickens. Serve over rice. *Makes 4 servings*

Baked Chicken and Garlic Orzo

Lemon-Ginger Chicken with Puffed Rice Noodles

Vegetable oil for frying
4 ounces rice noodles, broken in half
1 stalk lemongrass*
3 boneless skinless chicken breast halves, cut into 2½-inch strips
3 cloves garlic, minced
1 teaspoon finely chopped fresh ginger
¼ teaspoon ground red pepper
¼ teaspoon black pepper
¼ cup water
1 tablespoon cornstarch
2 tablespoons peanut oil
6 ounces fresh snow peas, ends trimmed
1 can (8¾ ounces) baby corn, drained, rinsed and cut lengthwise into halves
¼ cup chopped cilantro
2 tablespoons packed brown sugar
2 tablespoons fish sauce
1 tablespoon light soy sauce

*Or, substitute 1½ teaspoons grated lemon peel.

1. Heat 3 inches vegetable oil in wok or Dutch oven until oil registers 375°F on deep-fry thermometer. Fry noodles in small batches 20 seconds or until puffy, holding down noodles in oil with slotted spoon to fry evenly. Drain on paper towels; set aside.

2. Cut lemongrass into 1-inch pieces with utility knife, discarding outer leaves and roots.

3. Combine chicken, lemongrass, garlic, ginger, red pepper and black pepper in medium bowl; toss to coat. Combine water and cornstarch in cup; set aside.

4. Heat wok over high heat 1 minute or until hot. Drizzle peanut oil into wok and heat 30 seconds. Add chicken mixture; stir-fry 3 minutes or until no longer pink.

5. Add snow peas and baby corn; stir-fry 1 to 2 minutes. Stir cornstarch mixture; add to wok. Cook 1 minute or until thickened.

6. Add cilantro, brown sugar, fish sauce and soy sauce; cook until heated through. Discard lemongrass. Serve over reserved rice noodles.

Makes 4 servings

Lemon-Ginger Chicken with Puffed Rice Noodles

Chicken and Chili Stir-Fry

½ cup orange juice
4½ teaspoons oyster sauce
1 tablespoon minced fresh ginger
1 teaspoon cornstarch
Nonstick cooking spray
12 ounces boneless skinless chicken breasts, thinly sliced
4 ounces (about 6) jalapeño peppers,* stemmed, seeded and thinly sliced
4 ounces (about 3) poblano chili peppers, stemmed, seeded and thinly sliced
8 cloves garlic, thinly sliced
1 teaspoon olive oil
¼ cup slivered fresh basil or mint leaves
3 cups hot cooked white rice

*Jalepeño peppers can sting and irritate the skin; wear rubber gloves when handling peppers and do not touch eyes. Wash hands after handling.

1. Blend orange juice, oyster sauce and ginger into cornstarch in small bowl; set aside.

2. Spray large nonstick skillet with cooking spray; heat over medium-high heat. Add half the chicken; stir-fry 4 minutes or until chicken is no longer pink in center. Remove; set aside. Repeat with remaining chicken.

3. Add chili peppers, garlic and oil to same skillet; reduce heat to medium. Cook, partially covered, 8 minutes, stirring often, or until peppers are tender. (If skillet becomes dry and peppers stick, add 1 to 2 tablespoons water.) Return chicken to skillet. Add orange juice mixture. Cook and stir until sauce boils and thickens slightly. Remove from heat; stir in basil. Serve over rice. *Makes 4 servings*

Lemon Pepper Chicken

⅓ cup lemon juice
¼ cup finely chopped onion
¼ cup olive oil
1 tablespoon brown sugar
1 tablespoon cracked black pepper
3 cloves garlic, minced
2 teaspoons grated lemon peel
¾ teaspoon salt
4 chicken quarters (about 2½ pounds)

Combine lemon juice, onion, oil, sugar, pepper, garlic, lemon peel and salt in small bowl; reserve 2 tablespoons marinade. Combine remaining marinade and chicken in large resealable plastic food storage bag. Seal bag; knead to coat. Refrigerate at least 4 hours or overnight.

Remove chicken from marinade; discard marinade. Arrange chicken on microwavable plate; cover with waxed paper. Microwave at HIGH 5 minutes. Turn and rearrange chicken. Cover and microwave at HIGH 5 minutes.

Transfer chicken to grill. Grill covered over medium-hot coals 15 to 20 minutes or until juices run clear, turning several times and basting often with reserved marinade.

Makes 4 servings

Lemon Pepper Chicken

Roasted Rosemary-Lemon Chicken

1 whole chicken (3¼ pounds)
1 lemon, cut into eighths
¼ cup fresh parsley sprigs
4 sprigs fresh rosemary
3 leaves fresh sage
2 sprigs fresh thyme
½ teaspoon black pepper
1 can (about 14 ounces) chicken broth
1 cup sliced onion
6 cloves garlic
1 cup thinly sliced carrots
1 cup thinly sliced zucchini

1. Preheat oven to 350°F. Trim fat from chicken, leaving skin on. Rinse chicken and pat dry. Fill cavity of chicken with lemon, fresh herbs and pepper. Close cavity with skewers.

2. Combine broth, onion and garlic in heavy roasting pan. Add chicken. Bake 1½ hours or until juices run clear when pierced with fork. Remove chicken to serving platter.

3. Combine carrots and zucchini in small saucepan. Add ¼ cup water; bring to a boil over high heat. Reduce heat to medium. Cover and steam 4 minutes or until vegetables are crisp-tender. Drain vegetables.

4. Remove skewers. Discard lemon and herbs from cavity of chicken. Remove skin from chicken, if desired. Cut chicken into pieces; place in serving bowl. Remove onion and garlic from pan with slotted spoon to medium serving bowl. Add carrots and zucchini; mix well. Arrange vegetable mixture around chicken. Garnish, if desired. *Makes 6 servings*

Grilled Chicken Adobo

½ cup chopped onion
⅓ cup lime juice
6 cloves garlic, coarsely chopped
1 teaspoon dried oregano leaves
1 teaspoon ground cumin
½ teaspoon dried thyme leaves
¼ teaspoon ground red pepper
6 boneless skinless chicken breast halves
3 tablespoons chopped fresh cilantro

1. Combine onion, lime juice and garlic in food processor. Process until onion is finely minced. Transfer to resealable plastic food storage bag. Add oregano, cumin, thyme and red pepper; knead bag until blended. Place chicken in bag; press out air and seal. Turn to coat chicken with marinade. Refrigerate 30 minutes or up to 4 hours.

2. Spray grid with nonstick cooking spray. Prepare grill for direct cooking. Remove chicken from marinade; discard marinade. Place chicken on grid, 3 to 4 inches from medium-hot coals. Grill 5 to 7 minutes on each side or until no longer pink in center. Transfer to serving platter and sprinkle with cilantro. *Makes 6 servings*

Roasted Rosemary-Lemon Chicken

Thai Chicken with Basil

1 small bunch fresh basil, divided
2 cups vegetable oil
6 large shallots, coarsely chopped
5 cloves garlic, minced
1 piece fresh ginger (about 1 inch square), peeled and cut into thin strips
1 pound ground chicken or turkey
2 fresh Thai or jalapeño chilies (1 red and 1 green or 2 green), cut into thin slices*
2 teaspoons brown sugar
½ teaspoon salt
Boston lettuce leaves
Japanese mizuna, cherry tomatoes and additional Thai peppers for garnish

*Chili peppers can sting and irritate the skin; wear rubber gloves when handling peppers and do not touch eyes. Wash hands after handling.

1. Set aside 8 basil sprigs. Slice remaining basil sprigs into strips; set aside.

2. Heat oil in wok over medium-high heat until oil registers 375°F on deep-fry thermometer. Add 1 basil sprig and deep-fry about 15 seconds or until basil is glossy and crisp. Remove fried sprig with slotted spoon to paper towels; drain. Repeat with remaining 7 sprigs, reheating oil between batches.

3. Let oil cool slightly. Pour off oil, reserving ¼ cup. Return ¼ cup oil to wok and heat over medium-high heat 30 seconds or until hot. Add shallots, garlic and ginger; cook and stir 1 minute. Add chicken and stir-fry about 4 minutes or until lightly browned. Push chicken up side of wok, letting juices remain in bottom.

4. Continue to cook about 5 to 7 minutes or until all liquid evaporates. Stir in chili slices, brown sugar and salt; cook 1 minute. Stir in reserved basil strips. Remove from heat.

5. Line serving plate with lettuce. Spoon chicken mixture on top. Top with fried basil. Garnish, if desired.

Makes 4 servings

Chicken-Mango Stir-Fry

1 large (about 12 ounces) ripe mango
3 tablespoons lime juice
2 tablespoons reduced-sodium soy sauce
½ teaspoon hot pepper sauce
12 ounces boneless skinless chicken breasts
Nonstick cooking spray
4 teaspoons minced fresh ginger
3 cloves garlic, minced
1 medium red bell pepper, diced
3 green onions, thinly sliced diagonally
2 cups hot cooked white rice

1. Peel mango. Cut fruit away from pit; cut fruit into cubes. Combine lime juice, soy sauce and pepper sauce in small bowl. Slice chicken breasts crosswise into thin strips.

2. Spray large nonstick skillet with cooking spray; heat over high heat. Add chicken; stir-fry 4 minutes or until chicken is no longer pink in center. Add ginger and garlic; stir-fry 1 minute. Add lime mixture and bell pepper; stir-fry, scraping cooked bits from bottom of skillet. Add mango; stir-fry 1 to 2 minutes more, until heated through. Stir in onions. Serve over hot rice.

Makes 4 servings

Thai Chicken with Basil

Turkey Teriyaki with Grilled Mushrooms

- 1¼ pounds turkey breast slices, tenderloins or medallions
- ¼ cup sake or sherry wine
- ¼ cup soy sauce
- 3 tablespoons granulated sugar, brown sugar or honey
- 1 piece (1-inch cube) fresh ginger, minced
- 3 cloves garlic, minced
- 1 tablespoon vegetable oil
- ½ pound mushrooms
- 4 green onions, cut into 2-inch pieces

Cut turkey into long 2-inch-wide strips.* Combine sake, soy sauce, sugar, ginger, garlic and oil in 2-quart glass dish. Add turkey; turn to coat. Cover and refrigerate 15 minutes or overnight. Remove turkey from marinade; discard marinade. Thread turkey onto metal or wooden skewers, alternating with mushrooms and green onions. (Soak wooden skewers in hot water 30 minutes to prevent burning.) Grill on covered grill over medium-hot KINGSFORD® briquets about 3 minutes per side until turkey is cooked through. *Makes 4 servings*

*Do not cut tenderloins or medallions.

Butterball® Sweet Italian Sausage with Vesuvio Potatoes

- 1 package BUTTERBALL® Lean Fresh Turkey Sweet Italian Sausage
- 4 baking potatoes, cut lengthwise into wedges
- 2 tablespoons olive oil
- ½ teaspoon coarse ground black pepper
- 1 can (14½ ounces) chicken broth
- 6 cloves garlic, minced
- ½ cup dry white wine
- 6 tablespoons minced fresh parsley
- 2 tablespoons grated Parmesan cheese
- Salt

Grill sausage according to package directions. Combine potatoes, oil and pepper in large bowl. Spray large nonstick skillet with nonstick cooking spray; add potato mixture. Cook 15 minutes. Add chicken broth and garlic; cook, covered, 10 minutes or until potatoes are tender. Add wine and parsley; cook, uncovered, 5 minutes. Sprinkle with Parmesan cheese. Add salt to taste. Serve with grilled sausage.

Makes 6 servings

Preparation Time: 30 minutes

Turkey Teriyaki with Grilled Mushrooms

Turkey & Zucchini Enchiladas with Tomatillo-Green Chili Sauce

1¼ pounds turkey leg
Tomatillo-Green Chili Sauce (recipe follows)
1 tablespoon olive oil
1 small onion, thinly sliced
1 tablespoon minced garlic (5 to 6 cloves)
1 pound zucchini, thinly sliced and quartered
2 tablespoons water
1½ teaspoons ground cumin
½ teaspoon dried oregano leaves
¾ cup (3 ounces) shredded Monterey Jack cheese
12 (6-inch) corn tortillas
½ cup crumbled feta cheese
6 sprigs fresh cilantro for garnish

1. Place turkey in large saucepan; cover with water. Bring to a boil over high heat. Reduce heat to medium-low. Cover and simmer 1½ to 2 hours or until meat pulls apart easily with fork. Drain; discard skin and bone. Cut meat into small pieces. Place in medium bowl; set aside.

2. Prepare Tomatillo-Green Chili Sauce.

3. Heat oil in large skillet over medium heat. Add onion; cook and stir 3 to 4 minutes or until tender. Add garlic; cook and stir 3 to 4 minutes or until onion is golden. Add zucchini, water, cumin and oregano. Cook and stir over medium heat 10 minutes or until zucchini is tender. Add to turkey. Stir in Monterey Jack cheese.

4. Preheat oven to 350°F. Heat large nonstick skillet over medium-high heat. Place 1 inch water in medium bowl. Dip 1 tortilla in water; shake off excess. Place in hot skillet. Cook 10 to 15 seconds on each side or until tortilla is hot and pliable. Repeat with remaining tortillas.

5. Spray 13×9-inch baking pan with nonstick cooking spray. Spoon ¼ cup filling in center of each tortilla; fold sides over to enclose. Place seam side down in pan. Brush with ½ cup Tomatillo-Green Chili Sauce. Cover; bake 30 to 40 minutes or until hot. Top with remaining Tomatillo-Green Chili Sauce and feta cheese. Garnish with cilantro. *Makes 6 servings*

Tomatillo-Green Chili Sauce

¾ pound fresh tomatillos *or* 2 cans (18 ounces each) whole tomatillos, drained
1 can (4 ounces) diced mild green chilies, drained
½ cup chicken broth
1 teaspoon dried oregano leaves
½ teaspoon ground cumin
2 tablespoons chopped fresh cilantro

1. Place tomatillos in large saucepan; cover with water. Bring to a boil over high heat. Reduce heat to medium-high and simmer gently 20 to 30 minutes or until tomatillos are tender. Drain.

2. Place tomatillos, chilies, chicken broth (omit if using canned tomatillos), oregano and cumin in food processor or blender; process until smooth. Return mixture to pan. Cover; heat over medium heat until bubbling. Stir in cilantro.
Makes about 3 cups

Turkey & Zucchini Enchiladas with Tomatillo-Green Chili Sauce

Turkey Chili

- 1 pound extra-lean ground turkey breast
- 1 cup chopped onion
- 1 cup chopped green bell pepper
- 3 cloves garlic, minced
- 3 cans (14½ ounces each) chopped tomatoes, undrained
- ½ cup water
- 1 tablespoon chili powder
- 1 teaspoon ground cinnamon
- 1 teaspoon ground cumin
- ½ teaspoon paprika
- ½ teaspoon dried oregano leaves, crushed
- ½ teaspoon black pepper
- ¼ teaspoon salt
- 1 can (16 ounces) pinto beans, rinsed and drained

1. Spray large skillet with nonstick cooking spray. Cook turkey, onion, bell pepper and garlic over medium-high heat about 5 minutes or until turkey begins to brown, stirring frequently and breaking up turkey with back of spoon.

2. Stir in tomatoes; cook 5 minutes. Add water, chili powder, cinnamon, cumin, paprika, oregano, black pepper and salt; mix well. Stir in beans.

3. Bring to a boil; reduce heat to medium-low. Simmer about 30 minutes or until chili thickens. Garnish, if desired.

Makes 4 servings

Turkey Sausage Jambalaya

- 2 packages BUTTERBALL® Lean Fresh Turkey Hot Italian Sausage
- 2 tablespoons vegetable oil
- 2 cups chopped onion
- ⅔ cup chopped green bell pepper
- ⅔ cup chopped red bell pepper
- ⅔ cup chopped celery
- 4 to 6 cloves garlic, minced
- 4 cups chopped tomato
- ¼ to ½ teaspoon cayenne pepper
- ¼ teaspoon ground thyme
- 2 cans (14½ ounces each) chicken broth
- 2 cups uncooked long grain rice
- ⅓ cup chopped fresh parsley
- Salt and black pepper

Heat oil in large skillet over medium heat until hot. Brown turkey sausage in skillet 8 minutes, turning occasionally. Add onion, bell peppers, celery and garlic. Cook and stir 3 to 5 minutes. Stir in tomato, cayenne pepper and thyme. Add chicken broth; bring to a boil. Stir in rice; cover. Reduce heat to low; simmer 20 minutes. Remove from heat. Stir in parsley. Add salt and pepper to taste. Cover; let stand 5 minutes before serving.

Makes 10 servings

Preparation Time: 30 to 40 minutes

Turkey Chili

BBQ Turkey with Pineapple Relish

2 pounds boneless skinless turkey breast roast

MARINADE

- Grated peel and juice from 1 DOLE® Orange
- 2 tablespoons red wine vinegar
- 4½ teaspoons dried oregano leaves, crushed
- 1 tablespoon brown sugar, packed
- 2 teaspoons vegetable oil
- 5 cloves garlic, pressed
- Salt and pepper to taste

PINEAPPLE RELISH

- 1 DOLE® Fresh Pineapple
- 1 medium tomato, seeded and chopped
- 1 small red onion, minced
- ½ cup DOLE® Pitted Prunes, snipped
- ¼ cup chopped cilantro
- 2 tablespoons lime juice
- 1 tablespoon white vinegar
- 1 tablespoon drained capers

• Cut 4 (1-inch) slashes in both sides of turkey. Place in glass casserole dish.

• Combine marinade ingredients in small bowl. Pour over turkey. Cover; marinate in refrigerator 30 minutes or overnight, turning occasionally.

• Twist crown from pineapple. Cut pineapple in half lengthwise. Cut fruit from shells; core. Cut half of fruit crosswise into thin slices; reserve. Coarsely chop remaining fruit; combine with remaining relish ingredients in medium bowl.

• Drain turkey; heat marinade thoroughly. Place turkey 6 inches above medium hot coals. Grill, uncovered, turning and basting every 5 minutes with marinade 30 to 35 minutes or until meat thermometer registers 170°F. Let stand 5 minutes. Slice; serve with Pineapple Relish. Top with reserved pineapple. *Makes 6 servings*

Turkey Cutlets with Chipotle Pepper Mole

- 1 package BUTTERBALL® Fresh Boneless Turkey Breast Cutlets
- 1 can (14½ ounces) chicken broth
- ¼ cup raisins
- 4 cloves garlic, minced
- 1 chipotle chile pepper in adobo sauce
- 2 tablespoons ground almonds
- 2 teaspoons unsweetened cocoa
- ½ cup chopped fresh cilantro
- 2 tablespoons fresh lime juice
- ½ teaspoon salt

To prepare chipotle sauce, combine chicken broth, raisins, garlic, chile pepper, almonds and cocoa in medium saucepan. Simmer over low heat 10 minutes. Pour into food processor or blender; process until smooth. Add cilantro, lime juice and salt. Grill cutlets according to package directions. Serve chipotle sauce over grilled cutlets with Mexican polenta.*

Makes 7 servings

Preparation Time: 20 minutes

*To make Mexican polenta, cook 1 cup instant cornmeal polenta according to package directions. Stir in ½ teaspoon garlic powder, ½ teaspoon salt and 2 cups taco-seasoned cheese.

Turkey Cutlet with Chipotle Pepper Mole

Incredible Fish & Shellfish

Paella

¼ cup FILIPPO BERIO® Olive Oil
1 pound boneless skinless chicken breasts, cut into 1-inch strips
½ pound Italian sausage, cut into 1-inch slices
1 onion, chopped
3 cloves garlic, minced
2 (14½-ounce) cans chicken broth
2 cups uncooked long grain white rice
1 (8-ounce) bottle clam juice
1 (2-ounce) jar chopped pimientos, drained
2 bay leaves
1 teaspoon salt
¼ teaspoon saffron threads, crumbled (optional)
1 pound raw shrimp, shelled and deveined
1 (16-ounce) can whole tomatoes, drained
1 (10-ounce) package frozen peas, thawed
12 littleneck clams, scrubbed
¼ cup water
Fresh herb sprig (optional)

Preheat oven to 350°F. In large skillet, heat olive oil over medium heat until hot. Add chicken; cook and stir 8 to 10 minutes or until brown on all sides. Remove with slotted spoon; set aside. Add sausage to skillet; cook and stir 8 to 10 minutes or until brown. Remove with slotted spoon; set aside. Add onion and garlic to skillet; cook and stir 5 to 7 minutes or until onion is tender. Transfer chicken and sausage mixture to large casserole.

Add chicken broth, rice, clam juice, pimientos, bay leaves, salt and saffron, if desired, to chicken mixture. Cover; bake 30 minutes. Add shrimp, tomatoes and peas; stir well. Cover; bake an additional 15 minutes or until rice is tender, liquid is absorbed and shrimp are opaque. Remove bay leaves.

Meanwhile, combine clams and water in stockpot or large saucepan. Cover; cook over medium heat 5 to 10 minutes or until clams open; remove clams immediately as they open. Discard any clams with unopened shells. Place clams on top of paella. Garnish with herb sprig, if desired. *Makes 4 to 6 servings*

Paella

Baked Fish with Thai Pesto

- 1 to 2 jalapeño peppers,* coarsely chopped
- 1 lemon
- 4 green onions, thinly sliced
- 2 tablespoons chopped ginger
- 3 cloves garlic, minced
- 1½ cups lightly packed fresh basil leaves
- 1 cup lightly packed cilantro leaves
- ¼ cup lightly packed fresh mint leaves
- ¼ cup roasted peanuts (salted or unsalted)
- 2 tablespoons sweetened shredded coconut
- ½ teaspoon sugar
- ½ cup peanut oil
- 2 pounds boneless fish fillets (such as salmon, halibut, cod or orange roughy)
- Lemon and cucumber slices for garnish

*Jalapeño peppers can sting and irritate the skin; wear rubber gloves when handling peppers and do not touch eyes. Wash hands after handling.

1. Place peppers and seeds in blender or food processor.

2. Grate peel of lemon. Juice lemon to measure 2 tablespoons. Add peel and juice to blender.

3. Add green onions, ginger, garlic, basil, cilantro, mint, peanuts, coconut and sugar to blender; blend until finely chopped. With motor running, slowly pour in oil; blend until mixed.

4. Preheat oven to 375°F. Rinse fish and pat dry with paper towels. Place fillets on lightly oiled baking sheet. Spread solid thin layer of pesto over each fillet.

5. Bake 10 minutes or until fish flakes easily when tested with fork and is just opaque in center. Transfer fish to serving platter. Garnish, if desired. *Makes 4 to 6 servings*

Mock "Etouffee"

- ¼ cup butter or margarine
- 1 green bell pepper, chopped
- 1 medium onion, chopped
- 2 ribs celery, chopped
- 3 cloves garlic, minced
- 1 can (14½ ounces) diced tomatoes, undrained*
- 1 can (10¾ ounces) condensed golden mushroom soup
- 2 tablespoons FRANK'S® REDHOT® Hot Sauce
- 1 pound raw large shrimp, peeled and deveined
- ½ cup chopped parsley
- Cooked white rice or pasta (optional)

*You may substitute 1 can (14½ ounces) whole tomatoes, cut up, for diced tomatoes.

1. Melt butter in large nonstick skillet. Add bell pepper, onion, celery and garlic; cook and stir 3 minutes or until tender.

2. Stir in tomatoes with liquid, soup and REDHOT sauce. Bring to a boil. Simmer 5 minutes, stirring often. Add shrimp; simmer about 3 minutes or until shrimp turn pink, stirring occasionally.

3. Stir in parsley. Serve over rice or pasta, if desired. *Makes 4 servings*

Prep Time: 20 minutes

Cook Time: 15 minutes

Baked Fish with Thai Pesto

Baked Rockfish Veracruz

1 teaspoon olive oil
½ small onion, chopped
4 cloves garlic, minced
8 to 10 ounces tomatoes, cored and chopped *or* 2 cans (15 ounces each) whole tomatoes, drained and chopped
½ green bell pepper, chopped
½ to 1 jalapeño pepper,* seeded and minced
1 teaspoon dried oregano leaves
½ teaspoon ground cumin
¼ cup small pimiento-stuffed green olives
2 teaspoons drained capers
1 pound skinless rockfish, snapper or cod fillets
2 cups hot cooked rice

*Jalapeño peppers can sting and irritate the skin; wear rubber gloves when handling peppers and do not touch eyes. Wash hands after handling.

1. Preheat oven to 375°F. Heat oil in large nonstick skillet over medium-high heat. Add onion and garlic; cook and stir 3 minutes or until onion is tender. Add tomatoes, bell pepper, jalapeño pepper, oregano and cumin; cook over high heat, stirring occasionally, 2 to 3 minutes more. Stir in olives and capers; set aside.

2. Spray 11×7-inch baking pan with nonstick cooking spray. Place fish in single layer in pan, folding thin tail sections under to make fish evenly thick. Pour tomato mixture over fish. Cover with foil; bake 10 minutes or until fish is opaque and flakes easily when tested with fork. Serve with rice and garnish with fresh herbs, if desired. *Makes 4 servings*

Cajun Grilled Shrimp

3 green onions, minced
2 tablespoons lemon juice
3 cloves garlic, minced
2 teaspoons paprika
1 teaspoon salt
¼ to ½ teaspoon black pepper
¼ to ½ teaspoon cayenne pepper
1 tablespoon olive oil
1½ pounds shrimp, shelled with tails intact, deveined
Lemon wedges

Combine onions, lemon juice, garlic, paprika, salt and peppers in 2-quart glass dish; stir in oil. Add shrimp; turn to coat. Cover and refrigerate at least 15 minutes. Thread shrimp onto metal or wooden skewers. (Soak wooden skewers in hot water 30 minutes to prevent burning.) Grill shrimp over medium-hot KINGSFORD® briquets about 2 minutes per side until opaque. Serve immediately with lemon wedges. *Makes 4 servings*

Cajun Grilled Shrimp

Tunisian Fish with Couscous

5 medium carrots, peeled
¼ cup olive oil
2 cups chopped onions
8 cloves garlic, minced
2 tablespoons tomato paste
1 tablespoon ground cumin
1 tablespoon paprika
½ teaspoon ground cinnamon
8 cups canned chicken broth, divided
1½ pounds small potatoes, quartered
½ teaspoon salt
1 large red bell pepper, seeded and cut into ½-inch strips
1 can (15 ounces) chick-peas, rinsed and drained
6 grouper fillets (about 5 ounces each)
2 cups uncooked couscous

1. To cut carrots into julienne strips, cut lengthwise strip from carrot so that it can lie flat on cutting board. Cut carrot into 2-inch lengths. For each piece, place flat side down on cutting board. Cut lengthwise into thin strips with utility knife.

2. Stack a few strips. Cut down into ¼-inch-wide strips. Repeat with remaining carrots; set aside.

3. Heat oil in Dutch oven over medium heat; add onions and garlic. Cook and stir 3 minutes or until onions are tender. Stir in tomato paste, cumin, paprika and cinnamon. Cook 1 minute, stirring constantly.

4. Add 5 cups chicken broth to onion mixture. Increase heat to high. Bring mixture to a boil. Reduce heat to low; simmer, covered, 10 minutes.

5.Add potatoes and salt to broth; simmer, covered, 10 minutes.

6. Add carrots, bell pepper and chick-peas to broth; simmer, covered, 5 minutes.

7. Rinse fish fillets; pat dry with paper towels. Cut into 2×1-inch strips. Add fish to broth; simmer, covered, 5 to 7 minutes until fish flakes easily when tested with fork.

8. Bring remaining 3 cups broth to a boil in medium saucepan over medium-high heat. Stir in couscous. Remove from heat. Cover; let stand 5 minutes or until liquid is absorbed. Fluff with fork.

9. Spoon couscous into shallow soup plates. Top with fish and vegetables. Garnish, if desired.

Makes 6 servings

Tunisian Fish with Couscous

Grilled Shrimp Creole

½ cup olive oil, divided
3 tablespoons balsamic or red wine vinegar
3 cloves garlic, minced and divided
1½ pounds raw large shrimp, peeled and deveined
3 tablespoons all-purpose flour
1 medium green bell pepper, coarsely chopped
1 medium onion, coarsely chopped
2 ribs celery, sliced
1 can (28 ounces) tomatoes, undrained and coarsely chopped
1 bay leaf
1½ teaspoons dried thyme leaves, crushed
¾ teaspoon hot pepper sauce
1 cup uncooked white rice, preferably converted
1 can (about 14 ounces) chicken broth
1 can (15 ounces) red beans, rinsed and drained
¼ cup chopped fresh parsley

1. Combine ¼ cup oil, vinegar and 1 clove garlic in small bowl. Pour over shrimp; toss lightly to coat. Cover; marinate in refrigerator at least 30 minutes or up to 8 hours, turning occasionally.

2. For tomato sauce, heat remaining ¼ cup oil in large skillet over medium heat. Stir in flour. Cook and stir until flour is dark golden brown, 10 to 12 minutes. Add bell pepper, onion, celery and remaining 2 cloves garlic; cook and stir 5 minutes. Add tomatoes with juice, bay leaf, thyme and hot pepper sauce. Simmer, uncovered, 25 to 30 minutes or until sauce has thickened and vegetables are fork-tender, stirring occasionally.*

3. Meanwhile, prepare barbecue grill for direct cooking. While coals are heating, prepare rice according to package directions, substituting broth for 1¾ cups water and omitting salt. Stir in beans during last 5 minutes of cooking.

4. Drain shrimp; discard marinade. Place shrimp in grill basket or thread onto metal skewers. Place grill basket or skewers on grid. Grill shrimp, on uncovered grill, over medium coals 6 to 8 minutes or until shrimp are opaque, turning halfway through grilling time.

5. Remove and discard bay leaf from tomato sauce. Arrange rice and beans on 4 serving plates; top with tomato sauce. Remove shrimp from grill basket or skewers. Arrange shrimp over tomato sauce. Sprinkle with parsley.

Makes 4 servings

*If desired, tomato sauce may be prepared up to 1 day ahead. Cover and refrigerate. Reheat sauce in medium saucepan over medium heat while shrimp are grilling.

Grilled Shrimp Creole

Mediterranean Grilled Snapper

1 whole red snapper (about 4½ pounds), scaled, gutted and cavity cut open*
2 tablespoons fresh lemon juice
Salt and pepper
3 tablespoons olive oil, divided
2 tablespoons chopped fresh oregano leaves *or* 2 teaspoons dried oregano leaves, crushed
2 tablespoons chopped fresh basil leaves *or* 2 teaspoons dried basil leaves, crushed
4 slices lemon
3 whole heads garlic**
Fresh oregano sprigs (optional)
6 slices Italian bread, cut 1 inch thick
Additional olive oil (optional)

*This can be done by your fish retailer at the time of purchase or you may wish to do this yourself.

**The whole garlic bulb is called a head.

1. Prepare grill for direct cooking. Rinse snapper under cold running water; pat dry with paper towels. Open cavity of snapper; brush with lemon juice. Sprinkle lightly with salt and pepper. Combine 1 tablespoon oil, chopped oregano and basil in small bowl. Using small spatula, spread mixture inside cavity of snapper. Place lemon slices in cavity; close snapper. Secure opening by threading 6-inch metal skewer lengthwise through outside edge of cavity.

2. Cut off top third of garlic heads to expose cloves; discard. Place each head on small sheet of heavy-duty foil; drizzle evenly with remaining 2 tablespoons oil. Wrap in foil. Place packets directly on medium-hot coals.

3. Place snapper in oiled, hinged fish basket or directly on oiled grid. Grill snapper and garlic, on uncovered grill, over medium-hot coals 20 to 25 minutes or until snapper flakes easily when tested with fork, turning halfway through grilling time.

4. Soak oregano sprigs in water. Place oregano sprigs directly on coals during last 10 minutes of grilling.

5. Brush bread lightly with additional oil. During last 5 minutes of grilling, place bread around outer edges of grid to toast, about 4 minutes, turning once.

6. Transfer snapper to carving board. Carefully unwrap garlic. Peel off any charred papery outer skin. Using pot holder, squeeze softened garlic from heads into small bowl; mash to a paste with wooden spoon or potato masher, adding additional oil. Spread bread lightly with garlic paste.

7. Remove skewer from snapper. Slit skin from head to tail along back and belly of snapper; pull skin from top side of snapper with fingers. Discard skin. Using utility knife, separate top fillet from backbone; cut into serving-size pieces. Lift up tail; pull forward to free backbone from lower fillet. Cut lower fillet into serving-size pieces. Remove skin, if desired.

Makes 6 servings

Mediterranean Grilled Snapper

VERCHERIN & Cie

Shellfish Cioppino

- **12 cherrystone clams**
- **Salt**
- **4 tablespoons olive oil**
- **2 cups chopped onions**
- **2 red bell peppers, seeded and chopped**
- **1 green bell pepper, seeded and chopped**
- **8 cloves garlic, minced**
- **2 cups Fish Stock (recipe follows)**
- **2 cups vermouth or white wine**
- **2 cans (16 ounces each) tomatoes, drained and coarsely chopped**
- **1 tablespoon dried basil leaves, crushed**
- **1 teaspoon dried thyme leaves, crushed**
- **1 bay leaf**
- **¼ teaspoon red pepper flakes**
- **¾ pound raw large shrimp, peeled and deveined**
- **½ pound sea scallops**
- **8 crab claws or claw-shaped surimi**
- **Fresh bay leaves for garnish**

1. To prepare clams,* discard any clams that remain open when tapped. To clean clams, scrub with stiff brush under cold running water. Soak clams in mixture of ⅓ cup salt to 1 gallon water 20 minutes. Drain; repeat 2 more times.

2. To steam clams, place 1 cup water in large stockpot. Bring to a boil over high heat. Add clams. Cover stockpot; reduce heat to medium. Steam 5 to 7 minutes or until clams open. Remove from stockpot with tongs; set aside. Discard any clams that remain unopened.

3. Heat oil in stockpot over medium-high heat. Add onions, bell peppers and garlic. Cover; reduce heat to low. Cook 20 to 25 minutes or until tender, stirring occasionally.

4. Add Fish Stock, vermouth, tomatoes, basil, thyme, bay leaf and red pepper. Partly cover; simmer 30 minutes.

5. Add clams, shrimp, scallops and crab claws to tomato mixture. Cover; remove from heat. Let stand until shrimp turn pink and scallops turn opaque.

6. Remove bay leaf; discard. Ladle into large pasta or soup bowls. Garnish, if desired.

Makes 4 servings

*If fresh clams in shells are not available, substitute ½ pint shucked clams. Steam in vegetable steamer until firm. Omit steps 1 and 2.

Fish Stock

- **1¾ pounds fish skeletons and heads from lean fish, such as red snapper, cod, halibut or flounder**
- **2 medium onions**
- **3 ribs celery, cut into 2-inch pieces**
- **10 cups cold water**
- **2 slices lemon**
- **¾ teaspoon dried thyme leaves, crushed**
- **8 black peppercorns**
- **3 fresh parsley sprigs**
- **1 bay leaf**
- **1 clove garlic**

1. Rinse fish skeletons; cut out gills and discard.

2. Trim tops and roots from onions, leaving most of the dried outer skin intact; cut into wedges.

3. Combine fish skeletons and heads, onions and celery in stockpot or Dutch oven. Add water, lemon, thyme, peppercorns, parsley, bay leaf and

garlic. Bring to a boil over high heat. Reduce heat to medium-low; simmer, uncovered, 30 minutes, skimming foam that rises to the surface.

4. Remove stock from heat and cool slightly. Strain stock through large sieve or colander lined with several layers of dampened cheesecloth, removing all bones, vegetables and seasonings; discard.

5. Use immediately or refrigerate stock in tightly covered container up to 2 days or freeze stock in freezer containers for several months.

Makes about 10 cups

Crab and Corn Enchilada Casserole

Spicy Tomato Sauce (recipe follows), divided
10 to 12 ounces fresh crabmeat
1 package (10 ounces) frozen corn, thawed and drained
1½ cups (6 ounces) shredded reduced-fat Monterey Jack cheese, divided
1 can (4 ounces) diced mild green chilies
12 (6-inch) corn tortillas
1 lime, cut into 6 wedges
Sour cream (optional)

Preheat oven to 350°F. Prepare Spicy Tomato Sauce.

Combine 2 cups Spicy Tomato Sauce, crabmeat, corn, 1 cup cheese and chilies in medium bowl. Cut each tortilla into 4 wedges. Place one-third of tortilla wedges in bottom of shallow 3- to 4-quart casserole, overlapping to make solid layer. Spread half of crab mixture on top. Repeat with another layer tortilla wedges, remaining crab mixture and remaining tortillas. Spread remaining 1 cup Spicy Tomato Sauce over top; cover.

Bake 30 to 40 minutes or until heated through. Sprinkle with remaining ½ cup cheese and bake uncovered 5 minutes or until cheese melts. Squeeze lime over individual servings. Serve with sour cream, if desired.

Makes 6 servings

Spicy Tomato Sauce

2 cans (15 ounces each) no-salt-added stewed tomatoes, undrained *or* 6 medium tomatoes
2 teaspoons olive oil
1 medium onion, chopped
1 tablespoon minced garlic
2 tablespoons chili powder
2 teaspoons ground cumin
2 teaspoons dried oregano leaves, crushed
1 teaspoon ground cinnamon
¼ teaspoon crushed red pepper
¼ teaspoon ground cloves

Combine tomatoes with liquid in food processor or blender; process until finely chopped. Set aside.

Heat oil over medium-high heat in large saucepan or Dutch oven. Add onion and garlic. Cook and stir 5 minutes or until onion is tender. Add chili powder, cumin, oregano, cinnamon, red pepper and cloves. Cook and stir 1 minute. Add tomatoes; reduce heat to medium-low. Simmer, uncovered, 20 minutes or until sauce is reduced to 3 to 3¼ cups.

Baked Shrimp with Chili-Garlic Butter

1½ pounds medium fresh shrimp in shells
½ cup butter
¼ cup vegetable oil
8 cloves garlic, finely chopped
1 to 3 dried de arbol chilies, coarsely crumbled*
1 tablespoon fresh lime juice
¼ teaspoon salt
Green onion tops, slivered, for garnish

*For milder flavor, seed some or all of the chilies.

1. Preheat oven to 400°F. Shell and devein shrimp, leaving tails attached; rinse and drain well.

2. Heat butter and oil in small skillet over medium heat until butter is melted and foamy. Add garlic, chilies, lime juice and salt. Cook and stir 1 minute. Remove from heat.

3. Arrange shrimp in even layer in shallow 2-quart gratin pan or baking dish. Pour hot butter mixture over shrimp.

4. Bake shrimp 10 to 12 minutes until shrimp turn pink and opaque, stirring once. Do not overcook or shrimp will be dry and tough. Garnish, if desired. *Makes 4 servings*

Garlic Clams

2 pounds littleneck clams
2 teaspoons olive oil
2 tablespoons finely chopped onion
2 tablespoons chopped garlic
½ cup dry white wine
¼ cup chopped red bell pepper
2 tablespoons lemon juice
1 tablespoon chopped fresh parsley

1. Discard any clams that remain open when tapped with fingers. To clean clams, scrub with stiff brush under cold running water. Soak clams in mixture of ½ cup salt to 1 gallon water 20 minutes. Drain water; repeat 2 more times.

2. Heat oil in large saucepan over medium-high heat until hot. Add onion and garlic; cook and stir about 3 minutes or until garlic is tender but not brown. Add clams, wine, bell pepper and lemon juice. Cover; simmer 3 to 10 minutes or until clams open. Transfer clams as they open to large bowl; cover. Discard any clams that do not open. Increase heat to high. Add parsley; boil until liquid reduces to ¼ to ⅓ cup. Pour over clams; serve immediately. Garnish with parsley sprigs, if desired. *Makes 4 servings*

Garlic Clams

Grilled Swordfish with Hot Red Sauce

2 to 3 green onions
4 swordfish or halibut steaks (about 1½ pounds total)
2 tablespoons hot bean paste*
2 tablespoons soy sauce
2 tablespoons Sesame Salt (recipe follows)
1 tablespoon dark sesame oil
4 teaspoons sugar
4 cloves garlic, minced
⅛ teaspoon black pepper

*Available in specialty stores or Asian markets.

1. Spray grid of grill or broiler rack with nonstick cooking spray. Prepare coals for grill or preheat broiler.

2. Cut off and discard root ends of green onions. Finely chop enough green onions to measure ¼ cup; set aside. Prepare Sesame Salt; set aside.

3. Rinse swordfish and pat dry with paper towels. Place in shallow glass dish.

4. Combine green onions, hot bean paste, soy sauce, Sesame Salt, sesame oil, sugar, garlic and pepper in small bowl; mix well.

5. Spread half of marinade over fish; turn fish over and spread with remaining marinade. Cover with plastic wrap and refrigerate 30 minutes.

6. Remove fish from marinade; discard remaining marinade. Place fish on prepared grid. Grill fish over medium-hot coals or broil 4 to 5 minutes per side or until fish is opaque and flakes easily with fork. Garnish as desired.

Makes 4 servings

Sesame Salt

½ cup sesame seeds
¼ teaspoon salt

Heat small skillet over medium heat. Add sesame seeds; cook and stir about 5 minutes or until seeds are golden. Cool. Crush sesame seeds and salt with mortar and pestle or process in clean coffee grinder. Refrigerate in covered glass jar.

Shrimp Scampi

⅓ cup clarified butter*
4 tablespoons minced garlic
1½ pounds large shrimp, peeled and deveined
6 green onions, thinly sliced
¼ cup dry white wine
2 tablespoons lemon juice
8 large sprigs fresh parsley, finely chopped
Salt and black pepper
Lemon slices and fresh parsley sprigs, for garnish

*To clarify butter, melt butter over low heat. Skim off the white foam that forms on top, then strain clear golden butter through cheesecloth into container. Discard milky residue at the bottom of pan. Clarified butter will keep, covered, in refrigerator for up to 2 months.

Heat clarified butter in large skillet over medium heat. Add garlic; cook and stir 1 to 2 minutes or until soft but not brown. Add shrimp, onions, wine and lemon juice; cook until shrimp turn pink and firm, 1 to 2 minutes on each side. Do not overcook. Add chopped parsley; season to taste with salt and pepper. Garnish if desired.

Makes 4 servings

Grilled Swordfish with Hot Red Sauce

Tequila-Lime Prawns

- 1 pound medium shrimp, peeled and deveined
- 3 tablespoons butter or margarine
- 1 tablespoon olive oil
- 2 large cloves garlic, minced
- 2 tablespoons tequila
- 1 tablespoon lime juice
- ¼ teaspoon salt
- ¼ teaspoon red pepper flakes
- 3 tablespoons coarsely chopped cilantro
- Hot cooked rice (optional)

Pat shrimp dry with paper towels. Heat butter and oil in large skillet over medium heat. When butter is melted, add garlic; cook 30 seconds. Add shrimp; cook 2 minutes, stirring occasionally. Stir in tequila, lime juice, salt and red pepper flakes. Cook 2 minutes or until most of liquid evaporates and shrimp are pink and glazed. Add cilantro; cook 10 seconds. Serve over hot cooked rice, if desired. Garnish with lime wedges, if desired. *Makes 3 to 4 servings*

Grilled Snapper with Pesto

- 1½ cups packed fresh basil leaves
- 1½ cups packed fresh cilantro or parsley
- ¼ cup packed fresh mint leaves
- ¼ cup olive oil
- 3 tablespoons lime juice
- 3 cloves garlic, chopped
- 1 tablespoon sugar
- ½ teaspoon salt
- 4 (6-ounce) snapper or grouper fillets
- Black pepper

1. Combine basil, cilantro, mint, oil, lime juice, garlic, sugar and salt in food processor or blender; process until smooth.

2. Spread about ½ teaspoon pesto on each side of fillets. Sprinkle both sides with pepper to taste. Arrange fish in single layer in grill basket coated with nonstick cooking spray. Grill, covered, over medium-hot coals 3 to 4 minutes per side or until fish flakes easily when tested with fork. Serve with remaining pesto. Garnish with lime wedges if desired. *Makes 4 servings*

Prep and Cook Time: 20 minutes

Tequila-Lime Prawns

Curried Shrimp with Coconut Ginger Rice

Coconut Ginger Rice (recipe follows)
1 tablespoon vegetable oil
1 pound raw medium shrimp, peeled and deveined
3 cloves garlic, minced
1 cup finely chopped fresh pineapple *or* 1 can (8 ounces) crushed pineapple, drained
2 tablespoons packed brown sugar
1 tablespoon fish sauce
2 teaspoons curry powder
¼ teaspoon red pepper flakes
3 green onions, thinly sliced
Chives for garnish
¼ cup toasted coconut
¼ cup chopped roasted peanuts, salted or unsalted
¼ cup chopped cilantro
¼ cup diced red bell pepper

1. Prepare Coconut Ginger Rice.

2. Meanwhile, heat wok or large skillet over high heat. Add oil and swirl to coat surface. Add shrimp and garlic; cook and stir 2 to 3 minutes, until all shrimp turn pink and opaque. Transfer to bowl with slotted spoon.

3. Add pineapple, brown sugar, fish sauce, curry powder and red pepper flakes to wok; bring to a boil over high heat, stirring constantly. Reduce heat to medium; cook 2 minutes.

4. Stir in shrimp mixture and green onions; cook 1 minute or until shrimp are heated through.

5. Mound Coconut Ginger Rice on serving platter. Pour shrimp and sauce over rice; garnish, if desired. Serve toasted coconut, peanuts, cilantro and red bell pepper in small bowls to sprinkle on individual servings.

Makes 4 servings

Coconut Ginger Rice

3 cups water
2 cups long-grain white rice
1 cup unsweetened coconut milk
2 tablespoons sugar
2 teaspoons grated fresh ginger

Bring water, rice, coconut milk, sugar and ginger to a boil in medium saucepan over high heat. Reduce heat to low; cover and simmer 25 minutes or until liquid is absorbed. Fluff rice with fork. *Makes about 6 cups*

Curried Shrimp with Coconut Ginger Rice

Patrician Escargots

4 heads garlic, separated into cloves
½ cup olive oil
½ cup butter
1 onion, finely chopped
1 teaspoon finely chopped fresh rosemary leaves *or* ½ teaspoon dried rosemary leaves, crushed
¼ teaspoon dried thyme leaves, crushed
2 dashes ground nutmeg
Salt and black pepper to taste
24 large canned snails, drained
½ cup chopped fresh parsley
24 large fresh mushrooms
12 pieces thin-sliced white bread for serving

1. Trim off ends of garlic cloves. To loosen garlic peels, crush cloves with flat side of a large knife. Remove peels and discard.* Finely chop garlic.

2. Heat oil and butter in large skillet over medium heat until butter is melted. Add garlic, onion, rosemary, thyme and nutmeg; season with salt and pepper. Reduce heat to low. Add snails and parsley to garlic mixture. Cook 30 minutes, stirring occasionally.

3. Preheat oven to 350°F. Remove stems from mushrooms and discard.

4. Arrange mushroom caps upside down in 2-inch-deep baking dish; place 1 snail from garlic mixture in each mushroom cap. Pour garlic mixture over snails; cover with foil and bake 30 minutes.

5. Meanwhile, remove crusts from bread slices. Toast each slice and cut diagonally into 4 triangles. Serve with escargots.

Makes 4 servings

*To peel garlic cloves in microwave, place the desired number of cloves in small custard cup. Microwave at HIGH (100% power) until slightly softened, 5 to 10 seconds for 1 clove or 45 to 55 seconds for a whole head. Slip the cloves out of their skins.

Garlic Skewered Shrimp

1 pound large shrimp, peeled and deveined
2 tablespoons reduced-sodium soy sauce
1 tablespoon vegetable oil
3 cloves garlic, minced
¼ teaspoon red pepper flakes (optional)
3 green onions, cut into 1-inch pieces

Prepare grill or preheat broiler. Soak 4 (12-inch) skewers in water 20 minutes. Meanwhile, place shrimp in large plastic bag. Combine soy sauce, oil, garlic and red pepper in cup; mix well. Pour over shrimp. Close bag securely; turn to coat. Marinate at room temperature 15 minutes.

Drain shrimp; reserve marinade. Alternately thread shrimp and onions onto skewers. Place skewers on grid or rack of broiler pan. Brush with reserved marinade; discard any remaining marinade. Grill, covered, over medium-hot coals or broil 5 to 6 inches from heat 5 minutes on each side or until shrimp are pink and opaque. Serve on lettuce-lined plate. *Makes 4 servings*

Garlic Skewered Shrimp

Scallops, Shrimp and Squid with Basil and Chilies

1 pound small whole squid *or* 8 ounces cleaned body tubes (and tentacles, if desired)
8 ounces scallops
¼ cup water
2 tablespoons oyster sauce
1 teaspoon cornstarch
8 to 12 ounces raw medium shrimp, peeled
1 tablespoon vegetable oil
6 to 8 jalapeño peppers,* seeded and thinly sliced
6 cloves garlic, minced
½ cup roasted peanuts, salted or unsalted
2 green onions, thinly sliced
½ cup slivered fresh basil leaves
Hot cooked rice (optional)
Tomato wedges for garnish

*Jalapeño peppers can sting and irritate the skin; wear rubber gloves when handling peppers and do not touch eyes. Wash hands after handling.

1. Clean squid; discard head and contents of body. Set aside tubular body. Cut tentacles off head just behind eyes; remove and discard beak. Set tentacles aside.

2. Pull out and discard thin clear cartilage protruding from body. Rinse squid. Peel off and discard spotted outer membrane. Pull off side fins; set aside. Rinse well. Repeat with remaining squid.

3. Cut bodies crosswise into ⅓-inch rings; set aside. (Body rings, fins and reserved tentacles are all edible.)

4. Rinse and drain scallops. Slice large scallops (more than 1 inch across) crosswise into halves with utility knife.

5. Combine water, oyster sauce and cornstarch in small bowl; set aside.

6. To cook seafood, bring 4 cups water to a boil in medium saucepan over high heat. Add shrimp; reduce heat to medium. Cook 2 to 3 minutes or until shrimp turn pink and opaque. Remove with slotted spoon to colander.

7. Return water to a boil over high heat. Add squid; reduce heat to medium. Cook rings and fins 1 minute; cook tentacles 4 minutes. Remove with slotted spoon to colander.

8. Return water to a boil over high heat. Add scallops; reduce heat to medium. Cook 3 to 4 minutes or until opaque. Remove with slotted spoon to colander.

9. Heat oil in wok or large skillet over medium-high heat. Add jalapeño peppers; cook and stir 3 minutes or until slightly limp. Add garlic; cook and stir 2 minutes or until garlic is fragrant and peppers are tender.

10. Stir cornstarch mixture; add to wok. Cook and stir until bubbly. Add seafood, peanuts and green onions; cook and stir 2 to 3 minutes or until heated through. Stir in basil. Immediately transfer to serving bowl. Serve over rice and garnish, if desired. *Makes 4 servings*

Scallops, Shrimp and Squid with Basil and Chilies

ACKNOWLEDGMENTS

The publisher would like to thank the companies and organizations listed below for the use of their recipes and photographs in this publication.

A.1.® Steak Sauce

Butterball® Turkey Company

Del Monte Corporation

Dole Food Company, Inc.

Filippo Berio Olive Oil

Guiltless Gourmet®

The HV Company

The Kingsford Products Company

Kraft Foods, Inc.

McIlhenny Company (TABASCO® Pepper Sauce)

National Pork Producers Council

Reckitt & Colman Inc.

The J.M. Smucker Company

Index

T

V

W

Z

METRIC CONVERSION CHART

VOLUME MEASUREMENTS (dry)

1/8 teaspoon = 0.5 mL
1/4 teaspoon = 1 mL
1/2 teaspoon = 2 mL
3/4 teaspoon = 4 mL
1 teaspoon = 5 mL
1 tablespoon = 15 mL
2 tablespoons = 30 mL
1/4 cup = 60 mL
1/3 cup = 75 mL
1/2 cup = 125 mL
2/3 cup = 150 mL
3/4 cup = 175 mL
1 cup = 250 mL
2 cups = 1 pint = 500 mL
3 cups = 750 mL
4 cups = 1 quart = 1 L

VOLUME MEASUREMENTS (fluid)

1 fluid ounce (2 tablespoons) = 30 mL
4 fluid ounces (1/2 cup) = 125 mL
8 fluid ounces (1 cup) = 250 mL
12 fluid ounces (1 1/2 cups) = 375 mL
16 fluid ounces (2 cups) = 500 mL

WEIGHTS (mass)

1/2 ounce = 15 g
1 ounce = 30 g
3 ounces = 90 g
4 ounces = 120 g
8 ounces = 225 g
10 ounces = 285 g
12 ounces = 360 g
16 ounces = 1 pound = 450 g

DIMENSIONS

1/16 inch = 2 mm
1/8 inch = 3 mm
1/4 inch = 6 mm
1/2 inch = 1.5 cm
3/4 inch = 2 cm
1 inch = 2.5 cm

OVEN TEMPERATURES

250°F = 120°C
275°F = 140°C
300°F = 150°C
325°F = 160°C
350°F = 180°C
375°F = 190°C
400°F = 200°C
425°F = 220°C
450°F = 230°C

BAKING PAN SIZES

Utensil	Size in Inches/Quarts	Metric Volume	Size in Centimeters
Baking or Cake Pan (square or rectangular)	8×8×2	2 L	20×20×5
	9×9×2	2.5 L	23×23×5
	12×8×2	3 L	30×20×5
	13×9×2	3.5 L	33×23×5
Loaf Pan	8×4×3	1.5 L	20×10×7
	9×5×3	2 L	23×13×7
Round Layer Cake Pan	8×1½	1.2 L	20×4
	9×1½	1.5 L	23×4
Pie Plate	8×1¼	750 mL	20×3
	9×1¼	1 L	23×3
Baking Dish or Casserole	1 quart	1 L	—
	1½ quart	1.5 L	—
	2 quart	2 L	—

THE LEGEND OF NUCOR CORPORATION

THE LEGEND OF NUCOR CORPORATION

JEFFREY L. RODENGEN

Also by Jeff Rodengen

The Legend of Chris-Craft

IRON FIST: *The Lives of Carl Kiekhaefer*

Evinrude-Johnson and The Legend of OMC

Serving The Silent Service: The Legend of Electric Boat

The Legend of Dr Pepper/Seven-Up

The Legend of Honeywell

The Legend of Briggs & Stratton

The Legend of Ingersoll-Rand

The Legend of Stanley: 150 Years of The Stanley Works

The MicroAge Way

The Legend of Halliburton

The Legend of York International

The Legend of Amdahl

The Legend of AMD

The Legend of Applied Materials

The Legend of Echlin

The Legend of Goodyear: The First 100 Years

The Legend of AMP

The Legend of Cessna

The Legend of Pfizer

Publisher's Cataloging in Publication
Prepared by Quality Books Inc.

Rodengen, Jeffrey L.
The legend of Nucor Corporation /Jeffrey L. Rodengen.
p. cm.
Includes bibliographical references and index.
ISBN 0-945903-36-7

1. Nucor Corporation (Firm) 2. Steel industry and trade–United States. I. Title

HD9519.N8R64 1997 338.7'672'0973
QBI97-40259

GM Corporation Media Archives used with permission.

WRITE STUFF®

Write Stuff Enterprises, Inc.

1515 Southeast 4th Avenue • Fort Lauderdale, FL 33316
1-800-900-Book (1-800-900-2665) • (954) 462-6657

Library of Congress Catalog Card Number 96-61248
ISBN 0-945903-36-7

Completely produced in the United States of America
10 9 8 7 6 5 4 3 2

TABLE OF CONTENTS

When he conceived the design of the first Oldsmobile in the late 1800s, Ransom E. Olds could never have guessed that his venture into automobile manufacturing would lead to the growth of a state-of-the-art, world-class steel company.

But he surely would have appreciated the business philosophy and practices of Nucor. The company's commitment to egalitarian principles, dedication to quality at a fair price, and willingness to assume risk resemble the days when Olds tried, unsuccessfully, to convince his stockholders to build a good, low-priced car for the common man.

Here the resemblance ends, for Nucor continues to succeed as it marches toward becoming the nation's number one steel producer. The amazing thing about Nucor's success is that it is so simple: give employees a stake in the company's growth; focus on the business at hand; keep red tape and bureaucracy to a bare minimum.

While many other companies waste energy on internal politics, Nucor continues to make money by making steel and steel products. Revenues of $3.6 billion in 1996 prove the soundness of these ideals. Chairman F. Kenneth Iverson, who relinquished the post of chief executive officer in 1996, although he remains chairman, continues to be the best example of the principles he set down when he was appointed president of then-Nuclear Corporation of America in 1965: he doesn't mind answering his own phone.

In 1968, Iverson took on a huge gamble when Nuclear Corporation built its first minimill, essentially taking on both Big Steel and foreign steel at the same time. To achieve maximum efficiency, he elected to adapt technology developed outside the United States to Nuclear Corporation's needs. The result was the first three-high jumping mill to be built in the Western Hemisphere.

Working through the inevitable customization in such a project, the minimill proved to be the shot across the bow for Big Steel, which would soon find itself suffering from foreign competition in the 1980s, while Nucor reaped profits.

But more important than cutting-edge technology are the workers who use that technology. A unique bonus system links productivity directly to paycheck. Managers do not need to prod employees to improve performance and efficiency; they are self-inspired. Supervisors have the task of providing the tools and the environment. The rest is left up to the workers, who frequently find ingenious ways to boost productivity. Executives at Nucor's headquarters do not expect to be consulted before many of these ideas are implemented. In fact, the entire corporation runs with an executive staff of only 23.

The challenge for Nucor is — and always has been — to maintain this esprit de corps. CEO John Correnti knows that as Nucor grows, the risk of creating a cumbersome bureaucracy also grows. To combat this, Correnti insists on visiting every plant at least twice a year, to "shake everyone's hand and shoot the breeze. I want them to know if they have a problem, they can pick up the phone or write a letter and communicate with someone who is not a nameless, faceless stranger who's pulling the strings."

Correnti and all of the workers at Nucor know that they can lay the wreath of their company's success at their own feet. And the company as a whole will continue to follow the road to its inevitable place as the nation's number one steelmaker.

ACKNOWLEDGMENTS

RESEARCHING, WRITING and publishing *The Legend of Nucor* would not have been possible without the assistance and cooperation of many people.

The development of historical timelines and a large portion of the archival research was accomplished by my hard-working research assistant, Gina King. Her careful research made it possible to publish much new and fascinating information about the origins and evolution of this truly unique organization.

The candid insights of Nucor executives, both current and retired, were of particular importance to the project. I am especially grateful to Chairman F. Kenneth Iverson, Vice Chairman, President and Chief Executive Officer John Correnti and Vice Chairman and Chief Financial Officer Samuel Siegel for sharing so much of their valuable time with me and my staff.

Other executives and retirees who took time from their busy schedules to assist include Terry S. Lisenby, vice president and corporate controller; James M. Coblin, general manager of personnel services; H. David Aycock, who retired from Nucor in 1991 as president and chief operating officer; John Doherty, vice president in charge of engineering; Joe Urey, Nucor's advertising account representative since 1971; Richard Giersch, former assitant treasurer for Nuclear; Ernest Delaney, former outside counsel for Nucor; and his son, Ernest Delaney III, current outside counsel for Nucor. Rod Hernandez of the V. David Joseph Company also provided valuable insights.

Nucor's general managers, with "the best damn job in the world," were especially helpful and interesting. They include: Joseph A. Rutkowski, Jr., vice president and general manager of Nucor Steel — South Carolina; John J. Ferriola, general manager of Nucor Steel — Nebraska; Sam Huff, vice president and general manager of Nucor Steel — Texas; A. Jay Bowcutt, vice president and general manager of Nucor Steel — Utah; Larry A. Roos, vice president and general manager of Nucor Steel — Indiana; D. Michael Parrish, vice president and general manager of Nucor Steel — Arkansas; Rodney B. Mott, vice president and general manager of Nucor Steel — Berkeley County; Hamilton Lott, vice president and general manager of Vulcraft — South Carolina; Donald N. Holloway, vice president and general manager of Vulcraft — Nebraska; James E. Campbell, vice president and general manager of Vulcraft — Alabama; James R. Darsey, general manager, Vulcraft — Texas; James W. Ronner, vice president and general manager, Vulcraft — Indiana; Ladd R. Hall, vice president and general manager of Vulcraft — Utah; Jerry V. DeMars, vice president and general manager of Nucor Fastener — Indiana; Rick Campbell, plant manager, Nucor Fastener — Arkansas; Doug Jellison, plant manager, Nucor Bearing Products; Harry R. "Bob" Lowe, vice president and general manager, Nucor Building Systems — Indiana; T.W. "Bill" Baugh III, former plant manager of Nucor Wire; Daniel R. DiMicco, vice president and general manager of Nucor-Yamato Steel Company; and Gus Hiller, general manager of Nucor Iron Carbide.

Other Nucor employees and retirees who provided valuable insights include: Hank Carper of the Cold Heading Department at Nucor Fastener; David Chase, department manager at Nucor Steel — Arkansas; Michael Dunn, casting supervisor at Nucor Steel — Texas; Robert Foster, former inspector at Vulcraft — Alabama; Gene Harris, supervisor at Vulcraft — Indiana; Wally Hill, railroad yard supervisor at Nucor Steel — Nebraska; and Reginald Kercelus, shift superintendent at Nucor Iron Carbide; and LeRoy Prichard, manager of New Steel Technology. Cevyn Meyer of Vulcraft — South Carolina was kind enough to give me a tour of the facility.

Madge DeFosset, the widow of Vulcraft founder Sanborn Chase, was very generous with her time, as was Mabel Bristow, who began working at Vulcraft in 1946.

Valuable insights were also provided by Betsy Liberman, secretary and receptionist, who has been with the company since 1967, and Rose Daniel, who joined the company in 1966.

Cornelia Wells, executive secretary to F. Kenneth Iverson, was unfailingly kind and helpful.

Both the GM Media Archives and *Iron & Steel Maker* magazine provided additional images for the book.

Finally, a very special word of thanks to the staff at Write Stuff Enterprises, Inc., including Project Coordinator Karine N. Rodengen, Executive Assistants Bonnie Bratton and Dana Gierak, Executive Editor Karen Nitkin, Associate Editor Alex Lieber, Creative Director Kyle Newton, Art Directors Sandy Cruz and Jill Apolinario, Production Manager Fred Moll, Marketing and Sales Manager Christopher J. Frosch, Bookkeeper and Office Manager Marianne Roberts, and Logistics Specialist Rafael Santiago.

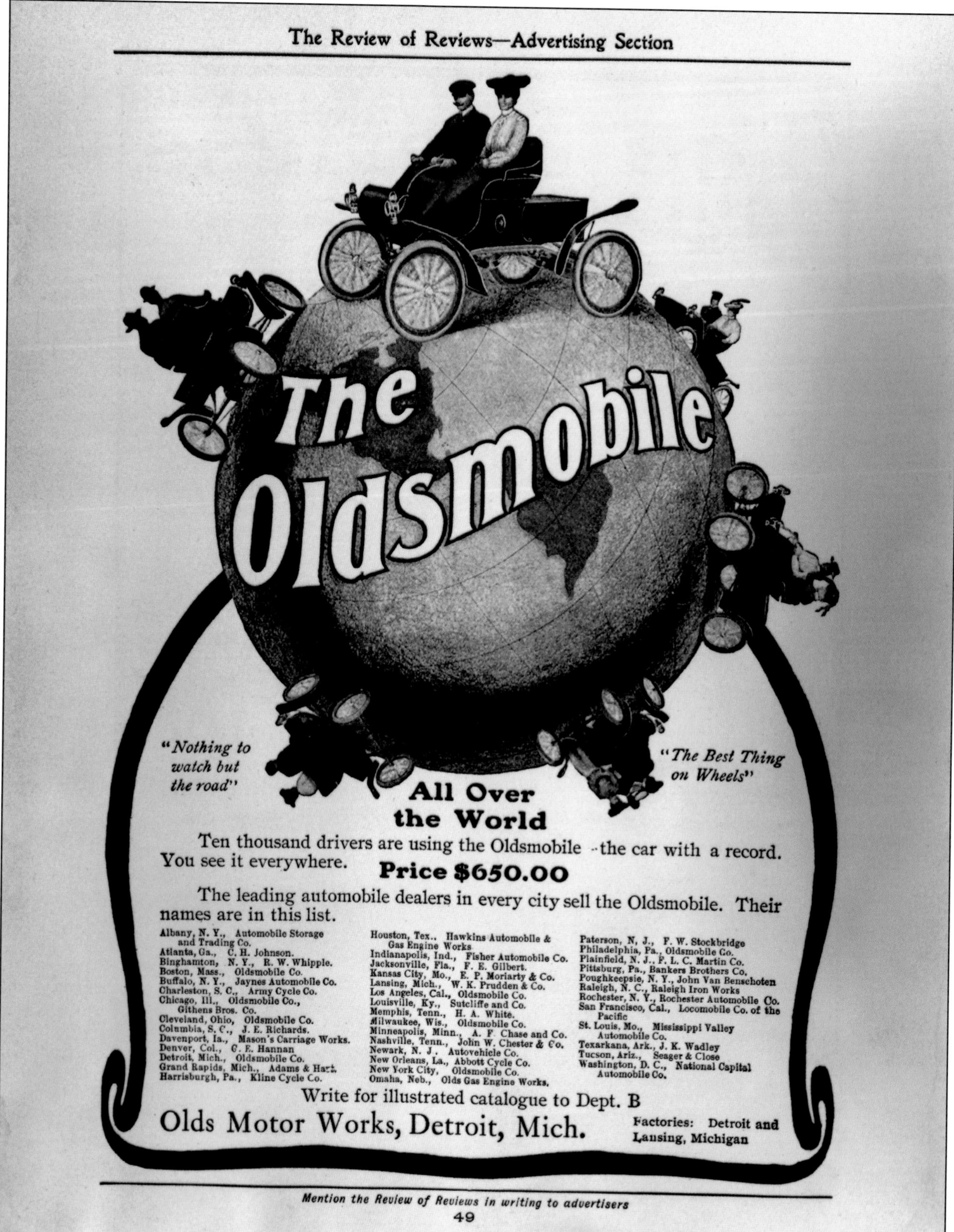

Touted as "The Best Thing on Wheels," the Oldsmobile rapidly gained a loyal following. The car company would eventually evolve into Nucor. (Photo courtesy of GM Media Archives.)

CHAPTER ONE

OLDSMOBILE

1886–1960

"Get a horse!"

— Shouted to one of the first
Oldsmobile drivers, 1901[1]

NUCOR'S STORY BEGINS in the workshop of Ransom E. Olds, namesake and inventor of among the most recognized automobiles in history, the Oldsmobile. From the Olds Motor Works in Lansing, Michigan, Nucor evolved through several different enterprises before its transformation into one of the largest steel manufacturers in the United States.

In 1886, Ransom Eli Olds took his first trip on a three-wheeled "land locomotive," then described in the popular press as the horseless carriage. Inspired by the experience, and convinced there was room for improvement in the newly developed internal combustion engine, Olds worked for years tinkering with engines in his father's machine shop, which produced stationary gas engines. His hard work paid off in 1891 when Olds was awarded a patent for a steam-powered engine. The engine ignited gasoline to heat steam, which in turn drove the pistons. Two years later he sold a steam-powered vehicle to the Francis Times Company of London for $400, probably the first American-made automobile to be shipped abroad.[2]

Olds was convinced that a bright and profitable future belonged to this novel method of transportation. By 1897, he was manufacturing light, gasoline-powered automobiles that he called "Oldsmobiles."[3] The cars were surprisingly reliable on the rough, unpaved roads of Lansing and the surrounding countryside. With backing from investors, Olds launched the Olds Gasoline Engine Works to mass-produce his vehicles for a quickly growing market. Unfortunately, the actual number of vehicles built is believed to be between four and six. A beautiful example of these four-passenger vehicles can be viewed at the Smithsonian Institution in Washington, D.C.[4]

In 1899, the company was reorganized, renamed Olds Motor Works, and moved to Detroit. Although Ransom Olds continued to secure new patents for the company, he was by then simply a minority shareholder. Ransom and his father, Pliny Olds, controlled only 7,625 shares of 35,000 issued.[5]

The prolifically inventive Olds secured patents for an electric ignitor for gas engines, a pneumatic cushion tire and an improved clutch mechanism. But his greatest invention was probably the Oldsmobile curved dash runabout, introduced in 1900. The car weighed 650 pounds and was powered by a one-cylinder, four-horsepower horizontal

Ransom E. Olds quickly grasped that the future would soon belong to the automobile. (Photo courtesy of GM Media Archives.)

Packed with enough spare parts to virtually build another engine, this early Oldsmobile Runabout was taken on a cross-country trip by a young Roy Chapin in 1901. (Photo courtesy of GM Media Archives.)

engine. Drivers had the luxury of two forward speeds, reverse, and a five-gallon fuel capacity.

The car was an international hit when it debuted in 1900. The Queen of Italy had one imported, as did Sir Thomas Lipton of Great Britain.[6] The Runabout proved its sturdiness when it traveled from Detroit to New York in the autumn of 1901 as part of a publicity stunt. Packed with spare parts, the vehicle was driven by a 21-year-old employee named Roy Chapin, who maintained the dizzying speed of 10 miles an hour during the eight-day trip.[7] Harassed by mule drivers who continually shouted, "Get a horse!" at the young man, Chapin proved that an automobile could — someday — become a practical vehicle for long-distance travel.[8]

Within two years of this feat, some 3,000 Oldsmobiles had been sold and annual sales were a respectable $2.3 million.[9] In order to meet the increasing demand, Ransom Olds searched for a more efficient way to manufacture. He hit upon an idea to move the vehicles along wooden platforms that were supported by rolling casters as workers attached the various components. His men helped to devise the system that was later adopted and modified by Henry Ford: the mass production assembly line.[10] Soon, the Olds Motor Works

1886: Ransom E. Olds takes his first trip in the "horseless carriage."

1893: Olds sells a steam-powered car, possibly America's first automobile export.

1897: First Oldsmobile is sold.

1899: The Olds Gasoline Works is reorganized into Olds Motor Works.

Henry Ford is often credited with developing the assembly line process. But it was Ransom Olds who pioneered many of the methods, which were later adopted by Ford. (Photo courtesy of GM Media Archives.)

1905: Frustrated with stockholders, Olds leaves to form Reo Motor Car Company.

1908: Without Olds, Olds Motor Works founders, and is bought by General Motors.

1938: Reo company files bankruptcy.

1955: Reo's assets merged with another company. Nuclear Corporation of America, Inc. is formed.

became the largest automobile manufacturer in the United States.

Although the car was a success, Olds soon became embroiled in a dispute with one of the principal stockholders. Olds wanted to increase the line of the low-priced automobiles, which in just three years of production had increased capital stock from $350,000 to $2 million.[11] The stockholders and company officers wanted to branch into more expensive cars for the very rich.

Frustrated, Olds sold his interest in the company in 1904. When he left, he took a small fortune and a large reputation with him. But he left behind something very valuable: the Oldsmobile name. When he tried to take it with him, he was threatened with a lawsuit. So instead he formed a new company using his initials, calling it the Reo Motor Car Company. Once again, Olds began to produce sporty, low-priced cars for the public. His new car, the Reo, was introduced in 1905 and was an immediate hit. Heavier than the Oldsmobile, the car sported a hooded bonnet and a new method of navigation: the steering wheel, which replaced the tiller steering bar that was in popular use. The car could accommodate five passengers and was priced at $1,250. Demand was so high that Olds, who started out with 150 men, soon had 2,000 employees turning out vehicles from his innovative assembly line process.[12] Meanwhile, the Olds Motor Works had foundered without Ransom Olds. In 1908 it was sold to newly formed General Motors, which continues to produce the Oldsmobile to this day.

In 1910, Ransom Olds embarked on another lasting venture, the production of a line of commercial trucks soon known as the Reo Speedwagon. Two types of Reo Speedwagons were built, a lightweight delivery vehicle that sold for $600, and a 1,500-pound truck that sold for $750.[13]

Above: In 1905, the Reo introduced the steering wheel as a way to steer, a revolutionary idea at the time. (Photo courtesy of GM Media Archives.)

Right: A Reo Speedwagon, probably from the 1920s. Following a dispute with Oldsmobile stockholders, Olds started the new venture in 1910. (Photo courtesy of GM Media Archives.)

The vehicle also inspired the name of a rock group in 1971, R.E.O. Speedwagon, known for such hits as "Take It On The Run," and "Keep On Loving You."

In 1915, Olds stepped down as general manager of Reo Motors, although he would remain president until 1923. Richard H. Scott, the factory superintendent, was named the new general manager. Reo became a leading innovator within the automobile industry, producing the first commercial vehicle to incorporate electric lights, an electric starter and pneumatic tires. The company was also the first to install constant mesh transmissions, chrome nickel engine blocks, dry-disc clutches, internal hydraulic brakes, automatic transmissions and aluminum alloy pistons. Reo was even the first to standardize left-hand drive.[14]

Reo manufactured motor cars through the middle of the 1920s. While retaining a seat on the board of directors, Olds resigned as president of Reo in 1923, turning his attention toward real estate speculation. He did not prosper, and in order to pay his bills was forced to sell off most of his assets in Reo.[15]

On October 29, 1929, the stock market crashed, ushering in the Great Depression of the 1930s, nearly destroying Reo Motors. Olds once again attempted to gain control of the company he founded by proposing that the company build the least expensive car on the market, one affordable to the struggling masses during the Depression. The board of directors demurred, and consequently Olds resigned from the board. He died on August 26, 1950, at the age of 86.

Metamorphosis

In December 1938, Reo filed for bankruptcy. A reorganization plan was filed by a trustee, approved by the stockholders and creditors, and confirmed by the courts within a year. Reo Motors, Inc. succeeded the Reo Motor Car Company in early 1940, and the company began restructuring with a $2 million capital loan. World War II provided the company with its biggest boost in years, as defense contracts poured in for Reo's trucks. Sales increased from $3.2 million in 1940 to a peak of $156.1 million in 1952. Additional defense contracts continued during the Korean War. When the conflict ended, so did Reo Motors, which owed 75 percent of its total sales from defense contracts. Production of Reo trucks rapidly declined in the postwar years.[16]

At the end of 1954, Reo Motors, Inc. sold off its assets to a subsidiary of Bohn Aluminum and Brass Corporation for the sum of $16.5 million. Reo Motors, now little more than a shell of its former self, once again changed its name, this time to the Reo Holding Corporation. The board of directors announced that the company would distribute $16.5 million in cash to stockholders and then liquidate its assets. Ten percent of the common stock was sold to TelAutograph, Inc., making that company its largest shareholder. TelAutograph opposed the complete liquidation of Reo Holding, favoring instead a merger of Reo Holding with one of TelAutograph's affiliates, Nuclear Consultants, Inc. of St. Louis, Missouri.[17]

TelAutograph had discovered that Reo had a hidden asset on its books, a $3 million loss that the company had sustained when it had sold its trucking business. TelAutograph wanted to capitalize on this loss to seek a tax advantage. In September 1955, TelAutograph initiated a proxy fight with Reo. The battle was short and TelAutograph emerged victorious, gaining six of the seven seats on Reo's board of directors, and forcing Reo into a

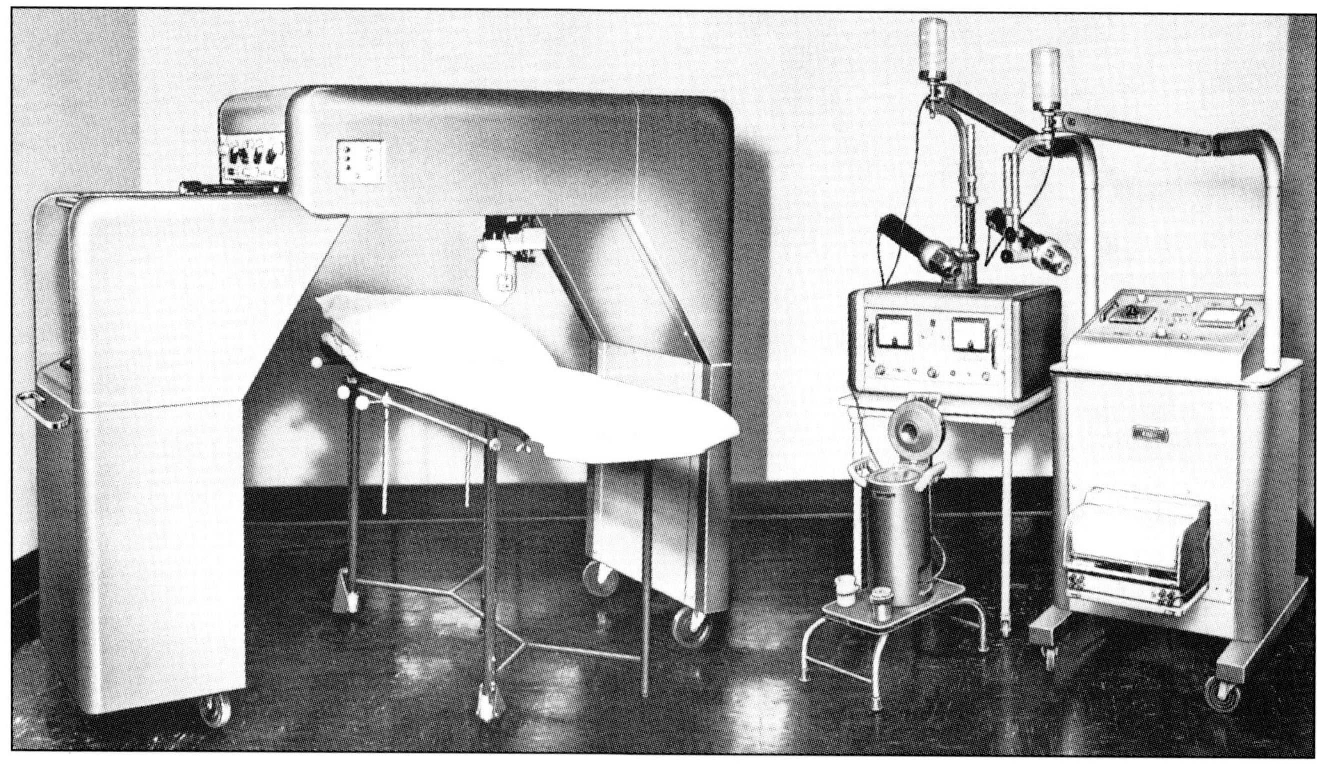

Straying far from its original product, Reo merged with Nuclear Consultants to begin supplying hospitals with nuclear-related equipment such as this mediscanner system.

merger with Nuclear Consultants, Inc.[18] According to the final proxy report, TelAutograph emerged in control of the new company with more than 292,000 shares of stock.

Nuclear Consultants, Inc. had been incorporated in St. Louis, Missouri, in 1950. Five years later, it would have net earnings of $22,338. The company had been somewhat vaguely formed to capitalize on the new possibilities of nuclear power. Its charter was to develop nuclear products and to offer consulting services to professions and industry. Eighty-five hospitals retained Nuclear for consulting work. Working with the medical profession, Nuclear Consultants offered a program that provided hospitals and physicians with radiation detection equipment, installation, and technical training. George M. Szabad, the secretary of Reo Holding Corporation's board of directors, informed stockholders on August 29, 1955, that a merger of Reo with Nuclear Consultants would enable the ailing corporation to move into a new, profitable direction.[19]

Nuclear Corporation of America

The result was a new company, renamed Nuclear Corporation of America, Inc. on October 7, 1955. Three days later, Nuclear's stock was admitted for trading on the American Stock Exchange in a glittering media presentation.

Nuclear Corporation was born in a sunny era of peace and prosperity. But it was also a time of deep fears. In 1945, Americans had used the first atomic bombs to bring an end to World War II. With the war over and the United States and the Soviet Union locked in the growing Cold War, Americans were terrified that the power of this new weapon would be unleashed against them. Bomb shelters were built in backyards and stocked with bottled water and canned foods. Families staged late-night drills, timed with a stopwatch, to see how long it would take them to reach safety in the terrifying event of a nuclear war. But nuclear energy also had peacetime applications, and Nuclear Corporation was eager to capitalize on this exciting and emerging new industry.

In a buzz of publicity, the company first used nuclear energy to power stock tickers at the American Stock Exchange in New York on October 10, 1955, when it recorded the first sale of Nuclear's stock. Radioactivity from a slug of cobalt 60 set the electronic circuit in action, temporarily replacing human energy at the keyboard of the Stock Exchange's ticker desk. Dr. Kennard Morgenstern, vice president of Nuclear Corporation, brought the cobalt 60 to the exchange encased in a lead jacket. Exchange President Edward T. McCormick manned a scintillation counter, an ultra-sensitive device similar to a Geiger counter, which, in turn, energized an electronic scaler. When enough energy was stored up, five magnetic coils were tripped, one at a time, thus depressing five keys on the Exchange's ticker keyboard. The atomic-activated quotes then went out on 959 stock tickers in 163 cities in the United States and Canada. The stunt seemed to work; investment in the company's stock grew.[20]

A Strategy of Acquisition

Nuclear Corporation's first president was Sam Norris, who had previously been president of Long Island-based Amperex Electronic Corporation, a unit of Philips' Incandescent Lamp Works, Ltd., in the Netherlands.[21] Norris's strategy was to purchase companies involved in atomic energy, nuclear development and electronics. However, nobody in the company seemed to give much thought to the overall direction of the company. His first purchase, in December 1955, was of Radioactive Products, Inc., of Ferndale, Michigan, which had been organized in 1948 as an industry and government consulting firm.

Two months later, Nuclear acquired Central Sales & Manufacturing Corporation, manufacturers of electron tubes; Garrett Engineering Company, Inc., of Denville, New Jersey; and Research Chemicals, Inc., dealers in rare oxides and metals, located in Burbank, California.

In March 1956, Nuclear acquired Isotope Specialties Co., Inc., also of Burbank, California, which manufactured radioactive isotopes, tagged biochemicals and radioactive handling equipment and techniques.[22] In March 1958, Nuclear merged these companies into a new Delaware corporation, called Nuclear Corporation of America.[23]

By January 1959, Nuclear's management had dissolved all subsidiary companies and organized them in divisions that worked out of two operating locations. Nuclear sold the radiopharmaceutical and x-ray divisions. That left the company with four divisions: the Rare Earth Division, Isotope Specialties Division, Electron Tube Division and Instrument Division.

President Norris assured stockholders in the 1958 Annual Report that the company was "in a position to play a noteworthy role in nuclear-electronics technology."[24] The company began to advertise itself as Nucor in its brochures, although its official name remained Nuclear Corporation of America.

Nuclear Corporation wanted to design new devices to "keep the United States ahead in the atomic age." The company emphasized to stockholders that its products would safely harness nuclear energy for "peaceful commercial purposes." Several of the devices being developed were to be manufactured as "aids to industrial production" and to "make nuclear research itself safer." One of those products was a Dosimeter. Powered by flashlight batteries, the instrument was intended to promote safety by providing an indication proportional to human tissue sensitivity to detect fast neutrons associated with nuclear radiation.[25]

Between 1956 and 1960, sales increased from $1.6 million to $2.1 million, but losses also grew, from $355,293 in 1956 to $628,977 in 1960.[26] If the first five years of Nuclear Corporation of America's existence seemed to indicate confusion as to the exact purpose of the enterprise, the beginning years of the 1960s would only add to this feeling. A change in management was imminent, which would create further disruption within the young company.

SCALER/RATEMETER DC-1900

- Fast Decade Scaler - 2.5 Microseconds
- Preset Time And Preset Count Features
- 1 Millivolt Sensitivity
- Precision Discriminator
- Scaler/Ratemeter Provision

The Model DC-1900 combines a fast resolving time with the stability required when studying living organisms, chemical reactions, or tracer phenomena. See data sheet on DC-1900 for complete details and specifications.

SCINTILLATION PROBE MODEL CS-100
A Directional Scintillation Probe For Medical Localizations

This fine directional scintillation probe consists of a shielded crystal and collimator assembly attached to a basic detection unit. Specifically designed for medical localizations, the CS-100 has proven superior in pinpointing tracer amounts of radioactivity, following the movement of radio-tagged compounds, delineating contours, etc. It offers a high acceptance-to-shielded zone ratio, maximum shielding per unit weight and a 1″ x 1″ NaI (Tl) crystal. This shielded crystal is provided with a hemispherical collimator which is completely removable by means of its simple bayonet connector. With the collimator removed, the crystal has a sensitive angle of 140°. With the collimator in place, the probe is highly directional. The nose section of the collimator has a ¾″ diameter aperture and is also removable.

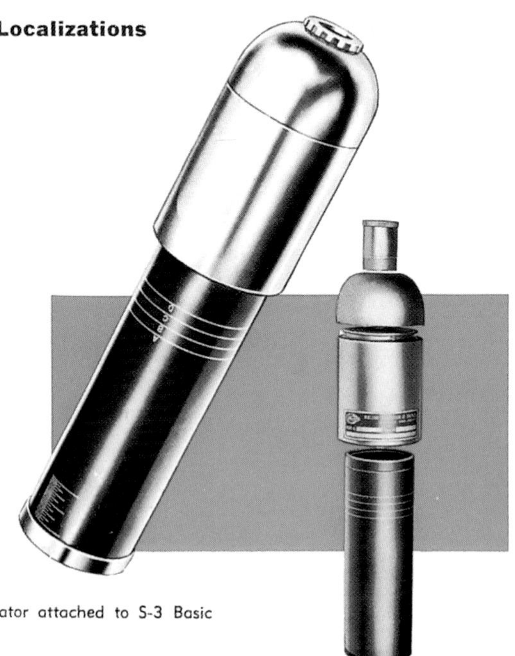

SPECIFICATIONS

The CS-100 consists of GS-44B shielded crystal and collimator attached to S-3 Basic Detection Unit.

GS-44B:
1″ x 1″ Sodium Iodide (Tl).

SHIELDING:
Minimum of 1″ over 290° forward solid angle except for collimator opening.

COLLIMATOR OPENING:
GS-4M has ¾″ standard diameter. Any size from ¼″ D to ⅝″ D on special order.

DIMENSIONS:
GS-44B 3″ O.D. x 5 7/16″ L. CS-100 12¾″ long (plus connector).

WEIGHT:
10¾ lbs. Shipping: 16 lbs.

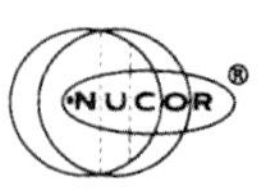

NUCLEAR CORPORATION OF AMERICA
Instrument & Research Division
DENVILLE, NEW JERSEY
Instrument & Research Division
Specialists in Nuclear Instrumentation

Built upon the remnants of two companies, Nuclear Corporation of America was launched with the vague purpose of becoming a leader in nuclear-related technology. The Nucor name and symbol were used from the beginning.

CHAPTER TWO

NEW DIRECTIONS

1960–1965

"Dave Thomas was tall, good-looking, articulate, charming and smart. He was a salesman and a promoter. About running a company, he didn't know beans. One of his problems was his fantastic ego."

— Sam Siegel, 1996[1]

FOR NUCLEAR CORPORATION of America, the early sixties were a time spent searching for an identity. The acquisitions continued, but there was no guiding vision for the company. The highlights during this period were the acquisition of the Vulcraft Corporation and the arrival of F. Ken Iverson. Although no one at Nuclear Corporation of America realized it at the time, these two events would eventually propel the company to leadership in the steel industry.

For the company, the decade began ominously. In July 1960, Engelhard Hanovia, Inc., led by Charles Engelhard, sold off its substantial interest in Nuclear Corporation. The company, engaged in the refining of rare and precious metals, had purchased Nuclear Corporation stock in May 1957, but became disillusioned following three years of substantial losses. On July 11, 1960, Engelhard sold his stock to the Martin Company (later renamed the Martin Marietta Corporation) of Baltimore, Maryland, and the New York investment banking firm of Bear Stearns.[2]

The sale prompted a reorganization of Nuclear's board of directors. Elected to lead the company as chairman of the board was David A. Thomas, a former vice president of Radio Corporation of America (RCA) and a friend of Martin Marietta's chairman, George Bunker. Two months later, Sam Norris resigned and Thomas succeeded him as president.

David A. Thomas

Thomas was an enthusiastic man, confident of his ability to run a major corporation. Tall and handsome, he had been a member of the Royal Canadian Air Force. His business experience was varied and interesting. Prior to 1947, Thomas had been an executive with Foute Brothers in New York City. From 1947 and 1957, he served in high-ranking positions at Bagley Sewell, American Insulators Corporation, Automatic Steel Products and the Babb Company. In 1957, he joined RCA as a corporate vice president, leaving in November 1960 to become chairman of Nuclear Corporation of America.

Thomas was a pilot and an adventurer. He leased his Beechcraft to Nuclear Corporation, then shuttled the entire board of directors around in it. Board members were terrified by his airborne exploits, worrying that a plane crash would wipe out the entire board at once. After several hair-raising trips, they hired a pilot for the plane.[3]

The Kachina Doll, representing an Indian spirit and traditional to Arizona, was featured on the cover of the 1961 Annual Report, heralding the purchase of a small Phoenix semiconductor company.

The run-down corporate headquarters of Nuclear Corporation in Denville, New Jersey. In 1962, the headquarters would be moved to a more aesthetically pleasing area in Arizona.

Yet for all his charm and energy, Thomas was in over his head. Sam Siegel, who joined Nuclear Corporation as an accountant in 1961 and would play a key role in the development of the company, once characterized Thomas as a charismatic man who didn't know enough about business.

> *"Dave Thomas was tall, good-looking, articulate, charming and smart. He was a salesman and a promoter. About running a company, he didn't know beans. One of his problems was his fantastic ego."*[4]

1960: Dave Thomas selected to lead Nuclear Corporation of America.

1961: In spite of misgivings, Sam Siegel goes to work for Nuclear Corporation.

1962: Nuclear acquires Valley Sheet Metal and Vulcraft Corporation.

1962: Ken Iverson hired by Nuclear to run Vulcraft Division.

Siegel, who joined Nuclear in 1961, would never forget his job interview with the company. He had just passed the CPA exam and needed a job, when he learned that Nuclear was hiring.

> *"I asked my brother and my brother-in-law, who were in different businesses, to find out what they could about the company, and both of them came back with a similar answer, which was, 'Don't go to work for them. They are a schlock company.' ... Anyway, I was looking to get my first job in industry, so I went to see their executive vice president at the Pennsylvania Hotel in New York. I got the room number and went up there. A man opens the door, and he's in his underwear. We talked for five minutes, and that was the interview. I was hired."*[5]

The concept of the conglomerate was in vogue, and Thomas and Siegel quickly became involved in a frenzy of acquisitions and divestitures. Thomas' first order of business was to sell off the Electron Tube Division, a decision that generated a capital loss of $683,323. Next to go was the Isotope Specialties Division, another losing venture.[6] Thomas then put the company on a program of growth by acquisition. Important purchases included U.S. Semiconductor Products in 1961, Valley Sheet Metal Company and Vulcraft Corporation in Florence, South Carolina, both in 1962. Valley Sheet Metal engaged in air conditioning, ventilating, pipe fitting, air purification and the operation of a large sheet metal shop.

Thomas decided to move Nuclear Corporation from its dilapidated quarters in New Jersey to better facilities in Phoenix, Arizona, where U.S. Semiconductor was based.

Vulcraft Corporation

The purchase of Vulcraft Corporation was by far Thomas' greatest achievement during his time at Nuclear. It was Vulcraft, manufacturer of steel joists and girders, that would sustain the company and lure in a future president who would one day lead it to become one of the nation's largest steel producers.

Vulcraft Corporation was incorporated on June 12, 1946 in Florence, South Carolina. Sanborn Chase, the company's president, had graduated from Auburn University in 1942 and worked for the federal government as a physicist during World

1962: Safety committee formed at Vulcraft; number of accidents drops dramatically.

1964: Teamsters union defeated in vote at Vulcraft Division.

1962: To foster productivity and cooperation, Iverson creates the Vulcraft Credit Association.

1965: Six divisions of Nuclear Corporation operating at a loss.

In the early days of Nuclear Corporation, the company manufactured air particulate monitors (left) and Geiger counters (below). Both machines detected the amount of radiation present in an area.

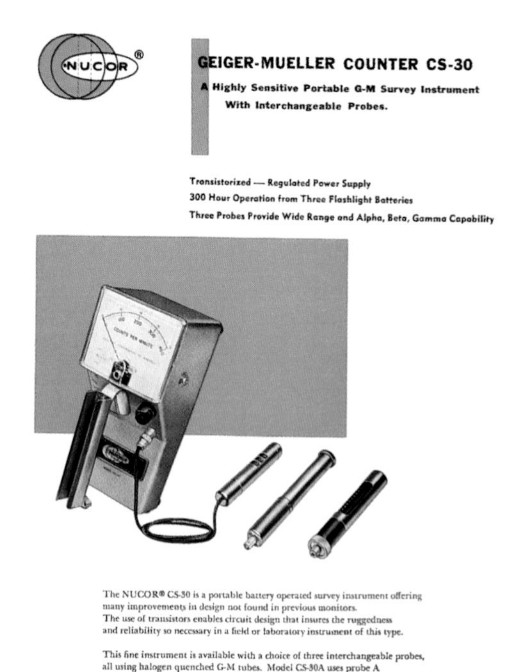

War II. Following the war, he joined with an old college friend, Frank W. Cayce, to found Vulcraft. Chase was president and Cayce was the secretary/treasurer.[7]

At first, the company manufactured steel for use in chain link fences, Quonset huts, outdoor movie screens and miscellaneous steel building supplies. To increase profits, Chase decided that the company should manufacture its own bar joists. The early fifties was a time of prosperity and growth for the United States. Shopping centers, schools and office buildings needed joists for their roofs, and Vulcraft was eager to provide them. Working with another engineer, Chase invented a machine that bent steel rods in the middle to produce the joists. With the success of the bar joist business, Vulcraft gave up its other fabricating lines.

Vulcraft was a small but bustling company, recalled Mabel Bristow, who went to work for Chase in 1947. In addition to secretarial work, Bristow did the books for the company, which at first consisted of only 15 to 20 people. She said Chase drove himself hard but was always fair with his employees. "He was a very smart, intelligent man, very good to his employees. We cared a lot for him and worked hard to make the business a success."[8]

David Aycock, who joined Vulcraft in 1954 and retired as president of Nucor in 1991, remembered Chase as a great man. "He loved people and would do anything for anyone. He was extremely intelligent and had a high-toned, scientific mind."[9]

Many people attribute Chase's three heart attacks to his work ethic. The first attack, which occurred at the office, was mild, and Chase recovered quickly. The second occurred in New York City, while Chase was there on business. The last attack, which proved fatal, occurred in 1961 at Chase's home.

At the time of his death, Vulcraft was devoted solely to the manufacture of steel joists. With four production lines and two more on the drawing board, the company was the nation's leading independent supplier of bar joists. It employed more than 200 people and enjoyed annual earnings of nearly $6 million.[10]

Sanborn's wife had to decide what to do with the growing company. "It was a most difficult decision," said the former Madge Chase, now Madge DeFosset.[11] To her fell the task of reassuring suppliers, the bank and most importantly, the workers.

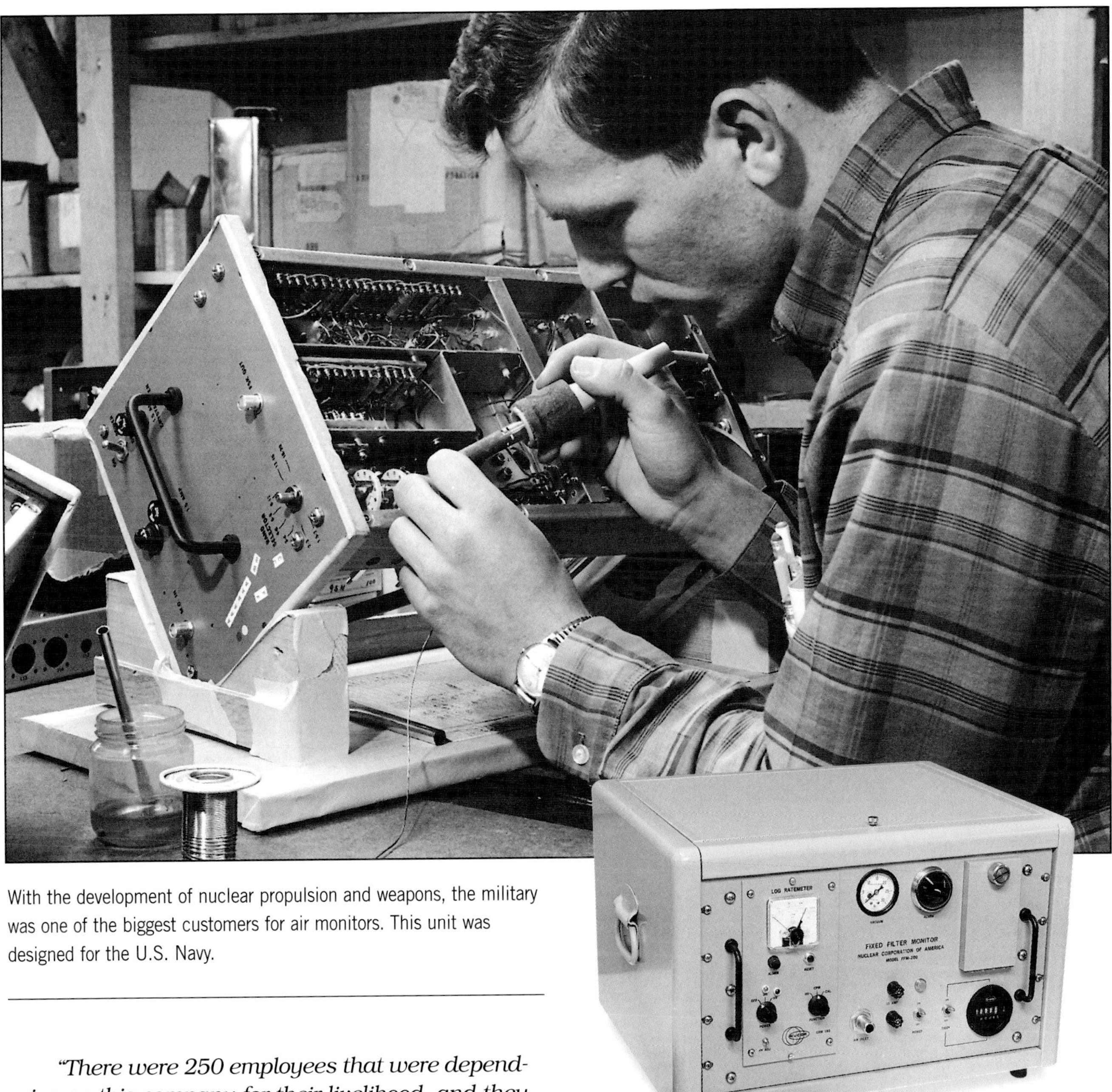

With the development of nuclear propulsion and weapons, the military was one of the biggest customers for air monitors. This unit was designed for the U.S. Navy.

> *"There were 250 employees that were depending on this company for their livelihood, and they had worked awfully hard to get it to where it was. And I will tell you that the last year of Sanborn's life, he did realize how successful he was, which was wonderful."*[12]

She received a call from Dave Thomas, who wanted to know if she was willing to sell the company. She was open to the idea, but only if he could assure her that the company would continue and that the employees would be able to keep their jobs. Thomas visited the facility and was impressed.

F. Kenneth Iverson

But Thomas didn't know anything about the steel joist business. Before Nuclear Corporation would agree to buy Vulcraft, it needed to find somebody to run it. On June 6, 1962, Clyde Y. Morris, an attorney for Nuclear Corporation, met with a young man named F. Kenneth Iverson in New York City to discuss Vulcraft.

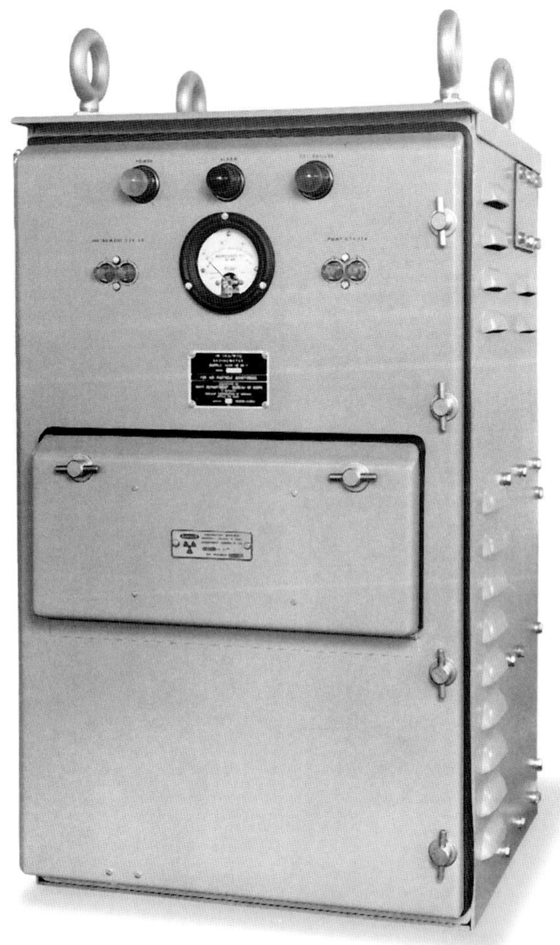

A continuous air particulate monitor manufactured by Nuclear Corporation for the Navy Department's Bureau of Ships.

F. Kenneth Iverson was born September 18, 1925 in Downers Grove, Illinois, a rural town just west of Chicago. From 1943 to 1946, he served in the U.S. Navy. He was discharged at the rank of lieutenant shortly after the end of World War II. In 1946, Iverson earned a bachelor of science degree in aeronautical engineering from Cornell University in New York. He went on to Purdue University in Indiana, where he received a master of science degree in mechanical engineering with a minor concentration in hot metal.[13]

When Iverson got his first look at the steel industry in Gary, Indiana, in 1947, the 22-year-old graduate student was less than thrilled with the work conditions. "We took a field trip to a big, integrated steel producer," Iverson told a Purdue alumni publication in 1987. "This was late afternoon. We were going through the plant, and we actually had to step over workers who were falling asleep there. I decided right then that I didn't ever want to work for a big steel company."[14]

Iverson's first job after graduate school was at International Harvester's manufacturing research center in Chicago. He remained there as a research physicist until 1951, when he was hired as the manager of engineering with Illium Corporation in Freeport, Illinois. Illium had been founded in a five-car garage by the former Burgess Battery Company. The company made a nickel-based alloy that was used to resist corrosion. Iverson's tenure with Illium lasted about two years. He decided to leave after he failed to persuade Illium's board of directors to invest in a state-of-the-art foundry.[15]

In 1953, Iverson was hired as assistant to the vice president of manufacturing at Indiana Steel Products Company in Valpariso, Indiana. A year later, he joined the Cannon Muskegon Corporation in Muskegon, Michigan. It was here that Iverson, the manager of Vacuum Metals and manager of Sales, developed two-inch slabs of Rene 41, a nickel-cobalt-iron alloy that was used as a high-temperature sheet material. Rene 41 was used as the outer shingle on the Mercury manned space capsule because it maintained strength in the 1,800-degree temperature of reentry.[16]

The final stop before Iverson landed at Nuclear Corporation was Coast Metals, Inc., in Little Ferry, New Jersey, where Iverson served as executive vice president. Among other things, the company made high-alloy welding rods. When he arrived, Iverson immediately noticed that the machinery was in an enormous room with terrible lighting. He decided to improve the lighting so that workers could see what they were doing. When the new lighting was in place, Iverson saw the room clearly for the first time. He almost wished he hadn't.

"Even I was startled. There was dust everywhere and dirt on the floor. Everything that you can imagine wrong with the old equipment showed up. One of the fellows who had been doing this for years suddenly shut off his machine and picked up a broom and started to sweep the floor. Production doubled overnight."[17]

While Iverson was at Coast Metals, Nuclear Corporation of America attempted to buy the company. That's when Iverson met Dave Thomas.

But Iverson left not long afterwards, following a disagreement with the company president. Several members of the board of directors were impressed with Iverson and wanted to offer him a substantial portion of stock in the company at a good price. The president objected, threatening to take the issue to court if the directors went ahead with their plan. Iverson didn't want to take the case to court, so he decided to leave the company instead.

In June 1962, executives at Nuclear asked Iverson to look at Vulcraft. Iverson traveled to Florence, met with its president, Madge Chase, and examined the facilities. He returned with the belief that Nuclear Corporation should buy Vulcraft. Nuclear agreed, but only if Iverson would become both general manager and a vice president of Nuclear Corporation of America. Vulcraft was sold to Nuclear Corporation of America for nearly $1 million.[18] Iverson joined Nuclear Corporation of America in September 1962 as a vice president of Nuclear and general manager of Vulcraft.

Moving to South Carolina

When Iverson joined Nuclear Corporation, his family experienced the culture shock of moving from New Jersey to South Carolina. Iverson's son Marc, who was in the fifth grade at the time, came home from school one day in tears because, he told his father, he couldn't understand the teacher, who apparently had a thick Southern accent.

Iverson himself found Southern ways, particularly Southern racism, hard to understand. Vulcraft, which had a fair number of black employees, engaged in practices that disgusted him. The company had separate bathrooms for blacks and whites, and even held separate Christmas parties. Iverson quickly eliminated the wall between the bathrooms and combined the parties.

He recalled one incident in 1963, when Vulcraft was celebrating the completion of a facility addition. Festivities that included a plant tour and refreshments were planned. But the public relations manager wanted to bring the black employees through at a different time. Iverson insisted that all employees and guests, black and white, enjoy the party together.

In those days, Southern towns had separate high schools for black students and for white students. Everyone assumed that the white high school was better, even though that wasn't always true. Since Nuclear hired a lot of black employees, Iverson was invited to the black school to speak about job opportunities. "I went out there and it was clean as a whistle. You could have eaten off the floor, and everything was just splendid."[19]

In Vulcraft's company newsletter for September 1962, employees were introduced to Iverson, who was given a glowing tribute. He was described as a man "endowed with personal magnetism, great aptitude and the qualities

Ken Iverson in 1962, the year he took over the recently-purchased Vulcraft Division.

Above: A 1962 picture of Vulcraft, soon to be run by Ken Iverson. He quickly introduced the egalitarian principles that have made Nucor famous.

Below: The Vulcraft logo at the time of its purchase by Nucor.

of leadership." Iverson told employees that the number one item on his agenda was to "perfect the Vulcraft joists." To do this, he said, "we must perfect not only production but every department at Vulcraft."[20]

David Aycock was a Vulcraft sales manager when Iverson arrived. He remembered that most employees were more curious than nervous about the change in leadership, since everybody knew and respected Sanborn Chase. Any doubts about Iverson were quickly put to rest.

"Ken was almost immediately a hit with the people. He was always very good with people. Iverson is probably a better businessman than Chase was, but Sanborn probably had a more scientific mind. Both had a strong compassion for people. That was a very similar thing between them."[21]

Iverson's first official duty as president of Vulcraft was to install a safety program. He appointed a safety committee and enacted rules, including strict enforcement of a policy requiring workers to wear safety equipment at all times at the plant. One month after the policy went into effect, the number of accidents dropped, with only "one mashed finger and one strained back" to report.

The Teamsters Union

From the time that laborers first banded together to protect their interests, steel unions had a long history of bitter and often violent labor difficulties. Big Steel workers and management clashed over wages, safety, benefits and other issues. Perhaps the worst such incident was in the summer of 1892. In the midst of contract negotiations between the Carnegie Steel Company and the Amalgamated Association of Iron and Steel Workers, Carnegie's plant manager, Henry Clay Frick, locked out all union members — 800 workers out of a total workforce of 3,800. The next day, July 3, many nonunion members walked off the job in support of the union. The company brought in 300 hired guards. A bloodbath ensued, with seven union workers and three guards losing their lives. Pennsylvania Governor Robert E. Pattison sent 8,000 militiamen to restore order. The situation grew so tense that on July 23, Russian-born anarchist Alexander Berkman shot and wounded Frick in an unsuccessful assassination attempt. The mill was eventually reopened, but the strike lingered until November 20, when the union accepted defeat.[22]

In the years after World War II, unions gained considerable power in the United States. The pent-up demand of the war years and the dominance of American industry created a golden time of prosperity, especially for large corporations. Workers wanted a piece of the pie. In automaker shops and steel mills, workers demanded, and received, steadily escalating wages and benefits. The increased cost of labor drove up consumer prices, which in turn drove wages even higher.

Iverson was determined to keep his shop union-free. It was a subject that needed no debate as far as Iverson was concerned. He didn't like unions, and he didn't want his shop to become a union shop.

Iverson went out of his way to treat employees with respect and dignity so that unions would not be necessary. In November 1962, he helped create the Vulcraft Credit Association, an undertaking viewed with enthusiasm by the plant employees. He wanted employees to feel responsible for the plant's overall productivity, and he reminded them that greater productivity meant greater job security.

Despite Iverson's opposition, it looked like a union might form at Vulcraft anyway. On August 31, 1964, the Teamsters union notified Vulcraft that it represented the majority of Vulcraft's truck drivers. The Teamsters then requested that Vulcraft recognize the union as the representative of the truck drivers.[23] Iverson acted quickly. In a memo dated September 2, 1964, he warned Vulcraft's truck drivers of the dangers of belonging to the union. He voiced concern over the tactics used by the Teamsters and warned the drivers not to be lured by false promises. "It would be well also for you to ask yourself where your present security lies," Iverson wrote.

> *"Does it lie with the Teamsters union, who has never provided you with a job or a single bit of security, or with this company, which has provided you with security and jobs in order for you to support yourself and your dependents? The Teamsters union will never provide you with a job and their main concern is the money they get from you in the form of dues. What the Teamsters union does with your money is something you should be concerned about. Certainly you would be concerned about giving the Teamsters union money in order to defend Mr. (Jimmy) Hoffa, who is the Teamsters boss and who has recently been found guilty of using Teamsters money for wrongful purposes. It is our positive intention to oppose the Teamsters union by every proper means to prevent it from coming here."*[24]

He warned the drivers that any employee caught organizing a union while on the job would be immediately discharged. Iverson was tenacious, but he could not prevent the drivers from voting on whether or not they wanted to be represented by the Teamsters union. The election was set for Monday, October 19, 1964. The question to be put to the drivers was simple: Do you want the Teamsters union or no union? The voting was to take place in private, with unsigned and unnumbered ballots to be dropped into a sealed box.

Until the very last minute, Iverson continued his campaign to win over the workers. Employees received another memo from their chief. "Union organizers are nothing more than salesmen selling union memberships," Iverson said. If the union were approved, an "out-of-town union man, who may or may not represent your interests" would create a bridge between driver and boss, instead of letting drivers and bosses work out issues directly. Unions moving into American towns meant that businesses would eventually go out of business or move to another part of the country, he asserted. "Having ruined one section of the country, they now want to ruin this section."[25]

Vulcraft, or any other company that dealt with union organization initiative, was by law without obligation to grant a single concession to the Teamsters union. The only way the Teamsters could get a concession from Vulcraft would be to strike. Iverson promised the drivers that any strikers at Vulcraft would find themselves out of work.

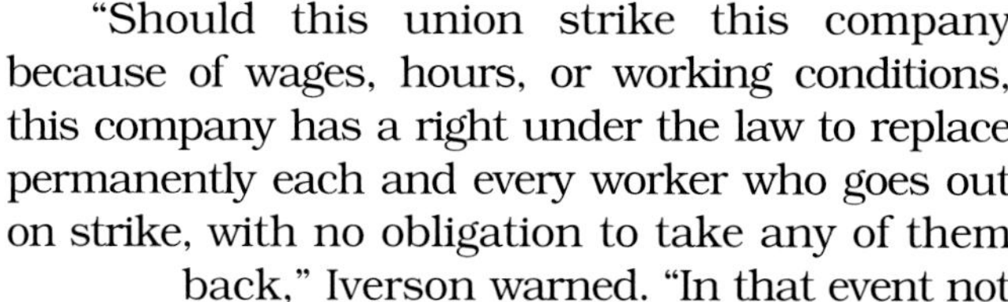

"Should this union strike this company because of wages, hours, or working conditions, this company has a right under the law to replace permanently each and every worker who goes out on strike, with no obligation to take any of them back," Iverson warned. "In that event not only do you fail to get what the union promised you, but you have lost your job as well."[26]

Finally, Vulcraft sent its workers home with coloring books depicting people associated with the Teamsters union. The Teamsters Coloring Book was published by the Communications Workers of America, AFL-CIO. The first caricature was of James R. Hoffa, president of the International Brotherhood of Teamsters. He was standing in front of a desk, his pockets overflowing with cash, and a dart-strewn picture of Bobby Kennedy on the wall behind him. The caption read, "My name is James R. Hoffa. The R. is for Riddle. Guess whether I will do as much for you as you will do for me. Color my pockets green." Another picture featured former Teamsters President Dave Beck, sitting in a jail cell wearing prison garb and holding up a check. The caption read, "My name is Dave Beck. I was President of the Teamsters before Hoffa. I am taking a five-year vacation at McNeil Island Federal Penitentiary. This letter contains my pension check for $50,000, which I receive every year. Color my touch golden."[27]

Iverson's campaign was successful and the union was voted down. To this day, Nucor is a completely union-free shop.

During Iverson's two-year tenure as Vulcraft's general manager, profits increased threefold. In 1962, Vulcraft's net sales were $3,068,847 and net earnings were $325,021. At the end of 1964, net sales topped $9,029,290 and earnings were up to $927,194.[28]

A coloring book circulated by the Communications Workers of America (logo above), did not paint a flattering picture of the Teamsters. The picture of Jimmy Hoffa (left), included instructions to "Color my pockets green."

On October 1, 1964, Iverson was called to Nuclear Corporation's headquarters in Phoenix, Arizona, where he was promoted to vice president. His new responsibilities included the Vulcraft of South Carolina division and a new Vulcraft of Nebraska division. Appointed to succeed Iverson in South Carolina was Charles N. Munn of Warren, Michigan. Prior to his move to Florence, Munn was factory and sales manager of Van-Dresser Specialty Corporation, supplier of automotive parts.

Searching for a Direction

In stark contrast to the overwhelming success at Vulcraft, Nuclear's other divisions were struggling to make profits. The company had continued to pursue a policy of expansion primarily by acquisition, without much thought concerning division compatibility. By 1965, the sprawling structure of Nuclear Corporation of America included a leasing company, an electromechanical development company, a general contractor, two steel joist plants and three other divisions manufacturing diodes, nuclear instruments and exotic metals.

By 1964, the company's earnings had decreased, mainly as the result of substantial operating deficits incurred by Valley Sheet Metal Division. In 1962, Valley Sheet Metal had net sales of $2.7 million and earnings of $182,918. Two years later, net sales were $3.8 million, but the division was operating with a net loss of $480,243. Chairman David Thomas was confident that the division would make a financial comeback in 1965, but things only got worse.

By 1965, six divisions of Nuclear Corporation of America were operating at a net loss. These divisions included the Nuclear Division, which designed and manufactured radiation detection instruments and systems; Research Chemicals, producers of rare earth products; U.S. Semcor, which produced such devices as tantalum capacitors and zener diodes which were marketed directly to the U.S. government and to electronic and space device companies; Valley Sheet Metal; Electromechanical Division, which developed an electrostatic office copier; and Southern Leasing Corporation, an equipment leasing company.[29]

The financial forecast for the company was grim, and its survival was in doubt.

Ken Iverson (left) and James White, of North Carolina National Bank, set up Nuclear's merit-based profit-sharing plan in 1966.

CHAPTER THREE

PICKING UP THE PIECES

1965–1966

"Ken was and is a thinker. ... Sam is one of the most brilliant financiers I've ever known. ... The two of them together were an effective crew. They would argue it out and somewhere they would come up with a plan."

— Ernest Delaney, 1996[1]

DESPITE THE PROBLEMS at Nuclear Corporation, the board of directors continued to exhibit support for David A. Thomas. At a special board meeting held January 28, 1965, his contract was extended for an additional 10 years, at an annual salary of $60,000.[2]

The board appeared satisfied with Thomas' leadership, but both Ken Iverson and Sam Siegel seriously doubted that the company would survive. Like many other Nuclear employees, they began looking for new jobs. One night they bumped into each other at a post office in Phoenix. They were both holding large stacks of résumés, which were ready to mail. The situation was so ridiculous that "they burst out laughing."[3]

Nuclear's misfortunes seemed to be caused mainly by the struggling Valley Sheet Metal Division. In a May 2, 1965 newspaper article, Thomas said the division was in default of its agreements with Valley National Bank and Marine Midland Trust Company in New York. Thomas said company officials were working on a refinancing agreement, prophetically adding that the solution "may well require drastic action."[4]

Martin Marietta Corporation, unhappy with its investment, wanted to divest all 1,439,924 shares of its Nuclear stock, representing 22 percent of the company. At this point, Donald Lillis, a director with a 2-percent shareholding in the company, intervened. Lillis, a savvy businessman with major interests in Bear, Stearns & Company and other important New York businesses, offered to buy Martin Marietta's stock for the bargain-basement price of a nickel a share. It didn't matter that Nuclear's common stock was trading on the American Stock Exchange for $1.60 a share. Martin Marietta's chairman, George Bunker, gratefully accepted the offer, along with a check for $72,000.

A special board meeting was convened on May 27, 1965. David A. Thomas offered his resignation, effective immediately, in a move that received unanimous approval from the board. To soften the blow, the directors agreed to retain Thomas as a "consultant," with an annual salary of $25,000, until December 31, 1970.[5] Lillis, with a 24-percent majority interest in the company's stock, was elected the new chairman.[6]

The bloodletting continued with the departure of board members Clark C. Vogel, the company's secretary; W. Murray Sanders; and Harrie T. Shea. Harold G. Shelton, appointed to the board just three weeks previously, was

·NUCOR

The Nucor logo from the mid-1960s. The company would radically change in focus after Iverson took over.

elected chief executive officer. The balance of the officers were Bernard W. Gilmore and F. Kenneth Iverson, group vice presidents; Elmo Di Ianni, vice president; Donald H. Bayles, general counsel and a vice president; Endicott Peabody Davis, assistant secretary; and Samuel Siegel, controller.[7]

But it was Chairman Lillis, at age 63, who faced the tough assignment of turning Nuclear Corporation of America into a profitable company. An avid football fan, Lillis was one of five partners who took over the bankrupt New York Jets football franchise in 1963. In 1968, he would become president and chief executive officer of the Jets, with one-fourth ownership of the team. Unfortunately, he would die of heart problems two months later.[8]

Donald Lillis, an owner of the New York Jets, revived Nuclear Corporation through a combination of personal and revolving credit lines.

On July 8, 1965, the board of directors met in New York for a second round of housecleaning. Bernard Gilmore, group vice president, and Donald Bayles, vice president, secretary and treasurer, both resigned. Shelton then won approval to sell the financially crippled Valley Sheet Metal Division. When it was sold a year later, Valley Sheet Metal was operating at a net loss of $200,000 while net sales were at their lowest ever, $1.6 million.

The ailing corporation needed a serious infusion of cash in order to survive. The board approved a secured revolving credit agreement with Southeastern Financial Corporation to provide Nuclear Corporation up to $3,850,000 of new financing. Lillis also agreed to personally loan the corporation $250,000.[9]

President Iverson

With the financial burden on Nuclear Corporation of America somewhat eased, there was still the question of who would lead the organization on a permanent basis. Siegel had quit his accounting job at Nuclear. But on July 30, 1965, he sent CEO Shelton a telegram. "I have

1965: Dave Thomas resigns as head of Nuclear, followed by several members of the board.

1965: Combination of credit line and a personal loan staves off disaster for Nuclear.

1965: Sam Siegel offers to stay at Nuclear if Ken Iverson is made president.

1965: Iverson appointed president; Siegel appointed treasurer and controller.

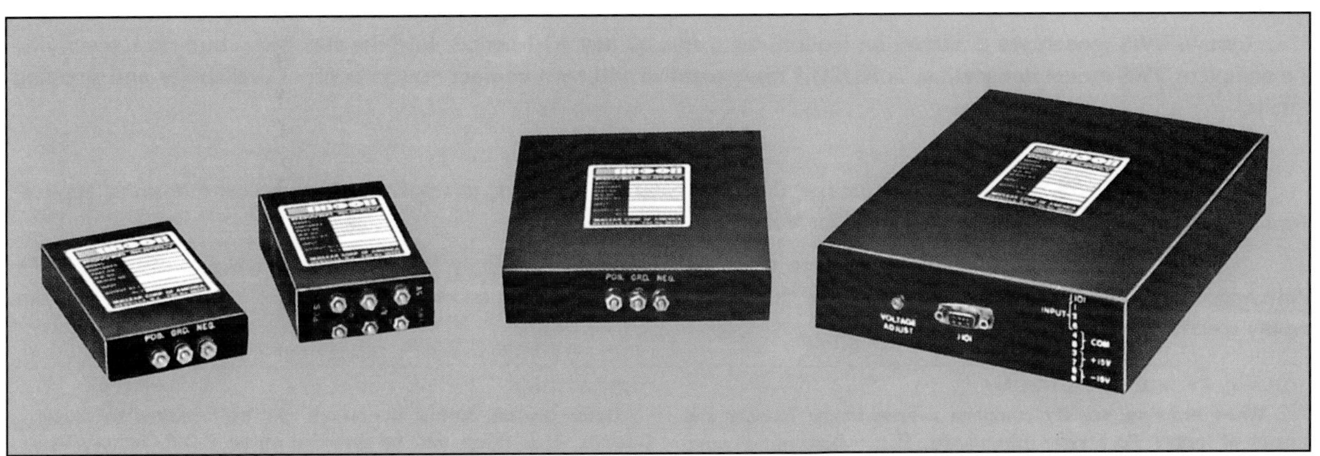

The Electromechanical Division, producer of products such as these DC power packs, was sold off soon after Iverson took over as president.

given careful thought to our telephone conversation tonight and would consider continuing with Nuclear if the following occurred: (1) Ken Iverson is given an employment contract as president of Nuclear. (2) I am given an employment contract as treasurer and controller of Nuclear."[10]

Shelton agreed, and on August 12, 1965, Lillis announced Iverson's appointment as president of Nuclear Corporation of America.[11]

Iverson wasted little time getting down to business. In a press release dated August 24, 1965, he announced that Nuclear Corporation was selling its Electromechanical Division, its U.S. Semcor Division, and, as had already been determined, the Valley Sheet Metal Division. Valley Sheet Metal and the Electromechanical Division had been losing money, Iverson said. U.S. Semcor, though profitable, "does not fit in with the future plans of the company." The com-

1965: Nuclear sells off ailing Valley Sheet Metal, U.S. Semcor and Electromechanical divisions.

1965: Siegel, David Aycock and Charles Munn appointed vice presidents of Nuclear.

1966: Corporate headquarters moved from Phoenix to Charlotte.

1966: Entire corporate support staff quits.

pany would consist of four divisions: the Vulcraft Division in Florence, South Carolina; the Vulcraft Division in Norfolk, Nebraska; the Nuclear Division in Denville, New Jersey; and the Research Chemical Division in Phoenix, Arizona.

Iverson also announced that a revolving credit agreement of $3.85 million was approved on August 12, 1965, with Southeastern Financial Corporation of Charlotte, North Carolina. Approximately $3.2 million was used to pay off existing debts.

Finally, Iverson announced the election of three vice presidents: Samuel Siegel; Charles M. Munn, who had been general manager of the Vulcraft Division in Florence, South Carolina; and H. David Aycock, who had worked his way up to general manager of Vulcraft Norfolk Division after 10 years at the Florence plant.[12]

But it was Iverson and Siegel who would rebuild the company. The two men had widely divergent styles that were uniquely complementary. Iverson had big ideas for the company, while Sam worried about the bottom line. They would argue loudly and often, always finding a way to resolve their differences. "Ken was and is a thinker, a visionary, I guess is the word I want to use," said Nucor attorney Ernest Delaney. Delaney, now retired, represented Nuclear Corporation and then Nucor until 1966. "Sam is one of the most brilliant

Service centers, which repaired and tested power supply units, were spread out across the country to service Nuclear's electrical products.

Samuel Siegel, the financial counterpart to Ken Iverson. Siegel would only continue at Nuclear Corporation if Iverson was appointed president.

financiers I've ever known. The two of them together were an effective crew. They would argue it out and somewhere they would come up with a plan."[13]

"It was Ken's drive that ran the company," said James Cunningham, who joined Nuclear in 1966 as general manager of the Research Chemical Division. "Sam Siegel was a very important part of it. He kept a firm hand on the money and didn't let us do anything foolish."[14]

The dramatic changes taking place at Nuclear Corporation of America left its employees in a state of shock. Many wondered if their jobs were secure. Iverson didn't forget about them. On November 1, 1965, he sent a letter to all employees, carefully outlining the company's direction. He began by noting that sales in 1964 were $17.5 million, an increase over 1963. This "rapid growth, coupled with other problems," Iverson wrote, resulted in a critical need for realignment of the company. The four divisions that remained possessed able leadership, he said. But Nuclear Corporation needed to adopt a new way of doing business. "We are confident that the company is now in a position to move forward with improved performance."[15]

A Unique Style of Management

In addition to restructuring the company's divisions, Iverson also put into place a unique and revolutionary management structure that would set Nuclear Corporation of America and its employees apart from mainstream corporate America in the years to come.

In an interview in *Management Review* magazine years later, Iverson explained that four basic principles formed the foundation for the company's success. "One is few management layers, which we believe in very, very strongly. The second is a minimum of staff people," he said. The third factor is to push responsibilities down to the lowest possible level. The final factor is the use of strong incentives to focus everyone on productivity and earnings. Iverson discounted the notion that there was a Ken Iverson management model. "There may be a Nucor management model," Iverson said. "But it is really based on and developed by the managers. They are probably the strongest single factor in determining our policies and programs."[16] Betsy Liberman, who has held a number of executive secretarial positions in the company since 1967, said decisions are made relatively quickly, compared to the usual torturous, meandering path taken by many-layered bureaucracies. "How do other companies ever make a decision?" she mused in a recent interview. "It must take weeks to come to a conclusion. Whereas here, with the four layers that we basically have, things aren't drawn out. They're done and they're usually done effectively."[17]

Iverson knew from experience what it was like to run an operating division while receiving bad, often inane, instructions from corporate headquarters. "We decided that the best thing to do was to place as much responsibility as possible in those managers, who were vice presidents of the company. They were free to operate the division within some basic parameters." Eventually, what evolved was a practice of senior officer compensation and production bonuses determined by explicit production and efficiency formulas. There would be no discretionary bonuses. The workers would know what the opportunities were and what the rewards would be, while senior management knew they had to foster an aggressive entrepreneurial spirit.

"It's not based on some idea how you did the last six months of the year, ignoring the first six months of the year," Iverson said in a recent interview. "I don't want anybody to sit as Solomon on me, and I don't want to sit as Solomon on anybody else. I want to know what the parameters are that you're working with."[18]

Iverson did not believe in the rigid hierarchy that characterizes many large organizations. "We really make an effort to eliminate the distinction between a management person and anyone else who works for the company. We all have the same vacations. We all have the same holidays. We all have the same health care program," Iverson said.[19]

As an example, Iverson explained that in many large heavy manufacturing companies, hard hats are usually color-coded according to rank. "People don't think about it, but color-coding a person's hard hat promotes a real hierarchy," Iverson said. After reading an article about a Canadian company in which all 400 people wore the same colored hard hat, Iverson sent out a memo decreeing that everyone in the company would wear a green hard hat, and visitors would wear white. It was one of the few unilateral directives ever issued from Iverson. The supervisors, who had traditionally worn white hats, were angry, but Iverson stuck to his guns. The company held training sessions, and told workers that their authority did not come from the color of their hat. However, Iverson had to make a minor change when he realized that, for safety reasons, maintenance people had to be easy to identify on a job site. They wore yellow hats, while all other employees wore green.[20]

Respect does not flow from the color of a hardhat. Therefore, Iverson mandated that all workers wear green hard hats while visitors wear white. Finding the right worker, however, became something of a challenge. So Iverson made a minor adjustment — maintenance workers wore yellow.

By the end of 1965, Iverson's actions appeared to have a positive effect on the company. Net sales had climbed nearly $5 million over the previous year, to $22.3 million. Net earnings, however, still showed a deficit of $431,013.[21]

Iverson and Siegel decided that it was time to leave Phoenix. It seemed clear that the company's headquarters should be closer to its most profitable division. In January 1966, Iverson and Siegel journeyed to Charlotte, North Carolina. There, they rented 2,000 feet of office space on the third floor of the Cotswold Building, located at 4425 Randolph Road. They unfolded a card table, brought in a few chairs and a telephone, and opened the new corporate headquarters of Nuclear Corporation of America in Charlotte.

The way Iverson and Siegel chose to make the move was characteristic of their no-frills management style. The entire corporation — desks, phones, chairs, filing cabinets, etc. — was loaded up in Phoenix and hauled to Charlotte in two moving vans. The move was completed by May 1, 1966.

Asked to move from Phoenix to Charlotte, all 12 corporate employees quit because they did not believe the company would survive. Iverson and Siegel were left alone to act in every administrative capacity until a new staff could be hired in Charlotte later that spring.

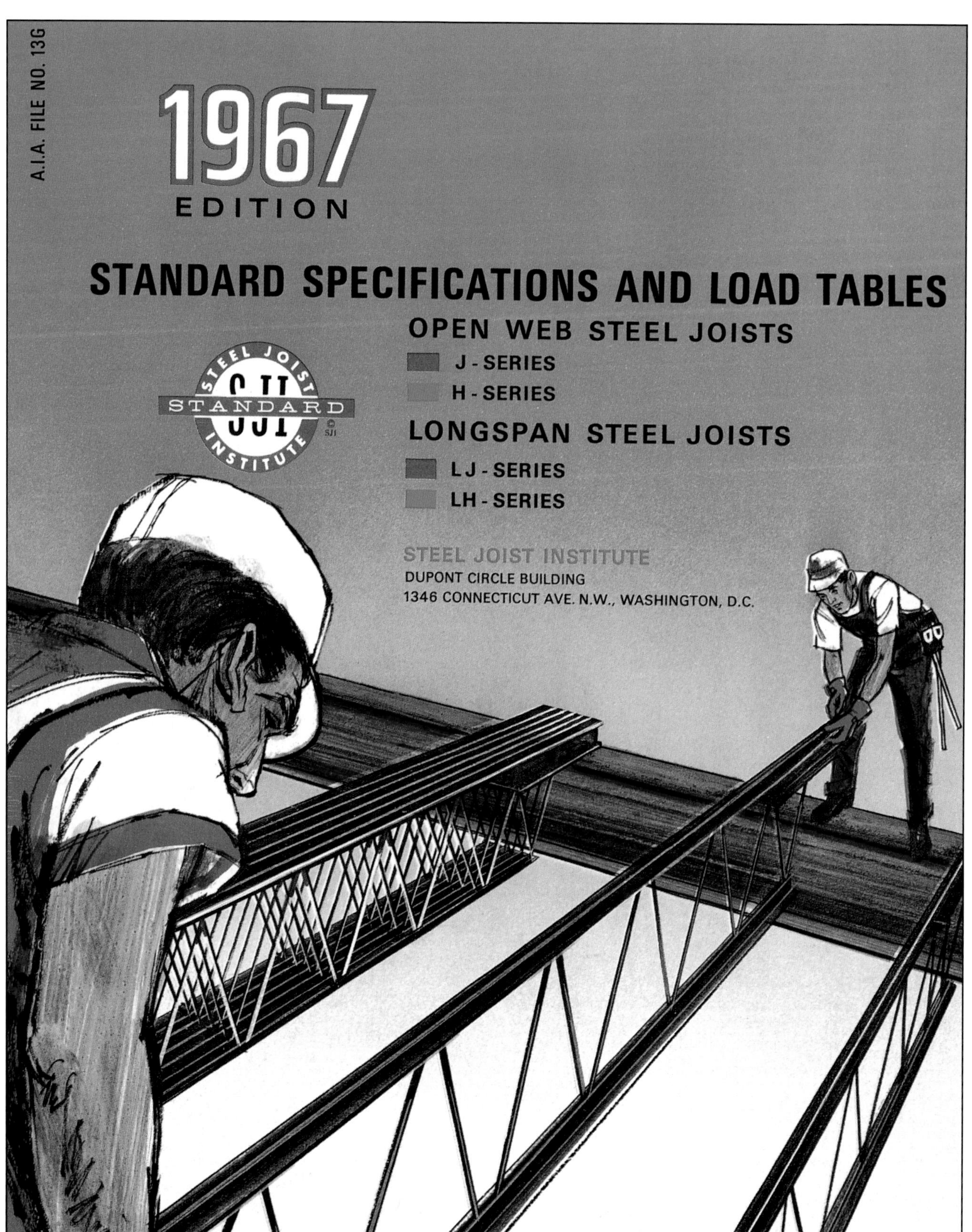

Under Ken Iverson's leadership, Nuclear's Vulcraft divisions became the nation's largest suppliers of steel joists by 1967.

CHAPTER FOUR

STEEL JOISTS SPELL SUCCESS

1966–1967

"Everybody was just so enthused in getting things going, and Ken and Sam are both such dynamic people. You can see that from talking to them. They haven't changed a bit."

— Betsy Liberman, 1996[1]

THE REBUILDING OF Nuclear Corporation of America began in earnest in 1966. Ken Iverson's philosophy called for placing nearly autonomous responsibility with the general plant managers. Twice a year, the managers would meet to grapple with the serious task of reinventing Nuclear Corporation. They were setting the policies that would determine the future of the company, and disagreements were common. "I remember that sometimes they'd get so violent they almost went across the table at each other," Iverson recalled.[2] Iverson himself acted simply as a participant, only taking charge when the group couldn't settle an issue.[3]

Along with new policies, the company needed new employees. The first was Rose March Edwards (now Daniel), who joined Nuclear on May 23, 1966 as executive secretary to the vice president and president. "I think the reason they hired me was not because of my secretarial expertise, but because I said I loved making order out of chaos," Daniel said in a recent interview. "There were so many boxes and cartons around that needed to be set up in a filing system."[4]

She recalled some of the arguments that would flare up between Iverson and Sam Siegel that year. "I remember that they were so frustrated with each other at times that Sam often would go back in Ken's office and they would yell and scream at each other. They had differences of opinion but they usually came together with a final conclusion they were both pleased with," she said.[5]

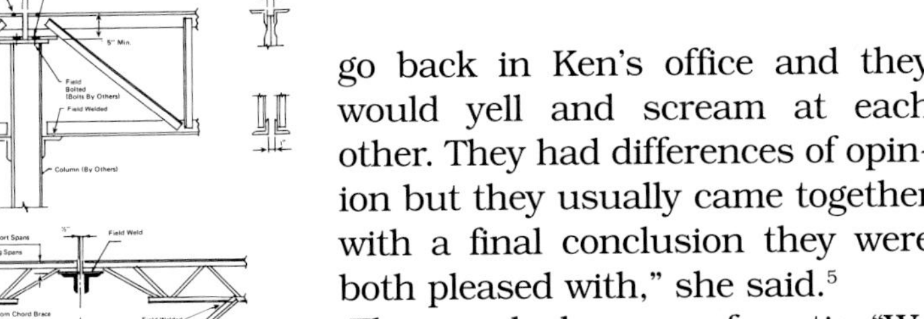

Those early days were frenetic. "We were constantly on the move," recalled Betsy Liberman, who joined the company in 1967 and still worked there in 1997. "Everybody was just so enthused in getting things going, and Ken and Sam are both such dynamic people. You can see that from talking to them. They haven't changed a bit."[6]

The Divisions of Nuclear Corporation

After Iverson's realignment, Nuclear consisted of four divisions: the Vulcraft Division in Florence, South Carolina; the Vulcraft Division in Norfolk, Nebraska; the Nuclear Division in Denville, New Jersey; and the Research Chemicals Division in Phoenix, Arizona. The Vulcraft divisions remained the most successful.

The Nuclear Division designed and manufactured radiation detection instruments and

A diagram from a Vulcraft catalog shows typical joist girders used to support a roof.

systems. These products were used mainly to evaluate the hazards of exposure to radiation from a variety of sources, including nuclear reactors. In 1966, about 90 percent of the division's business was derived from military contracts. The radiation detection equipment produced for the Navy and Air Force varied in size from pocket detection instruments to permanent installations weighing several hundred pounds. The division also marketed its products to hospitals, industries and universities. By 1966, the Nuclear Division had about 75 employees. Most products were custom in nature and had to be manufactured by hand.

The Research Chemicals Division, based in Phoenix, produced rare earth oxides and metals that were extracted from ores known as "yttro-fluoride" and sold to the federal government, universities, research laboratories and industry. The division purchased mined ores primarily from sources in Colorado, undertaking no mining of its own. The materials were used primarily in electronic, nuclear and laser applications, including the phosphors in color television tubes. The division had a comparatively large number of small customers, with five larger contracts accounting for approximately 50 percent of annual sales. The division had a history of poor financial performance, posting losses every year from 1962 through 1966. The loss for 1966 was $103,921.[7]

By far the most profitable divisions were the Vulcraft plants in South Carolina and Nebraska, which manufactured steel joists used almost exclusively in construction of industrial, commercial and institutional buildings. The joists were rarely used for the construction of private homes, which did not require heavy-duty support for the floors and roofs. Because the joists were built to

The 1966 logo for the Research Chemicals Division.

1966: Realignment leaves four divisions comprising Nuclear Corporation of America.

1966: Lagging behind the rest of the company, Research Chemicals posts its fourth consecutive loss.

1966: By the end of the year, Nuclear Corporation is back on its feet.

1966: With new capital, Nuclear searches for the right acquisition in steel joist industry.

customers' specifications, the division did not have to maintain costly inventory.

Using carbon steel, the Vulcraft divisions manufactured both long- and short-span joists, with lengths varying from 10 feet to 130 feet. The raw materials for the joists consisted of steel angles and rounds, paint, welding and other materials, which were purchased from a number of manufacturers.

Throughout the sixties, the steel joist business was characterized by fierce competition among many manufacturers for many small customers. But with its streamlined focus and unique production incentive programs, Nuclear Corporation of America became the leading steel joist manufacturer in the United States by the end of 1967, capturing 25 percent of the market. Nuclear's next largest competition was Ceco Corporation, which produced about half the amount Nuclear did.[8]

But competition gradually lessened as the large steel companies began to abandon the steel joist business. U.S. Steel stopped making joists in 1968. Bethlehem Steel closed down its Florida joist plant in 1969. Republic Steel left the joist business, then went back into it, then left it again. Laclede Steel, a large joist producer in St. Louis, also left the business.[9] The trend would continue even though the steel joist market would grow every year for 10 years.[10]

Nuclear's strategy was straightforward. Provide a good product, offer the best price, and market aggressively. From the beginning, the company focused on quality. Nuclear emphasized its design flexibility and customer service. Each

In the late sixties, Charles Munn (left) was general manager of the Vulcraft Division in Florence, South Carolina, and Dave Aycock (right) was general manager in Norfolk, Nebraska.

1967: Streamlining enables Vulcraft Division to net 25 percent of steel joist market.

1967: Nuclear acquires M & S Steel Company in Alabama.

1967: Iverson announces proposal to build fourth steel joist plant, located in Grapeland, Texas.

1967: Nuclear earns record profits as all divisions improve financial performance.

Vulcraft plant maintained its own engineering department, which was computerized to help generate customized designs for customers' specialized needs. Vulcraft engineers designed about 20 percent of the orders in cooperation with the customers' construction engineers or architects. The remaining 80 percent were ordered from Vulcraft's own design specification catalogs.[11]

The company aggressively worked to reduce its costs wherever possible. It maintained its own fleet of trucks to guarantee on-time delivery to all 50 states. By controlling shipping, Nuclear Corporation generated loyalty from contractors, who didn't have to worry about their workers standing idly by, waiting for a commercial carrier to arrive. Another strategy was to locate the joist plants in rural areas near the markets they served.[12]

As a result of such foresight, the company saw an increase in profits during the first half of 1966, even though revenues actually dropped slightly. Nuclear Corporation posted net earnings of $755,440, up from $114,777, while sales dropped from $10.94 million to $10.5 million.

M & S Steel Company

By the end of 1966, Nuclear Corporation of America was back on its feet again. Working capital had increased from $1.8 million on December 31, 1965, to $43 million on December 31, 1966. Stockholders' equity had tripled during the same period, from $762,380 to $2.2 million. Iverson informed stockholders in the 1966 Annual Report that Nuclear was actively working to expand its successful steel operation through either construction or acquisition.[13]

Iverson acted quickly, and on April 3, 1967, Nuclear announced that it had purchased M & S Steel Company of Fort Payne, Alabama, a company with sales of approximately $4.5 million in 1966. M & S would become Vulcraft Alabama, the company's fifth division and one of the few Vulcraft divisions that Nuclear would acquire instead of building from scratch. The purchase allowed Nuclear to increase its production capacity for steel joists by more than 25 percent. "The acquisition of M & S Steel marks an important step in the expansion of our company's steel fabrication," Iverson said in a press release. "M & S Steel, a manufacturer of long-span steel joists since its organization, is strategically located in the industrial south. With our other facilities, Nuclear can now profitably ship joists to every state in the union."[14] Although M & S had manufactured only long-span joists, Nuclear modernized the facilities so that short-span joists could be produced as well.[15]

ONGSPAN STEEL JOIST LJ-SERIES

STANDARD LOAD TABLE, LJ-SERIES

Based on Allowable Stress of 22,000 psi

Joist Designation	Approx. Wt. in Lbs. per Linear Ft.	Depth in Inches	Maximum End Reaction Lbs.	CLEAR OPENING OR NET SPAN IN FEET															
				65	66	67	68	69	70	71	72	73	74	75	76	77	78	79	80
40LJ09	23	40	8602	262 / 237	255 / 227	248 / 217	241 / 207	235 / 198	229 / 190	223 / 182	217 / 175	212 / 168	207 / 161	202 / 155	197 / 149	192 / 143	188 / 138	183 / 133	179 / 128
40LJ10	26	40	9521	290 / 263	282 / 251	274 / 240	267 / 230	260 / 220	253 / 211	246 / 202	240 / 194	234 / 186	228 / 179	223 / 172	217 / 165	212 / 159	207 / 153	202 / 147	198 / 141
40LJ11	28	40	10375	316 / 291	308 / 278	299 / 266	291 / 255	284 / 244	276 / 233	269 / 224	262 / 215	256 / 206	249 / 198	243 / 190	237 / 183	232 / 176	226 / 169	221 / 163	216 / 157
40LJ12	30	40	12181	371 / 317	361 / 303	351 / 290	341 / 277	332 / 265	323 / 254	315 / 244	307 / 234	299 / 224	291 / 216	284 / 207	277 / 199	270 / 191	264 / 184	257 / 177	251 / 171
40LJ13	36	40	14479	441 / 384	429 / 367	417 / 351	406 / 336	395 / 321	385 / 308	375 / 295	365 / 283	356 / 272	347 / 261	338 / 251	330 / 241	322 / 232	314 / 223	307 / 215	300 / 207
40LJ14	38	40	16219	494 / 407	479 / 389	465 / 372	452 / 356	439 / 341	426 / 327	415 / 313	403 / 300	392 / 288	382 / 277	372 / 266	362 / 256	353 / 246	344 / 237	335 / 228	327 / 220
40LJ15	41	40	17664	538 / 458	522 / 438	507 / 419	492 / 401	478 / 384	464 / 368	452 / 352	439 / 338	427 / 324	416 / 312	405 / 299	394 / 288	384 / 277	375 / 266	365 / 256	356 / 247
40LJ16	48	40	19468	592 / 537	584 / 513	575 / 491	567 / 470	558 / 450	551 / 431	535 / 413	521 / 396	507 / 380	493 / 365	480 / 351	468 / 337	456 / 324	444 / 312	433 / 300	422 / 289
40LJ17	54	40	20884	636 / 610	626 / 583	617 / 557	608 / 533	599 / 511	591 / 489	582 / 469	574 / 450	566 / 432	559 / 415	552 / 399	537 / 383	524 / 368	510 / 355	498 / 341	485 / 329
40LJ18	60	40	22506	685	675 / 656	665 / 627	655 / 600	646 / 575	636 / 551	628 / 528	619 / 506	611 / 486	602 / 467	594 / 448	587 / 431	579 / 415	572 / 399	565 / 384	558 / 370

Joist Designation	Approx. Wt. in Lbs. per Linear Ft.	Depth in Inches	Maximum End Reaction Lbs.	73	74	75	76	77	78	79	80	81	82	83	84	85	86	87	88
44LJ10	26	44	8913	242 / 227	236 / 218	230 / 209	225 / 201	219 / 194	214 / 186	209 / 179	205 / 173	200 / 166	196 / 161	191 / 155	187 / 149	183 / 144	179 / 139	175 / 134	172 / 130
44LJ11	27	44	9687	263 / 237	257 / 227	251 / 218	245 / 210	239 / 202	234 / 194	228 / 187	223 / 186	218 / 174	213 / 167	208 / 161	204 / 156	199 / 150	195 / 145	191 / 140	187 / 136
44LJ12	30	44	11565	314 / 274	306 / 263	299 / 253	292 / 243	285 / 234	278 / 225	271 / 217	265 / 209	259 / 201	253 / 194	248 / 187	242 / 180	237 / 174	232 / 168	227 / 163	222 / 157
44LJ13	35	44	13517	367 / 313	357 / 301	348 / 289	339 / 278	330 / 267	322 / 257	314 / 248	306 / 239	299 / 230	291 / 222	285 / 214	278 / 206	271 / 199	265 / 192	259 / 186	253 / 180
44LJ14	38	44	15617	424 / 353	413 / 339	403 / 325	393 / 313	384 / 301	375 / 290	366 / 279	357 / 269	349 / 259	341 / 249	334 / 241	326 / 232	319 / 224	312 / 216	305 / 209	299 / 202
44LJ15	41	44	17422	473 / 396	460 / 381	448 / 366	436 / 352	425 / 338	414 / 325	404 / 313	394 / 302	384 / 291	375 / 280	366 / 270	358 / 261	349 / 252	341 / 243	333 / 235	326 / 227
44LJ16	48	44	20626	560 / 465	545 / 446	531 / 429	517 / 412	504 / 396	491 / 381	479 / 367	467 / 354	456 / 341	445 / 329	434 / 317	424 / 306	414 / 295	405 / 285	395 / 275	387 / 266
44LJ17	54	44	22105	600 / 528	592 / 507	584 / 487	576 / 469	569 / 451	562 / 434	548 / 418	536 / 402	523 / 388	511 / 374	499 / 360	487 / 348	476 / 336	465 / 324	454 / 313	444 / 303
44LJ18	60	44	23749	644 / 595	636 / 571	627 / 549	619 / 528	611 / 508	603 / 488	596 / 470	588 / 453	581 / 437	574 / 421	567 / 406	561 / 392	548 / 378	535 / 365	523 / 353	511 / 341
44LJ19	68	44	25669	696 / 674	687 / 647	678 / 622	669 / 598	661 / 575	652 / 553	644 / 533	636 / 513	628 / 494	621 / 477	613 / 460	606 / 444	599 / 428	592 / 414	585 / 399	579 / 386

Joist Designation	Approx. Wt. in Lbs. per Linear Ft.	Depth in Inches	Maximum End Reaction Lbs.	81	82	83	84	85	86	87	88	89	90	91	92	93	94	95	96
48LJ11	27	48	9024	221 / 208	216 / 201	212 / 194	207 / 187	203 / 180	199 / 174	195 / 168	191 / 163	187 / 157	183 / 152	179 / 147	176 / 142	172 / 138	169 / 133	166 / 129	162 / 125
48LJ12	30	48	10984	269 / 241	263 / 233	257 / 224	251 / 217	246 / 209	241 / 202	236 / 195	231 / 188	226 / 182	221 / 176	217 / 171	213 / 165	208 / 160	204 / 155	200 / 150	196 / 145
48LJ13	35	48	13025	319 / 276	312 / 266	305 / 257	298 / 248	292 / 239	286 / 231	280 / 223	274 / 215	268 / 208	263 / 201	257 / 195	252 / 189	247 / 183	242 / 177	237 / 171	233 / 166
48LJ14	36	48	14618	358 / 299	350 / 288	341 / 278	333 / 268	326 / 259	318 / 250	311 / 242	304 / 234	297 / 226	291 / 218	284 / 211	278 / 205	272 / 198	267 / 192	261 / 186	256 / 180
48LJ15	41	48	17190	421 / 349	411 / 336	401 / 325	392 / 313	383 / 302	374 / 292	365 / 282	357 / 273	349 / 264	342 / 255	334 / 247	327 / 239	320 / 231	313 / 224	307 / 217	300 / 210
48LJ16	48	48	19926	488 / 409	477 / 394	466 / 380	456 / 367	446 / 354	437 / 342	427 / 331	418 / 320	409 / 309	401 / 299	393 / 289	385 / 280	377 / 271	370 / 262	362 / 254	355 / 246
48LJ17	54	48	22376	548 / 465	536 / 449	524 / 433	513 / 418	502 / 403	491 / 389	480 / 376	470 / 363	460 / 351	451 / 340	442 / 329	433 / 318	424 / 308	416 / 299	407 / 289	399 / 280
48LJ18	60	48	24871	609 / 525	601 / 506	594 / 488	587 / 471	580 / 454	573 / 439	567 / 424	561 / 410	548 / 396	536 / 383	524 / 371	513 / 359	502 / 348	492 / 337	481 / 326	472 / 316
48LJ19	68	48	26364	645 / 594	637 / 573	630 / 552	622 / 533	615 / 515	608 / 497	601 / 480	594 / 464	588 / 449	581 / 434	575 / 420	569 / 406	562 / 394	557 / 381	545 / 369	534 / 358

*Section 104.10 of the "Standard Specifications for Longspan Steel Joists, LJ- and LH-Series" limits the design LIVE load deflection as follows: Floors, 1/360 of span. Roofs, 1/360 of span where a plaster ceiling is attached or suspended; 1/240 of span for all other cases.

Above: The logo of the Steel Joist Institute, an organization for United States joist manufacturers who meet the institute's exacting specifications. Vulcraft was accepted into the institute in 1959.

Left: A chart of standards from the Steel Joist Institute's 1967 specifications guide.

Above: The M & S Steel Company in 1963, four years before it was acquired by Nuclear Corporation.

Right: The Steel Joist Institute's 1967 standards for J-Series joists and H-Series joists.

One problem with the M & S facility was that the ceiling was too low. "We couldn't get any productivity because there was no adequate dimension from the floor up to the crane," explained James Campbell, who joined Vulcraft Alabama in 1972 and had been vice president and general manager of it since 1986. Nuclear couldn't afford the expense of dismantling the building and raising the roof, so Iverson and Sam Siegel came up with an ingenious plan. Instead of raising the roof, they decided to lower the floor. "It took several years to complete because they never stopped producing joists during that time. They just closed a section, brought in equipment, cut out the floor and dug down about five or six feet."[16]

On November 30, 1967, Iverson announced that the company would build its fourth steel joist plant in Grapeland, Texas. The 150,000-square-foot plant would be up and running by April 1, 1968, he said, and would employ approximately 100 people. Nuclear invested more than $1 million on the new plant, underscoring its policy of developing new operations in rural areas.

The changing fortunes at Nuclear Corporation of America were attracting the attention of investors. In October 1967, the American Stock Exchange asked Nuclear why the company's stock had accelerated. In a press release dated October 20, 1967, Iverson responded that the management at Nuclear simply did not know why the stock price was going up.[17]

However, the answer was obvious. In 1967, Nuclear experienced a record year in sales and earnings, with every division showing a profit. Sales topped $23.6 million, a healthy 12 percent

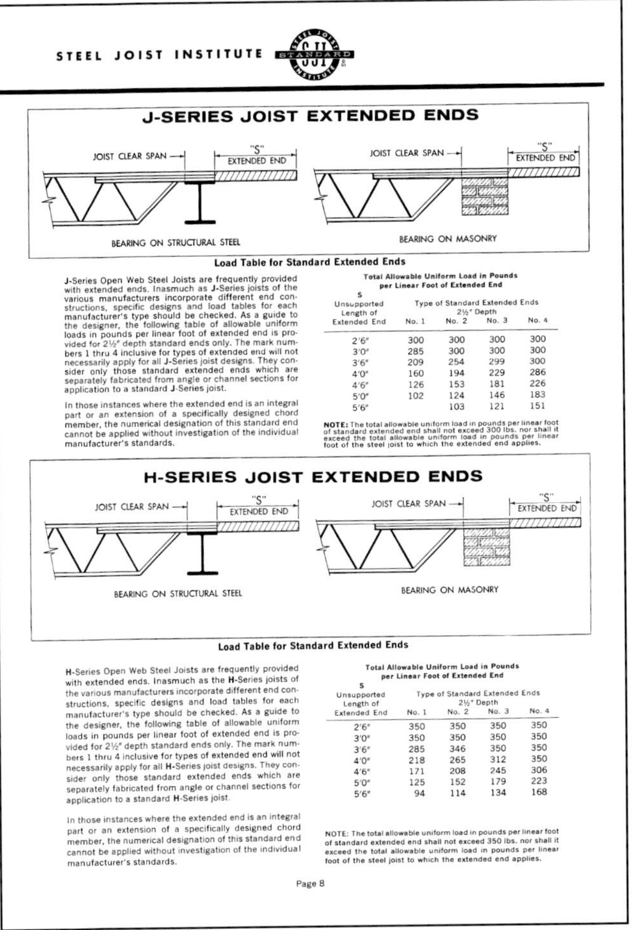
STEEL JOIST INSTITUTE

J-SERIES JOIST EXTENDED ENDS

JOIST CLEAR SPAN — "S" EXTENDED END

BEARING ON STRUCTURAL STEEL

BEARING ON MASONRY

Load Table for Standard Extended Ends

J-Series Open Web Steel Joists are frequently provided with extended ends. Inasmuch as J-Series joists of the various manufacturers incorporate different end constructions, specific designs and load tables for each manufacturer's type should be checked. As a guide to the designer, the following table of allowable uniform loads in pounds per linear foot of extended end is provided for 2½" depth standard ends only. The mark numbers 1 thru 4 inclusive for types of extended end will not necessarily apply for all J-Series joist designs. They consider only those standard extended ends which are separately fabricated from angle or channel sections for application to a standard J-Series joist.

In those instances where the extended end is an integral part or an extension of a specifically designed chord member, the numerical designation of this standard end cannot be applied without investigation of the individual manufacturer's standards.

Total Allowable Uniform Load in Pounds per Linear Foot of Extended End

S Unsupported Length of Extended End	Type of Standard Extended Ends 2½" Depth No. 1	No. 2	No. 3	No. 4
2'6"	300	300	300	300
3'0"	285	300	300	300
3'6"	209	254	299	300
4'0"	160	194	229	286
4'6"	126	153	181	226
5'0"	102	124	146	183
5'6"		103	121	151

NOTE: The total allowable uniform load in pounds per linear foot of standard extended end shall not exceed 300 lbs. nor shall it exceed the total allowable uniform load in pounds per linear foot of the steel joist to which the extended end applies.

H-SERIES JOIST EXTENDED ENDS

JOIST CLEAR SPAN — "S" EXTENDED END

BEARING ON STRUCTURAL STEEL

BEARING ON MASONRY

Load Table for Standard Extended Ends

H-Series Open Web Steel Joists are frequently provided with extended ends. Inasmuch as the H-Series joists of the various manufacturers incorporate different end constructions, specific designs and load tables for each manufacturer's type should be checked. As a guide to the designer, the following table of allowable uniform loads in pounds per linear foot of extended end is provided for 2½" depth standard ends only. The mark numbers 1 thru 4 inclusive for types of extended end will not necessarily apply for all H-Series joist designs. They consider only those standard extended ends which are separately fabricated from angle or channel sections for application to a standard H-Series joist.

In those instances where the extended end is an integral part or an extension of a specifically designed chord member, the numerical designation of this standard end cannot be applied without investigation of the individual manufacturer's standards.

Total Allowable Uniform Load in Pounds per Linear Foot of Extended End

S Unsupported Length of Extended End	Type of Standard Extended Ends 2½" Depth No. 1	No. 2	No. 3	No. 4
2'6"	350	350	350	350
3'0"	350	350	350	350
3'6"	285	346	350	350
4'0"	218	265	312	350
4'6"	171	208	245	306
5'0"	125	152	179	223
5'6"	94	114	134	168

NOTE: The total allowable uniform load in pounds per linear foot of standard extended end shall not exceed 350 lbs. nor shall it exceed the total allowable uniform load in pounds per linear foot of the steel joist to which the extended end applies.

Page 8

increase over 1966 revenues of $21 million. Net earnings were $1.7 million, up from $1.3 million in 1966.[18]

Even Nuclear's less successful divisions, Research Chemicals and Nuclear, had increased sales in 1967. Research Chemicals had obtained an exclusive contract with the Dow Chemical Company for a patented process of separating rare earth elements into extremely pure components. One of Dow Chemical's products, the neutron radiograph, had been successfully marketed to the military, which used it to ensure the reliability of military and aerospace components and devices. The neutron radiograph was able to image certain low-atomic-weight materials that were undetectable by X-ray. The converter screen used in the neutron radiography consisted of a thin sheet of the rare earth metal Gadolinium.[19]

By the end of 1967, Research Chemicals had net sales of $399,743, and a profit of $33,305, a refreshing contrast to 1966's operating loss of $103,92.[20]

At the Nuclear Division in Denville, New Jersey, earnings were up by $15,000 over 1966, and sales had increased more than $200,000. Fifteen percent of the division's sales were generated by its modular power supplies, which were used as power sources in a broad range of sophisticated electronic equipment. Nuclear expected the modular power supplies to do even better in 1968.[21]

The following year, Nuclear Corporation of America would announce plans to build its first minimill, a move that would eventually pay enormous dividends as Big Steel faltered. As news reports began to chorus the death of American steel, Nuclear was poised to become the darling of the industry.

Left: Nuclear's Vulcraft divisions dominated the steel joist market by providing high-quality products at low prices.

The Darlington steel mill, of the Eastern Carolina Steel Division, released Nucor from the fluctuating steel market.

CHAPTER FIVE

THE TRIUMPH OF THE MINIMILL

1967–1968

"The single most important event in shaping the future of the company has been the construction of [the Darlington] steel mill. This is no ordinary mill. It has been described as a forerunner of a new generation of minimills."

— Ken Iverson, 1972[1]

FOR SOME TIME, F. Kenneth Iverson had been mulling over a thought in the back of his mind. Even while he was enjoying Nuclear Corporation's increasing success, Iverson believed the company would become even more profitable if it would manufacture its own steel. Iverson, a trained metallurgist, had never gotten the love of steelmaking out of his blood, and he believed that the company could save money by supplying its own steel for its joist operations.

Iverson and Charles Munn, vice president and general manager of Vulcraft in Florence, asked the board of directors at its August 16, 1966, meeting to consider building an electric furnace steel mill like the ones that were already being used in Europe. Iverson had worked out a detailed proposal with projected financial statements for an electric furnace steel mill with a capacity of 60,000 tons per year. Known as a minimill, the facility would be smaller and less expensive than the large mills used by most of the major steel companies.

The board enthusiastically approved the plan to form the Eastern Carolina Steel Division, which would manufacture steel angles and rounds that would be used by the Vulcraft divisions.[2] It was an enormous gamble for a company that had just recently found its footing, but it had many attractions.

In 1967, nearly 60 percent of each Vulcraft sales dollar was spent on materials, with steel representing the vast majority of the materials. Furthermore, around 60 percent of the steel purchased by Vulcraft was imported from abroad.[3] In the previous four years, the average price of foreign steel had ranged from $104.40 a ton to $121.80 a ton.[4]

"They were really at the mercy of foreign steel," said Rod Hernandez, of the V. David Joseph Company. As the largest scrap steel broker in the country, the company has supplied scrap steel to Nuclear since the construction of the Darlington minimill. "You had to buy several months in advance, and it didn't really give you a chance to have your market situation work. The prices could fall on your finished products, and you had commitments to live up to."[5]

Iverson was confident that Nuclear Corporation could manufacture steel at a lower cost than it would pay on the open market. Minimills were relatively inexpensive to construct and operate. They were energy-efficient and they produced a high-quality product. Unlike large steel opera-

Cover of employee's handbook. In welcoming new Darlington plant employees, the handbook emphasized teamwork and dedication.

tions, minimills didn't require enormous blast furnaces to melt iron ore. Instead, they were equipped with smaller electric furnaces and continuous casters. The furnace would quickly melt scrap metal and iron ore, and the molten product would be poured into the top of a continuous caster. As it settled through the caster, it slowly solidified, emerging as a solid piece of steel ready to be rolled into a finished product.[6]

The blast furnaces that had been developed in the fifties and sixties required enormous throughput in order to be profitable. A mill with two furnaces might produce between 3 million and 5 million tons of steel each year. Minimills, by contrast, were much more efficient. The electric arc furnace proposed by Iverson had three inherent features that made it attractive to small producers: it could operate efficiently on scrap alone; it could be built to produce relatively small quantities of metals; and it could produce high-quality steel in batch quantities, as well as produce small batches of special types.[7]

The large steel companies had recently started using basic oxygen furnaces (BOFs) to mix pig iron with oxygen to convert it to molten steel, which was then shaped into large slabs of steel to make automobiles, appliances and other products. These furnaces could use only about 35 percent scrap, a situation that spurred the development of minimills, which could make use of the excess material.

The first minimills had been built in the 1930s by Northwestern Steel and Wire Company, which used electric furnaces to produce carbon steel. Before that time, electric furnaces had been used mainly for refining steel and producing specialty steel that required slow heating. Northwestern and other companies improved the furnace technology and brought it to larger-scale operations.[8] The electric furnace was unique among steelmaking processes in that it was possible to control the chemistry of the steel independent of the temperature. For that reason, electric furnaces could produce the highest quality of steel.

Logo of the Eastern Carolina Steel Division.

1966: Ken Iverson and Charles Munn propose entering steelmaking industry.

1967: Nuclear's board receives study recommending construction of a minimill.

1967: Study recommends South Carolina as site for the plant.

1968: Company announces plan to build a minimill in Darlington, South Carolina.

By the fifties, these facilities dotted the landscape of the Sun Belt states, often in small, rural areas. Minimills were essentially regional, usually shipping within a radius of less than 300 miles.

But embarking on any steelmaking project in the late sixties was considered extremely risky. In the early 1960s, steelmakers in the United States began to suffer from international competition. Labor unions and outdated technology had caused domestic prices to skyrocket as cheaper foreign steel began to invade the market.[9] American steel, which had long dominated the world market, was losing market share and by 1969 was no longer a world leader.[10]

The Darlington Minimill

On April 18, 1967, Nuclear Corporation's board members received a feasibility study on the construction of a continuous casting electric furnace steel mill with a capacity of 60,000 tons per year. This was a minuscule quantity, compared to the output of the large integrated mills of between 3 and 5 million tons a year.[11] According to the study, steel consumption in the form of angles and rounds in 1967 was approximately 60,000 tons per year at the Florence plant and 20,000 tons per year at the Norfolk plant. "There is ample supply of scrap available in the South Carolina area to support a small electric furnace scrap conversion mill, producing the rounds and angles required by the Florence Division. Such a mill would provide the following advantages: The joist plant would be assured of a continuing economical supply of steel for its production requirements, and the steel mill would have a captive market and could operate profitably."[12]

Controller Sam Siegel gave the board an analysis of capital requirements that totaled $3,367,500. The building and property would cost approximately $848,000, while the continuous casting unit and tower would be around $228,500. The most expensive area would be the rolling mill, estimated to exceed $1 million. The mill would be constructed 16 miles away from the Florence plant, in the small town of Darlington, South Carolina.[13]

On July 10, 1968, amid much fanfare and media coverage, Nuclear Corporation of America formally announced that it would build a $4.5 million steel mill in Darlington, which would employ 125 people at start-up and produce 60,000 tons of steel rounds and angles per year. The Darlington

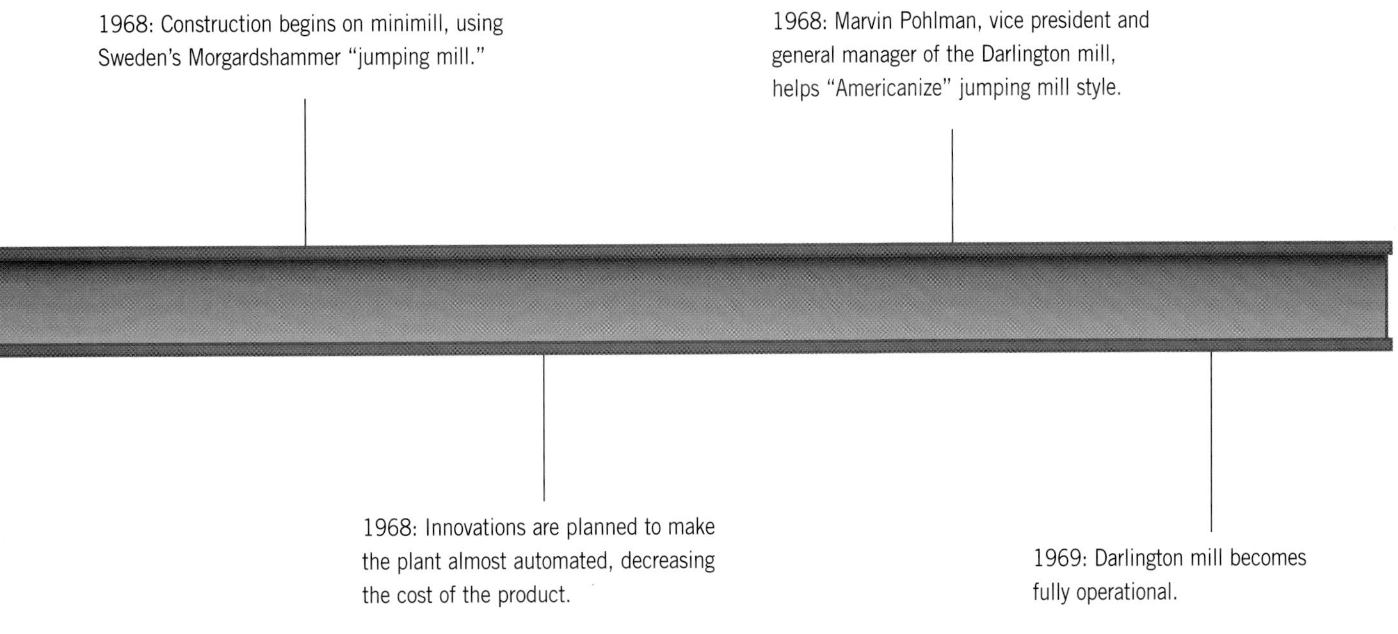

Designed with the most modern equipment available, the Darlington minimill could quickly turn scrap into finished steel.

mill would be located on an 111-acre site. At completion, it would be one of the county's largest electric and gas consumers, using an estimated 15 million British Thermal Units (BTUs) of gas per hour and buying more than $350,000 worth of electricity per year.[14] The mill would be the seventh division of Nuclear Corporation and would operate under the name Eastern Carolina Steel Division.

The financing for the new mill came from Wachovia Bank and Trust Company, American Credit Corporation and the State Bank of Alabama. The mill would be highly automated, containing a 20-ton electric furnace capable of melting steel at the rate of approximately 15 tons per hour. A two-strand continuous casting machine would be used to convert the molten steel into 600-pound, four-inch-square billets. The billets would be reheated and processed through a rolling mill for conversion into rounds and angles, the final product.

Construction began in August 1968 on two buildings with a total area of more than 100,000 square feet. Nuclear planned to start the melt shop in June 1969 and the rolling operations in August. Iverson explained that the mill was designed so that it could be readily expanded from 60,000 tons per year to more than 100,000 tons per year. He estimated that the Eastern Carolina Steel Division would purchase close to $2 million in scrap steel per year.[15]

Like most minimills already in existence, the Darlington mill would be located in a rural area, making it a "community" steel mill. In the past, the location of a steel mill was usually dictated by the requirement for nearby blast- and open-hearth furnaces, raw ore, fuel supplies and the necessary waterways for inexpensive bulk shipment. But an abundant supply of low-cost scrap, the modern electric arc and other technological advances made it possible to locate these new minimills in communities far from the principal steel-producing regions of the country, in areas where steelworker unions were non-existent.

Perhaps the most exciting thing about Darlington was the fact that it would be the first three-high "jumping mill" in the Western hemisphere. "Jumping" described the electric motors, which raised and lowered the mill as rectangular steel billets — up to four at a time — were passed back and forth between rolls. The jumping mill was actually a 25-ton giant, so delicately balanced on air chambers that a mere 15-horsepower motor raised and lowered the mill. Billets would then require seven to nine passes through the rolling stands as they were gradually shaped into angles or rounds of steel. Vertical movement of the mill between passes eliminated having to raise or lower the billets on tilting tables.[16]

Iverson had traveled with Marvin Pohlman, who later became general manager of Eastern Carolina Steel, and Bill White, construction manager, to more than a dozen mills in nine countries to analyze European mill technology. The group finally solicited proposals for three rolling mill bids from Morgardshammer AB and Moehler Neuman in Europe and Birdsboro in the United States.[17] John Doherty arrived at Nuclear Corporation in 1968, in time to help set up the Darlington minimill, and would become its first rolling mill manager. "We had a lot to learn about the Morgardshammer jumping mill. We got it Americanized," said Doherty, vice president in charge of engineering in 1996.[18]

> *"The conventional three-high mill stayed stationary. So that meant that your pass line between the center roll and the bottom roll was your table level. It meant that to make your return between the center roll or the top roll you had to lift the work, bringing the work to the tool. The Swedes came up with a jumping mill ... where the mill would rise to the height of the middle roll, and then go the other way, bringing the mill to the work. It worked fine for them, but they didn't fully understand how to apply that mill to making shaped products. With angles and flats and channels, the mill wasn't made for that. It almost drove us crazy."*[19]

Doherty said a consultant, a "fine old gentleman who had retired from Armco Eastern Stainless," was brought in to help work out the details. The plant was soon up and running. E. Michael Delaney III, son of Nucor attorney Ernest Delaney and a Nucor attorney himself, said Iverson told him he wasn't nervous about the risk the company was taking. "Iverson said he slept like a baby all through the project — he woke up and cried every 30 minutes."[20]

Before Nuclear Corporation came to town, Darlington was known chiefly for its stock car racing. The arrival of the minimill meant not only recognition in a different form — the first to operate the three-high "jumping mill" steel plant — but it also meant good news for the economy. *The Darlington News and Press* welcomed the newcomer in an editorial.

> *"Darlingtonians have justifiable reason for rejoicing today after the announcement that Nuclear Corporation of America will build a $4.5 million steel mill here. Darlington and Nuclear Corporation are already friends; so that sometimes difficult period of 'getting to know you' happily can be dispensed with. Many*

John Doherty, who helped bring the Darlington minimill on line, inspects the steel billets that were the fruit of his labor.

Above: Electric arc furnaces, such as the one shown here from the company's Berkeley County mill, operate more cheaply and efficiently than the traditional blast furnace and basic oxygen furnace.

Right: Basic oxygen furnace, showing a lance injecting oxygen to refine the hot metal.

Darlingtonians have had contact with Nuclear Corporation through the Florence plant, which it has owned for six years, and we know it as a stable industry of the highest caliber. Confident of a long and prosperous relationship, Darlington welcomes Nuclear Corporation of America."[21]

Town officials had every reason to expect good things from Nuclear. The company was growing at a steady pace and enjoying its largest profits ever. A fourth Vulcraft Division, located in Grapeland, Texas, had opened its doors in March 1968. Additional production facilities had been constructed at the Vulcraft divisions in Florence, South Carolina, and Fort Payne, Alabama. The Florence and Fort Payne plants would purchase all the steel produced at the Darlington mill. Net sales for 1968 exceeded $35.5 million, up from $23.6 million in 1967. Net earnings in 1968 were $2.3 million, up from $1.7 million the year before.

Up and Running

The steel-pouring process began when a workman used an oxygen lance to cut the refractory plug on a huge electric furnace, releasing some 30 tons of 2,950-degree molten steel into a waiting ladle. From here the ladle took the steel to a 30-foot-high tower, where it was poured into continuous four-inch-square strands. This particular furnace produced 30 tons of steel every two hours. The strands were then cut into 12-foot, 650-pound billets. Next, they went to a 40-ton-per-hour reheat furnace that brought them back up to 2,000 degrees for entry into the roughing mill.

After making the required number of passes between rolls of the jumping mill, billets were fed through five 16-inch intermediate rolling mills in a straight line operation. Billets to be shaped into steel rods then went through

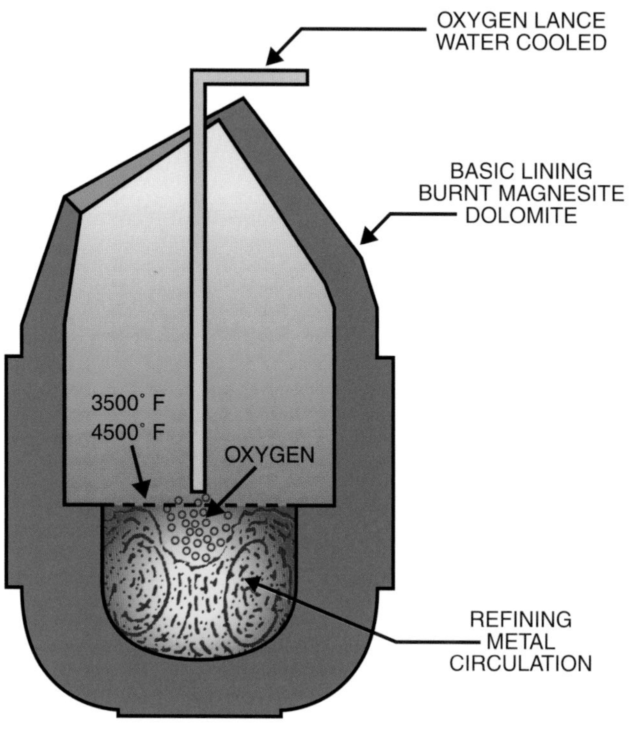

The Electric Arc Furnace

WITH ABOUT 50 percent of the world's steel generated from scrap metal, the electric arc furnace has become indispensable to reincarnating such junk as old bicycles, worn-out refrigerators and crushed cars into useful products.[1]

Scrap metal is sorted as it arrives at the minimill and conveyed into the electric arc furnace, which typically has a capacity of 80 to 200 tons. The furnace is a large steel melting pot lined with fire brick. There are two types of electric furnaces — AC and DC. An AC furnace uses three large carbon electrodes, between 16 inches and 24 inches in diameter, which carry massive amounts of electricity into the scrap. The lightning bolts arc between the electrodes, melting the scrap at temperatures exceeding 3,000 degrees Fahrenheit. A DC furnace relies on one large electrode, 28 to 30 inches in diameter, and a bottom anode to melt the scrap. Other methods of heating, such as oxygen, carbon and natural gas, sometimes supplement the electrical energy.[2]

In both cases, the electrodes are lowered until they almost touch the scrap, and then are drawn away, creating the electric arc. The charge usually runs between 200 and 300 volts, with somewhere between 20,000 and 30,000 amps.[3]

The quality of the steel can be carefully controlled because the temperature of the furnace can be maintained precisely. Once the scrap has been melted, the material is tested to verify its chemistry and then poured into a ladle, where it is mixed with other additives and brought to the correct temperature. The liquid is then poured into the continuous casting machine to be reverted to a solid.[4] The liquid steel is made solid by firing high-velocity water jets at the mold, a process that forms the material into billets. The billets are cut into the proper length and then sent to the rolling mill.

four continuous loop finishing mills. Rods, moving at 30 miles an hour, bypassed the first mill, made a narrow loop and then looped back through the first only to then go on to a second set of contiloops. (The contiloop consisted of strands set up in pairs in an alternating two-high arrangement in such a way that the lower, two-high strands could be used for straight continuous rolling. Each strand was driven by a separate motor and the loop was controlled in each repeater. Throw-outs and whip-ends were eliminated.)[22]

Photoelectric cells controlled the electric motors that regulated the speed of the steel so that it would not whip out of line as it looped through the mills. The mills could roll steel at speeds from 700 to 1,700 feet per minute. From the last of the finishing mills, the shaped steel went into a walking cooling bed. As metal fingers pushed the steel across the sawtooth-surfaced bed, the steel was cooled. Three technicians and a foreman controlled the steel from the time the billets came out of the reheat furnace until it reached the end of the cooling bed. There it would be sheared to length and stored for shipment.[23]

Another special feature at the Darlington plant was a Swiss-patented sliding gate valve at the bottom of each ladle that poured molten steel into the casting machine. The valve kept steel from overflowing. It emptied the ladle so efficiently that it eliminated the usual 4 percent of residue which normally would have to be laboriously chipped from older-type pouring ladles. This and other factors meant fewer ladles could do quicker work. By the end of 1969, the Darlington plant had poured more steel through these valves than any other plant in the world.[24]

An artist's conception of the L-shaped Darlington minimill. The actual construction of the building differed from the drawing.

The mill possessed other unique features: gas inspiration preheaters for ladles, designed by Marvin A. Pohlman, general manager at Eastern Carolina Steel and a Nuclear Corporation of America vice president, built at about one-fifth the cost of a commercial model; and a walking-beam reheat furnace, designed by John Doherty and built by Nuclear Corporation of America. The facility was automated to an exceptional degree. Three workers and a foreman could do what required 10 to 20 men in a conventional rolling mill. The men, stationed in monitoring pulpits, could override automatic controls should anything go wrong. Finally, the mill had the capability to produce high-quality angles and rounds at low cost.[25]

No Ordinary Mill

The first steel was poured on June 26, 1969. In *American Steel*, Richard Preston explained what happened.

> *"At the top of the casting machine there was a furnace for gathering the flow of liquid steel. The funnel captured the flow as it drained from the ladle. Then from the base of the funnel a strand of solidifying steel began to emerge. Suddenly, the casting machine melted down. It drenched itself with liquid steel. That is, it broke out. A hot metal cascade splashed down three stories through the casting tower with a great uproar and a cloud of smoke."*[26]

It took until October 1969 for the Darlington plant to become fully operational. Even before the facility was constructed, Nuclear Corporation had plans to eventually expand it. The original building was laid out in an L-shape, with more than 100,000 square feet of space. Foundations were laid at the time of construction for a second melting furnace and a second continuous casting machine, both of which would be installed by 1970.[27]

With the addition of the second continuous casting machine, Eastern Steel could increase its annual output to 130,000 tons of carbon steel, providing approximately half of the total steel needed by the Vulcraft division.[28]

Iverson was confident that the Darlington plant would pay big dividends. He believed that the facility at Darlington would assure the Vulcraft divisions of an economical supply of steel and create an opportunity for future expansion. He was right. The Darlington mill would provide Nuclear Corporation of America with access to extensive markets in a variety of steel products such as alloy steels, stainless steels and high temperature alloys as well as the carbon steels already produced.

Speaking to the Phoenix Society of Financial Analysts in 1972, Iverson said the Darlington mill had put the company on a path for future success. "In recent years, the single most important event in shaping the future of the company has been the construction of a highly automated steel mill at Darlington, South Carolina," Iverson said. "This is no ordinary mill. It has been described as a forerunner of a new generation of minimills."[29]

Welders producing steel joists at Nuclear's Vulcraft Division in Norfolk, Nebraska, in 1968.

CHAPTER SIX

Fighting Against Unions

1968–1969

"No union has the right to run M & S Steel Division and tell us what we have to do. We will never have to bow down to any demand which is unsound and unreasonable."

— General Manager H.M. Crapse, 1968[1]

As with the rest of the nation, the late sixties was an eventful time for Nuclear Corporation of America. While the Vietnam War, peace protests, political assassinations and man's first walk on the moon dominated the national agenda, Nuclear grappled with a problem that had plagued the steel industry for decades: the growing power of organized labor.

In January 1968, employees at Nuclear Corporation of America's M & S Steel Division in Fort Payne, Alabama (soon to become a Vulcraft division), were recruited by members of the Ironworkers International Union and Shopmen's Local 539 of Birmingham, Alabama. General Manager H.M. Crapse sent employees a memo on January 8, 1968, asking them to carefully consider the implications of unionization.

"Look at Schedule 8 on the International Union's latest financial report for the year ending June 30, 1967. You will notice that twelve bigwigs of that union divided among themselves $481,753.90 in that one year. Are these men interested in your welfare or are they looking for your dues money to continue to pay themselves such astronomical salaries? Now, do you see why these men want you to sign up with them so much? Are they in this business out of brotherly love or to drag down those tremendous salaries? ... Now, I do not know about you but this is not the kind of people I would like to have safeguarding my interests."[2]

This pro-union brochure explains why some people join unions and others do not.

Crapse asked the workers to again go over the benefits Nuclear Corporation of America provided and compare them with what a union could do. The only power a union had, he pointed out, was that it could call a strike. "No union has the right to run M & S Steel Division and tell us what we have to do. We will never have to bow down to any demand which is unsound and unreasonable."[3]

No other Nuclear division had a union contract. Vulcraft of Florence, Vulcraft of Norfolk and the Nuclear Division in Denville were all nonunion. Research Chemicals in Phoenix had held a National Labor Relations Board (NLRB) election in April 1967, in which the Packing House Workers had been voted in. Thirteen people were eligible to vote in that election. Eight favored the union and five voted against it. Although the election had been held in April 1967, no contract was ever signed.

M & S Steel Division was notified by the NLRB on December 21, 1967 that the election

would be held on January 19, 1968. When employees were notified of the date, Crapse told them, "We are confident that our people will reject this union overwhelmingly, and we want to get this matter behind us as soon as possible."

Crapse's campaign failed and the union was voted in. The final tally was 96 ballots for the Ironworkers Union, 61 against. There were also 12 challenged ballots, seven by the union and five by the company.

This cartoon was circulated at the Nuclear Corporation before the union vote at M & S.

1967-1968: Local Ironworkers union tries to unionize recently-purchased M & S Steel.

1968: Union voted in, the first for any division of Nuclear Corporation.

January 1968: Election in dispute. M & S alleges coercion by union.

1969: Union files six claims against M & S over firing of workers.

The Aftermath

On January 25, M & S filed a petition before the NLRB, seeking to have the election set aside. The company charged that the Ironworkers Union had engaged in coercive conduct, including threats against employees if they did not vote for the union. According to M & S, the union had threatened physical harm to employees who didn't sign the union authorization cards and told them they would not be able to get jobs elsewhere. M & S also said that a Ku Klux Klan officer had threatened workers with bodily and property damage if they did not join the union.

Finally, M & S charged that the NLRB representative who conducted the election "failed to conduct herself as required and furthermore, appeared in a short, short miniskirt and other attire that would bring question to employees as to whether or not the U.S. government was actually conducting this election. The gravity and seriousness of the whole election process thus lost import and perspective."[4]

Another cartoon showing the Nuclear Corporation's strong opposition to unions.

The union retaliated by filing a complaint with NLRB charging that M & S Steel fired several of its employees because they had joined the union. M & S, in a letter fired off to the NLRB, denied this was the case. One employee had been fired because "he disrupted and slowed down production by failure to remain at his station and do his work as instructed."[5] Two other employees were also fired shortly thereafter, one because he "deliberately slowed down production by wiring CO_2 gas hoses, closed and turned gas off to cause, and did cause, welding problems on the line in the plant." The other employee was terminated sim-

1969: Union gives up fight before a hearing can be held. M & S is non-union once again.

1969: Nuclear Corporation's revenues rise by $15 million over 1968.

1969: Fueled by unique incentive programs, sales increase 1,000 percent compared to 1962.

1969: Engineering computers are installed in all Vulcraft divisions.

ply because of continued absences, in violation of company policy.[6]

The battle continued into 1969. On April 21, six unfair labor charges were filed against M & S Steel in which the union challenged the termination of six employees. In the end, M & S Steel emerged the winner in both the terminations and its fight with the union. On July 15, 1969, a hearing was set for August 7 to go over a petition against the union that had been filed by the plant's attorneys. On August 1, Shopmen's Local Union No. 821, the certified bargaining representative, filed a written disclaimer of interest in the employees of M & S Steel. The union was gone.[7]

In 1981, Iverson told *The Wall Street Journal* that unionization efforts had proved to be unsuccessful because even the most lucrative basic steel agreement with a union couldn't match Nuclear's combination of wages and job security.[8]

Above: The Vulcraft Division in Grapeland, Texas, depicted in Nuclear Corporation's 1968 Annual Report.

Right: The Vulcraft Division in Florence, South Carolina, 1968.

Below: By 1968, the Nuclear Corporation was operating in seven states.

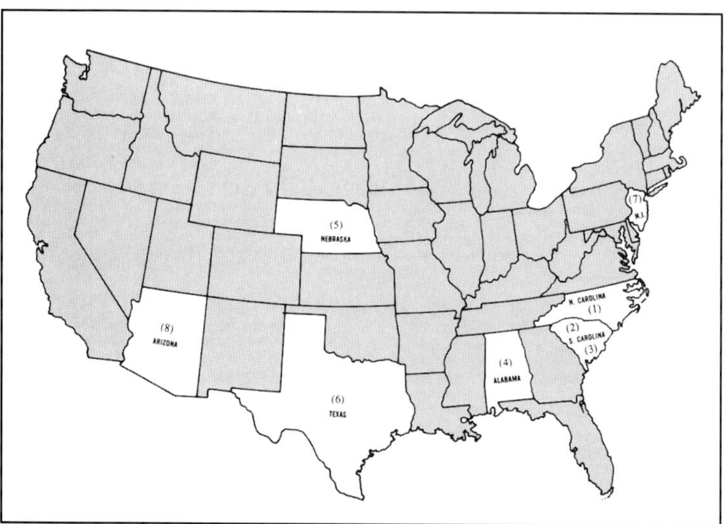

A Unique Management Structure

Nuclear's management structure would eventually become the envy of the corporate world. The

company had only four levels of management. The chairman and vice president were at the top. The next level included vice presidents and general managers, and the level below consisted of department managers. The final management level was supervisors. With the exception of the financial management, any of these divisions could operate as independent companies.[9] "In the traditional corporate culture, the general manager would be the president," noted Nucor Fastener General Manager Jerry DeMars.

> *"We do everything at the divisional level other than federal and state income taxes and cash management. I'm responsible for the marketing, sales, production, engineering, accounting, credit and collection. It's like having your own business. You've got to meet certain corporate goals of return on assets and profitability, but you keep driving to do better because your money is invested heavily in the stock, not to mention the profit-sharing plan. Everyone has an incentive to make the division grow."*[10]

Iverson believed that the general manager position was the best one in the company because the person who held that job was responsible for day-to-day operations. The general managers seemed to agree. "I'm responsible for the bottom line, and as long as the contribution is there for the company, I don't get many phone calls," said James Ronner, general manager of Vulcraft Indiana in St. Joe. "Basically, I'm my own president."[11]

Donald Holloway, vice president at Vulcraft in Nebraska, agreed. "I know that there's a corporate office in Charlotte, and if I have a major problem, somebody will talk to me and give me some advice. But aside from that, it's almost as if I'm running my own business."[12]

Three times a year, the general managers met in Charlotte. In the early years, the meetings could be quite acrimonious, as several strong-willed people, used to working with very little supervision, shared their ideas and visions. But over time, the gatherings grew calmer. November

was the preliminary budget meeting, which generally lasted about three days. Each manager would predict sales and plan expenditures for the coming year. "You make a 10-minute presentation, and at the end you know whether you've got your new furnace or not," explained Hamilton Lott, vice president and general manager of Vulcraft in Florence.[13]

Incentive Programs

Ken Iverson worked hard to keep his employees happy so they would not be tempted to join unions. Iverson didn't object to the pay scales set by the unions; he hated the work rules, which set strict requirements on the specific requirements of each job category. He believed these rules hobbled workers and stifled productivity.[14]

He never forgot that the productivity and profit of the corporation came not from management, but from the general workforce. Nuclear, and later Nucor, had four simple principles that guided employee relations.

1. Management is obligated to manage Nucor in such a way that employees will have the opportunity to earn according to their productivity.

2. Employees should feel confident that if they do their jobs properly, they will have a job tomorrow.

3. Employees have the right to be treated fairly and must believe that they will be.

4. Employees must have an avenue of appeal when they believe they are being treated unfairly.[15]

The pace was challenging and the work was difficult and dirty. Workers had to deal with ear-splitting noise and air thick with the stench of molten steel. The turnover rate in a new plant tended to be high during the first year but usually dropped to nearly zero after

Vulcraft divisions in Fort Payne, Alabama (left), and Norfolk, Nebraska (below), as they looked in 1968.

Nuclear's incentive programs encouraged productivity and allowed employees to earn higher-than-average wages. These welders are hard at work in Norfolk, Nebraska.

that. Once the workforce stabilized, productivity rose dramatically.[16]

Employees knew that working hard at Nuclear Corporation meant more money in their own pockets. John Savage, Nucor's director of personnel until 1985, noted that the company operated under the philosophy that "money is the best motivator." As he explained, "Most of our workers are unskilled or semiskilled when they begin working for us. In the past, their earnings normally have not been high, and many have had real problems maintaining even a modest standard of living."[17]

The company also prided itself on equality. All employees, from the president down to the lowest-paid hourly workers, had the same insurance, holiday and vacation benefits. There were no company cars, company boats or company planes. Everybody flew coach. There were no executive restrooms or reserved parking spots.

Furthermore, no pension plan existed. Instead, the company established a profit-sharing program with a deferred trust. Under the plan, 10 percent of the company's pretax earnings was put into profit-sharing annually. Out of this amount, approximately 20 percent was set aside to be paid to employees once per year. The rest was put into a trust to be allocated to employees based on a percentage of earnings.

By 1982, the company had four incentive compensation programs to correspond to the levels of management. The programs all relied on formulas that were based on performance because Iverson considered discretionary bonuses intrinsically unfair. The production incentive program was the most important to employees.

This program put employees in groups of 20 to 40 people and paid them weekly bonuses based on either anticipated production time or tonnage produced. To calculate the bonus, the company took the complete paycheck, including overtime, and multiplied it by the bonus factor. Each shift and each production line was in a separate bonus group.

The second incentive plan, for department managers, was based on the contributions of particular divisions. They were based primarily on return on assets for that facility.

The third incentive program applied to employees not involved in the production end and who were not at the department manager level, including accountants, engineers, secretaries, receptionists and others. Their bonuses were based on the division return on assets and the corporate return on assets.

Finally, there was the senior officer's incentive program. True to Iverson's egalitarian principles, senior officers had no employment contracts, profit sharing, pension, retirement plans or other fairly standard executive perks. Base salaries were lower than in comparable companies, but a significant part of compensation was related to the company's return on stockholder's equity. A portion of pre-tax earnings was placed into a pool that was divided among the officers as bonuses that were part cash and part stock.

The incentive program required employees to stick together, and encouraged them to find ways to improve productivity, since the results would directly affect their paychecks. "We're always looking for ways to make things better, and we pride ourselves in letting our men do that," said Gene Harris, who joined Vulcraft Indiana in 1974 and has been shift supervisor since 1978.

> *"If they come up with an idea, unless it's a tremendous amount of money, we'll try it. If it doesn't work, we'll go back to something else. But even if the original idea doesn't work, it gets a lot of other people thinking. When you have 25 guys thinking about something, somebody usually comes up with something that is really helpful."*[18]

Employees thought about the company in almost personal terms. Sam Huff, general manager of the Grapeland Plant, recalled how workers toiled throughout one miserable night to get the facility running after a flood.

> *"In the winter of 1971, we were doing some expansion when we were hit with a flood. We had taken some walls off a building, and water came in*

Above: Ken Iverson touts the benefits of doing business in Nebraska in this 1968 *Business Week* advertisement.

Right: Pouring the foundation for the Norfolk, Nebraska, joist facility on January 23, 1964.

from everywhere. People were all over squeegeeing, pushing and pumping the water out. Then the power went out. People waded in knee-deep water to string new power lines from the station outside to get the plant running again so we could produce joists."[19]

In addition to the incentive programs, the company occasionally issued bonuses to all employees when the company was doing exceptionally well. Since bonuses could account for more than half of their paychecks, employees became almost obsessed with productivity, and they would apply a lot of pressure on each other. Iverson recalled one employee who arrived for work in sunglasses rather than safety glasses. Furious because they could not do any work, the other members of his team chased him around the plant with a piece of angle iron.[20]

Competition within each plant spurred productivity to even greater heights. Michael Dunn, who joined Nucor in 1976 and is now a casting supervisor, said that his team of nine always strives to be the most productive at the Jewett facility. "You can see the weekly results of each crew. It's an unspoken thing. Whoever is in the lead is the team that we want to beat."[21]

Employees were allowed up to five absences during the calendar year, in addition to five holidays: New Year's Day, Independence Day, Labor Day, Thanksgiving and Christmas. Records were kept on all employees and their schedules. Any absences were noted. Excessive tardiness was cause for dismissal. Unexcused absences were not tolerated. If an employee was absent without excuse four times, the punishment was termination. [22]

Employees were expected to be honest and conduct themselves in a considerate way while at work. They were also cautioned to maintain good personal hygiene. Finally, this reminder was drilled into every employee's head: The customer furnishes the money for all their paychecks.[23] Employees prided themselves on high productivity and low absentee rates. Robert Foster, who joined M & S Steel in 1955 and retired from the same location in 1996, missed only seven days of work in 41 years of service. "That's the goal I set for myself," he said. "Some days, I would feel bad but I'd come to work anyway. Later in the day, I'd feel better."[24]

About half of the mill employees had never finished high school, and few had any steel mill experience. When the Darlington mill opened, the staff consisted mainly of tobacco farmers, carpenters and sharecroppers. The base starting wage at the Vulcraft's Florence plant in 1968 was $1.95 per hour at Grade I. Grade II workers could expect $2 per hour. The next grade up, a machinist's helper, made $2.25 per hour. The wages were standard for the time period, but Nuclear employees were paid a bonus for productivity, boosting wages well beyond the industry average.[25]

In a 1985 interview, Iverson noted that when the company found good workers, it went out of its way to keep them. He pointed out that the

Contractors and engineers survey the future site of the Darlington Mill in 1968.

company had had only one layoff in the 20 years Iverson had headed the company and that was in 1970. At that time, he recalled, a general manager laid off 40 employees because business was slow. This infuriated Iverson, even though his policy was normally to give managers latitude in their respective divisions. After ordering the general manager to never lay off a worker again, Iverson saw to it that within a year most of the employees were back at work at Nuclear Corporation. The general manager wasn't one of them.[26]

Big Steel vs. Nuclear

With the threat of unionization over, Nuclear continued to prosper. The four Vulcraft divisions entered 1969 with an annual production capacity that would surpass by $15 million the capacity at the beginning of 1968.[27] The divisions also entered the computer age with the addition of an IBM 1021A engineering computer at the Florence plant. By the end of 1969, computers would be installed in all four Vulcraft divisions. Sales in the Vulcraft divisions had increased more than 1,000 percent since 1962, the year Nuclear purchased the first Vulcraft in Florence.

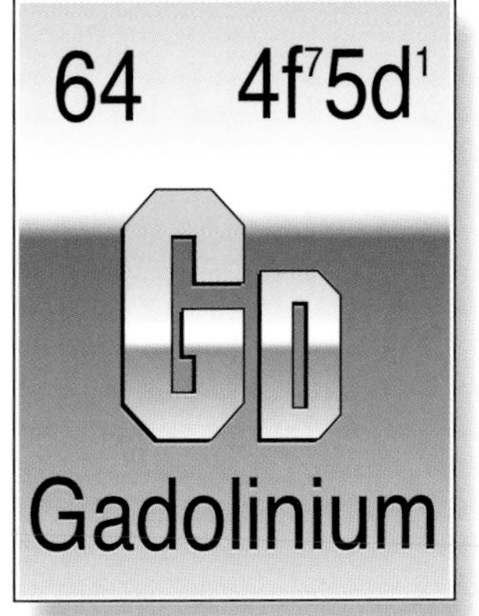

Even the Research Chemicals Division had been profitable in 1969, with sales increasing by more than 60 percent. Nuclear was optimistic that the uses of rare earths would continually expand. By this time, the division was a major supplier of such rare earth metals as lanthanum, cerium, praseodymium, neodymium, samarium, europium, gadolinium, terbium, dysprosium, holmium, erbium, thulium, ytterbium, lutetium, yttrium and scandium. Samarium was one of the more important products because it could be combined with cobalt to produce a magnet with higher field strength at less than one-tenth the cost of cobalt-platinum magnet materials. Samarium-cobalt magnets could be included in virtually any application where size, weight and dependability were important factors.

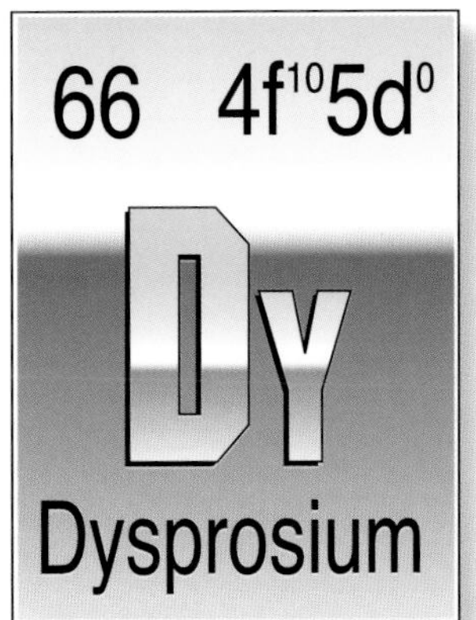

Research Chemicals supplied samarium metals in ingots, special shapes, powder, chips or distilled form to industries around the world. Gadolinium was used for effective control of nuclear power reactors. Gadolinium and dysprosium were used for neutron radiographic imaging screens. Lutetium and thulium were used for tracers. Yttrium and gadolinium oxides were used for garnets.[28]

The Nuclear Division was also turning a profit, having doubled its sales of modular power supplies, which accounted for more than 35 percent of total sales in 1968.[29]

Nuclear's success was especially striking when compared to the struggles of Big Steel. Iverson attributed the problems of Big Steel — and other large corporations — to top-heavy management that was reluctant to change. "The Big Steel companies tend to resist new technologies as long as they can. They only accept a new technology when they need it to survive."[30]

The decade, which had begun with Nuclear Corporation of America struggling to develop as a corporation, ended with success. Dick Giersch, former Nuclear assistant treasurer from 1968 to 1978, witnessed the corporation's turnaround. "Sam [Siegel] did a tremendous job on the finances, keeping the company straight on the financial end," he said.[31]

The Research Chemicals Division sold rare earth metals such as Samarium, Gadolinium and Dysprosium.

For achievement of outstanding success and adherence to the finest business standards in the true American tradition, this

Certificate of Recognition

is awarded to

Nucor Corporation

by

National Commercial Finance Conference, Inc.

at its Annual Convention this 31 st day of October, 1972.

Chairman of the Board

President

Secretary

As a rising star in industry, Nucor won many awards in the seventies. In 1972, the company was honored with a Certificate of Recognition from the National Commercial Finance Conference, Inc.

CHAPTER SEVEN

TAKING ON BIG STEEL

1970–1975

"If we have excess capacity when our competitors are constrained, and if we can maintain our lower costs, we will be unstoppable."

— Ken Iverson, 1975[1]

Designed and partially written by Sam Siegel, Nucor's 1972 Annual Report was named the best in its category by *Financial World* magazine.

THE SEVENTIES WAS a decade defined by an energy crisis, a shattered presidency, inflation and disco. It was also a period of excess. In the late sixties and early seventies, the steel industry enjoyed a brief euphoria as demand surged. Plants were expanded, with large new basic oxygen furnaces replacing open hearths. These new facilities provided greater capacity, but also had much higher operating costs. The big companies could only justify the investment by even more investment in blast furnaces, continuous casters and modern rolling mills.[2] Squeezed between a cycle of investment and the growing power of their stranglehold unions, the largest steel companies steadily raised prices. Between 1969 and 1976, the list price of steel jumped 106 percent, from $165 per short ton in December 1969 to $339 in December 1976.[3]

Meanwhile, Nuclear Corporation of America was in an enviable position. The company's minimill, with its efficient electric furnace, represented the very latest in steelmaking technology. Nuclear Corporation of America had shifted its focus from the nuclear industry (in which it had never excelled) to the steel industry. It was time to acknowledge the obvious. On December 28, 1971, stockholders at a special meeting voted to change the company's name to Nucor Corporation. The name was proposed by Sam Siegel. Nucor had been a registered trademark of the Nuclear Instruments Division since 1959, and the Nucor name and logo already appeared on stock certificates. After considerable discussion, the new name was approved, effective January 1, 1972. Said Iverson: "We feel that Nucor Corporation, our new name, not only is simpler but also more accurately reflects the nature of our business today, since the nuclear end of it accounts for less than 5 percent of our sales."[4]

When it announced the new name, Nucor also announced plans to file an application with the New York Stock Exchange to list its common shares. On July 12, 1972, Nucor's stock began trading on the New York Stock Exchange represented by the symbol NUE. At the time, Nucor was listed by *Fortune* magazine as the nation's 954th largest industrial firm. Out of the top 1,000 companies listed by *Fortune*, Nucor ranked 95th in return on stockholders' equity and 94th for 10-year growth in earnings per share.[5]

Although these rankings were impressive, they were not good enough for Iverson. His goal

Nucor stock began trading on the New York Stock Exchange on July 12, 1972. From left to right: New York Stock Exchange Executive Vice President Richard B. Howland; Nucor President Ken Iverson; and Nucor Vice President Sam Siegel.

1971: Board of Directors change name of Nuclear Corporation of America to just Nucor.

1972: Nucor stock listed on the New York Stock Exchange for the first time.

1972: Plans unveiled to build minimill in Norfolk, Nebraska.

1972: Nucor's fifth steel joist plant goes into operation in St. Joe, Indiana.

was nothing less than to position Nucor in the upper echelon of the steel industry. He took a calculated gamble and decided to expand the company's steelmaking facilities. "We are very confident that it's going to be a very fine business for those people who are efficient low-cost producers," Iverson said. "I think that we can compete in the steel business with anybody, anywhere in the world. And from all present indications, there may be a shortage of steel between 1975 and 1980. And I think it's going to be a great opportunity for good, efficient, low-cost producers."[6]

On August 10, 1972, the company announced that it would build a second minimill at Norfolk, Nebraska, the first steel mill to be built in that state. At a projected cost of $11 million, the mill would have a capacity of 160,000 tons of steel angles and rounds annually, compared to the Darlington mill's capacity of 120,000 tons. Like the Darlington mill, the Norfolk mill would make steel exclusively from scrap metal.

Also in 1972, Nucor's fifth steel joist plant went into operation in St. Joe, Indiana. By then, Nucor had launched an advertising campaign to promote the high-quality, reliable and low-cost joists streaming out of Vulcraft facilities. Joe Urey of Price-McNabb, who became Nucor's advertising account representative in 1971, said joist manufacturers hadn't bothered to advertise before. But he and Iverson concluded that Nucor offered distinct advantages to its customers that set it apart.

> *"We advertised how Vulcraft has its own trucks, which was unusual at the time. So we advertised about our ability to deliver. We also talked about our engineers who, when a problem occurs in the field, will jump in a plane or car, get to the job site and resolve the problem quickly. Now other companies might be willing to do that, but no other company advertised it. And we talked about our size, which was growing, and our locations."*[7]

In another triumph that year, the company's 1972 Annual Report was selected by *Financial World* magazine as best in its category for design and content. Between 1965 and 1978, the reports were designed by Sam Siegel, a graphic arts buff who had won art awards from *Scholastic* magazine. Siegel also did much of the writing.

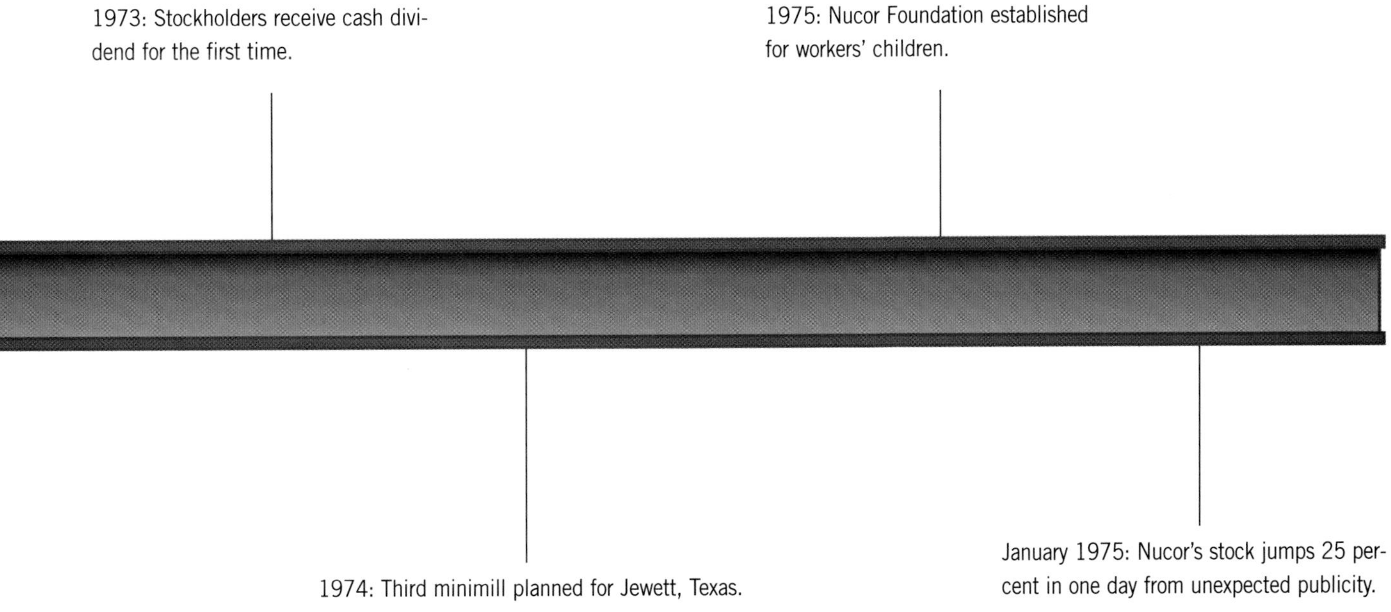

High Demand for Steel

In 1973 and 1974, the demand for steel peaked, producing a short-term shortage. Analysts predicted that raw steel capacity would be 22 million to 35 million tons short by 1980 unless new facilities were built. But the big steel companies were unwilling or unable to invest more, especially since Japanese steelmakers had found ways to produce steel at lower prices. The industry lobbied the federal government for protection from imports while it tried to improve its competitive position, as *Industry Week* explained.

> *"The script would read like this. Either investment in new steel facilities is made potentially profitable — by stabilizing foreign steel's share of the market, by liberalizing the investment tax credit and depreciation allowance, and by some kind of break on pollution control spending — or steel won't play."*[8]

The article quoted Edwin H. Gott, who had recently retired as chairman of U.S. Steel Corporation, addressing steel's joint productivity conference with the United Steelworkers of America: "I can also tell you that we have reached the time when no steel company in America can afford to invest in new raw steelmaking facilities, unless it can foresee that facility operating at 90 percent or better."[9]

Nucor, unlike other steel producers, perceived opportunity. Iverson convened a meeting with Sam Siegel and Marvin Pohlman, then vice president and general manager of the Darlington plant, to discuss construction of a third minimill. Siegel said potential steel shortages were a powerful incentive. The minimills would give Nucor its own supply of steel, so it would not have to rely on outside sources with escalating prices. Iverson also noted that the shortages would create a market for any excess steel produced by the mill. "If we have excess capacity when our competitors are constrained, and if we can maintain our lower costs, we will be unstoppable."[10]

In 1974, Nucor announced plans for construction of its third minimill, near Jewett, Texas. Like the mills at Darlington and Norfolk, it would be located near a Nucor joist plant, this one 60 miles away in Grapeland, Texas. The Jewett mill, at a cost of $17 million, would have an annual capacity of 200,000 tons of steel angles and rounds. Nucor touted the new minimill as one of the most modern and efficient mills in the United States. Although it would use more than 2,000 gallons of water per minute, no water would be taken from any river or stream, nor would any water be discharged. The dirty water from the mill would go into a settling pond where it would be filtered, reconditioned and recirculated. Nucor also planned to spend more than $1 million on dust and smoke control equipment.[11]

Because it owned its own fleet of trucks, Nucor was able to guarantee delivery.

The Jewett facility was built to supply the Grapeland joist plant with rods and angles. But the mill had enough capacity to allow Nucor to begin soliciting steel orders from outside customers. The company targeted medium-sized service centers that had formerly purchased Japanese steel.

While most domestic steel producers were calling for government restrictions on imports, Iverson did not support such measures. In December 1975, Iverson and other heads of the steel industry were asked to share their thoughts on imports at the Electric Furnace Conference held in Houston, Texas. Richard P. Simmon, president of Allegheny Ludlum Steel Corporation, and Martin H. Ornitz, president of Crucible Stainless Steel Division of Colt Industries, Inc., claimed their companies had been damaged by imports. Iverson, however, surprised the audience with his opposition to duties on steel imports.

"I am confident that any benefits that the industry derives will be more than offset by additional controls and restrictions on prices and earning," Iverson told the stunned crowd. Domestic steelmakers were in better shape than they realized, Iverson said, citing increased labor and energy costs facing offshore producers, costs that were increasing more rapidly than those in the United States. The problem with the domestic industry, he continued, was that in some respects it no longer led in new inventions and techniques.

"For many years we Americans have been conditioned to believe in our technical superiority," Iverson said. "But in the last two decades almost all of the major developments in steelmaking were made outside of the United States."[12]

Iverson believed that government interference was more detrimental than helpful. "I would be negligent if I did not recognize the significant contribution that the government has made toward the technological deterioration of the steel industry," Iverson said in another speech. "Unrealistic depreciation schedules, high corporate taxes, excessive regulation and jawboning for lower steel prices have made it difficult for the steel industry to borrow or generate the huge quantities of capital required for modernization."[13]

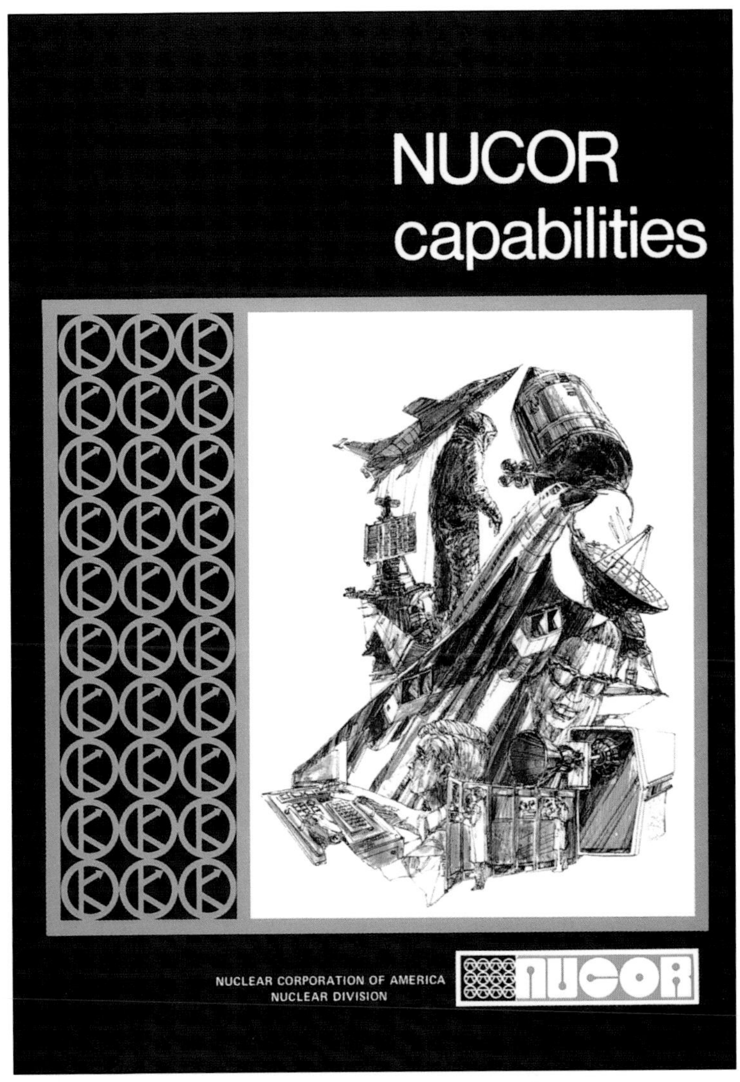

The company's Nuclear Division, in Denville, New Jersey, accounted for less than five percent of Nucor's sales in the early seventies.

Other small firms began to enter the minimill market with the same expectations as Nucor. Georgetown Steel and Eastern Carolina Steel had both opened minimills, according to *33 Magazine*, a trade publication for the steel industry.[14]

With Nucor's energy and focus on its steel mills, the emphasis shifted further away from the company's other two divisions. The Nuclear Division at Denville, New Jersey, and the Research Chemicals Division at Phoenix, Arizona, were afforded little more than a paragraph each in the company's annual reports from 1970 to 1974. Iverson had stated in 1973 that Nucor would continue to expand the two divisions, which accounted for less than 5 percent of the company's sales and earnings, as market conditions permitted. Compared to the steel business, however, the two divisions were small potatoes.

"The markets in which they participate are small when measured beside the markets for steel or steel joist, and it would be unreasonable to anticipate that either business would approach the size of our other operations in the foreseeable future," Iverson said. "In the next several years, the expansion of our business will be primarily in the steel and steel joist area."[15]

The Benefits of Success

Nucor's successes were noticed by stockholders. On May 10, 1973, Iverson announced at the annual meeting that it would issue a cash dividend. This first dividend would be 5 cents per share on Nucor's common stock. The company's success also meant bigger paychecks for employees, and more opportunities for those committed to hard work.

One example highlighted what perseverance and commitment could accomplish at Nucor. In 1969, James Samuel, a 47-year-old former sharecropper, applied for a job at the Darlington, South Carolina Vulcraft plant. The pay was $1.90 an hour for trainees. He had never been inside a steel mill, didn't even know what exactly to do, but he was willing to learn and he was willing to work hard. Four years later, Samuel, like many of his fellow Nucor employees, was earning $12,110 a year, good wages for the time and for a man who never made it to high school and had never earned more than $4,000 a year before.

Samuel became a strand-tender, controlling the level of molten steel poured into a casting machine which spit out more than 20 tons of steel billets an hour. The job was hard but Samuel was happy to do it. After four years, he was able to buy a new car and a house for his family of seven. By 1973, he was surprised when he received a bonus of more than $4,000 in cash a year for producing a bumper crop of steel billets.[16]

Nucor employees earned more than the industry standard — and they did it without unions. The secret, according to a 1973 *Wall Street Journal* article, was productivity. Workers at the Darlington plant turned out 150,000 tons a year at a cost per ton of less than four labor hours — only $3.48 in one recent week — in contrast to a national average of more than eight labor hours and an average of six in Japan, one of the most efficient foreign producers at that time.

"The pay at Nucor amazes a lot of people," noted the article. "It's a big topic of conversation on paydays at nearby beer parlors. After one session of beer guzzling and check comparing, union employees at a metalworking plant down the road, reportedly in sheer envy, staged a wildcat strike. There isn't much chance of their going to work for Nucor, however. The backlog of applicants numbers 100 or so, and only some eight jobs a year open up."[17]

Wally Hill, hired by Nucor at the Vulcraft plant, said the system encourages shifts to compete with each other and against themselves. "You get paid only for the good production you make on a shift. It's highly competitive with the next shift. It pays off for all of us."[18]

The Nucor Foundation

A fatal accident at the Darlington steel mill in 1974 prompted the company to establish the Nucor Foundation, designed to help employees send their children to college. A ladle sprung a leak, pouring molten metal over the casting platform. Four men were killed and two others were seriously injured. Nucor wanted to help the families of the men who had been killed, especially the 12 children who had been left behind. "We knew they had good insurance so we weren't so concerned with paying expenses and the like," Iverson told the *Charlotte News* in 1975. "Eventually, we came up with the idea of a college scholarship program for those children."[19]

David Aycock, then one of Nucor's vice presidents, pointed out to Iverson that the company

Right: Steel joists manufactured by Nucor can be found in retail stores, warehouses, manufacturing buildings, hospitals, churches, schools and multi-story apartments and single-family dwellings.

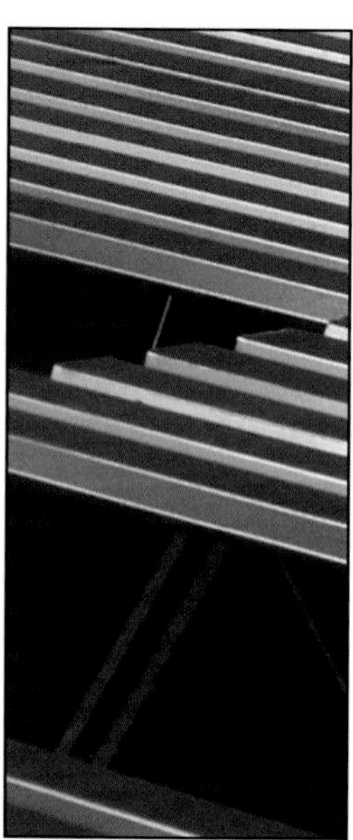

Above: Nucor Steel, a division of Nucor Corporation, manufactured a wide range of steel products at facilities throughout the United States.

had a policy of equality, so the program was expanded to cover the children of all employees. The only requirement was that a worker be employed at Nucor for at least two years. Nucor employees were given up to $1,000 per year per child for four years to attend college. The child could use the scholarship money to attend college, vocational school or a training school of his or her choice.

Left: Nucor's logo in 1972, after it changed its name from the Nuclear Corporation of America.

In 1975, Nucor conducted a survey showing that there were five or six employees' children in college every year before the scholarship program began. In 1974, there were 76 attending college full-time. By 1996, the program had expanded to more than 600 children and the scholarship had risen to $2,200.[20] Since its inception, the program has been a source of pride to everyone connected with Nucor. Said E. Michael Delaney III, an independent counsel representing Nucor:

"When you say the reason America gets behind in the world is the failure of education, and we don't have skilled workers, here's a company that's ensuring that its workers' children get to go to college. To me, it's just remarkable."[21]

A Wild Day on Wall Street

By 1975, Nucor Corporation had 2,300 employees, up from 1,420 at the start of the decade. Net sales were $121 million and net earnings were $4.1 million.

On January 19, 1975, Sheila Baird, of New York's Kimelman and Baird, appeared on the PBS series, *Wall Street Week*, and mentioned that a little-known steel mill based in, of all places, Charlotte, North Carolina, was one of her favorite companies from an investor's standpoint. What followed Baird's remarks would become known as 'White Monday.' On January 20, Nucor's stock closed at 15⅝, up 3⅛, having traded as high as 16¾. By Wednesday of that week, it was trading in the 15 to 16 range. It was unusual for a company to gain 25 percent in one day's trading, especially when analysts following the steel industry knew little, if anything, about the company.

Smith Barney's steel analyst, Peter Anker, said of Nucor, "I'd say it's not widely followed, it's not even narrowly followed, it's not even distantly followed." Even Steve Hires of Charlotte's Interstate Securities was surprised, despite the fact that he had been following Nucor for years and had recommended it to his customers.

The media speculated that one reason Nucor had been ignored by many institutional analysts was the fact that it had slightly less than 2 million shares outstanding. Not bad for a company whose shares were traded for $1.40 in 1971.[22]

Nucor's leap in shares left the New York Stock Exchange baffled. An official from the NYSE telephoned Sam Siegel asking if there was any news about the company that they should be aware of. Siegel calmly assured them that there had been no developments within the company that should have affected trading. He could only attribute it to Baird's remarks and perhaps, to a favorable article about Iverson that had appeared in the latest issue of *Forbes* magazine.[23]

The remainder of the decade would be fraught with difficulties for the steel industry. The shortage predicted in the early seventies would not materialize, and the big steel companies would find themselves in a losing battle with foreign competition. But stockholders who put their faith in Nucor Corporation would not be disappointed.

Refusing to follow Big Steel's retreat from the steel market, Nucor went on the offensive and kept its prices below those of the Japanese.

CHAPTER EIGHT

COMPETING ON ITS OWN TERMS

1976–1980

"We are not a special mill deal and won't get pushed into making deals. ... We're not interested in selling to big brokerage firms who broker steel sold to them at huge discounts."

— Ken Iverson, 1975[1]

NUCOR'S SUCCESSFUL foray into steel was all the more striking because the steel industry in general was in a state of turmoil. Demand for steel dropped sharply in 1975 and didn't improve the following year. U.S. Steel and National Steel both canceled plans to build new plants, while other projects were canceled or postponed. Between 1977 and 1981, Bethlehem Steel, U.S. Steel, National Steel and Cyclops either shut down plants or reduced operations. A few went into bankruptcy; some merged with other companies to save themselves. By 1980, the steel industry in the United States had less capacity than in 1974.[2]

"I could see them starting to fail even before I got involved in steelmaking," said David Aycock, who retired as president and chief operating officer of Nucor in 1991. "We were a very large purchaser of steel, so we could easily see it. They were very archaic and seemed to be always one generation of equipment behind Europe and Japan."[3]

At the same time, competition from overseas picked up the slack. Imported steel had first become a factor in the domestic steel market in 1959, when a nationwide steel strike shut down the industry for four months. During the next decade, the influence of imports grew slowly but steadily. Imports, which had accounted for less than 1.5 million tons of steel before the strike, totaled 18 million tons in 1968.[4] Foreign competitors had bypassed the expensive investments in basic open furnaces and integrated facilities, finding more cost-effective ways to produce steel.

Steel had become an important commodity in international trade, which made it a key issue in the debate about imports. In 1977, imported steel was a significant part of the total domestic supply, while steel exports had stagnated. In 1971, imported steel reached a high of 17.9 percent of domestic supply, and the steel trade deficit was $2.1 billion, more than 75 percent of the U.S. merchandise trade deficit of $2.7 billion. In 1973, imports had fallen back to 12.4 percent of domestic supply, but in 1976, they reached a high of 19.6 percent.[5]

Rather than retreat — the strategy followed by Big Steel — Nucor went on the offensive against foreign steel producers. "We feel there is a good chance we can keep foreign steel out," Iverson said in an interview with *American Metal Market* in 1975. "We're not paying attention to domestic mills. We're trying to keep prices beneath the Japanese."

Nucor offered many steel products at competitive prices.

Ten-strand intermediate and finishing mill. Nucor kept steel prices low by using virtually automated processes. (Photo courtesy *Iron & Steel Maker.*)

1976: Nuclear division sold off.

1977: Nucor matches price of foreign steel as it continues to drop.

1977: Imports continue to rise as Big Steel stagnates from lack of modernization.

1977: Trigger Pricing System proposed by Carter Administration to halt falling prices.

Controlling the Price Structure

Nucor beat its competition by meeting foreign prices. In mid-1974, Nucor's published prices on large orders of more than 1,000 tons were as low as $60 per ton less than domestic competitors' quality bar prices. Nucor, with minimills in Darlington and Norfolk, forced several other minimills and several major mills to begin discounting bar prices. The biggest difference in Nucor's published prices, in the summer of 1975, and those of other mills were on orders of more than 200 tons. As the amount customers purchased increased, the per-ton price decreased.

Nucor's one-inch bars, for example, were $205 per ton on orders up to 200 tons, $180 on 200- to 1,000-ton orders, and $170 on orders for more than 1,000 tons. Other domestic mills published base prices on bars between $202 and $214 per ton. On an order of 1,000 tons or more of one-inch bars, most domestic mills' published prices were $217 per ton compared to Nucor's $170. However, Nucor's competitive pricing narrowed its profit margins.[6]

Although there had been some talk of Nucor increasing its price at the end of the summer of 1975, executives decided to stick to a firm price list.

"We are not a special mill deal and won't get pushed into making deals," Iverson maintained in a 1975 interview. "We're trying to set our prices so they appeal to service centers. We're not interested in selling to big brokerage firms who broker steel sold to them at huge discounts. That (discounting) is not in the best interests of building integrity in the steel business."[7]

Although discounting to brokers was a common practice among the major mills and some minimills, Nucor would have no part of it. Iverson didn't believe in maintaining a fictitious base price during a soft market, while actually selling steel at various cut-rate levels.

"If we have to come down in price to meet the market, we'll do it across the board by issuing a new lower price list," Iverson said in 1975. "Then when the market firms up, we'll raise our base prices."

According to one article, Nucor's prices were as low as any domestic mill could go and still make a profit. At the time, Nucor's steel prices were 10 to 15 percent below foreign prices. As a result, sales increased despite early reluctance on

1978: In spite of protests from steel industry segments, Trigger System goes into effect.

1979: Construction begins on new minimill in Plymouth, Utah.

1978: Bonus given to workers to reward better-than-expected profits.

1979: Nucor enters cold-finish market.

The conveyor system brings billets from the continuous casting machine to the conductive billet heater. (Photo courtesy of *Iron & Steel Maker.*)

the part of service centers to take on Nucor Steel, according to the American Metal Market firm.

"Our major problem was that we had to convince service centers that we wouldn't go back to just producing joists in our own plants when the market firmed up," Iverson explained.[8]

Nucor's price reductions fueled competition from the smallest producers to the largest steel giants. In an open letter to steel customers December 19, 1975, Iverson wrote:

"In the last several weeks a number of larger steel companies have decided, almost simultaneously, to match Nucor Steel's prices. You might ask how they are going to do this since we do not equalize freight nor do we have the same pricing structure. Obviously they intend to match our prices on a customer-by-customer basis. (It is interesting to note that in most cases their reductions are only on the products and sizes made by Nucor.)

"At Nucor Steel we place great emphasis on building mills economically and running them efficiently. I suggest you ask some of the larger producers if they can build plants, as we do, with a capital cost under $90 per ton of annual capacity. Can they produce steel with less than five man-hours per ton? Last year the seven largest steel companies in the United States had total employment costs that averaged more than $110 per ton. Ours were under $45. Our yields from hot metal to finished product are in the range of 90 percent. Our prices are based on these lower costs, and we operate profitably.

"Chances are our salesman won't call on you very often. He probably doesn't play golf. The odds are he won't take you to dinner. And I am sure he won't offer you a ride on an ore boat. But he will provide high-quality steel angles, rounds, channels, flats, special shapes and forging billets at economical prices.

"My only regret is that we don't make an even wider range of products and sizes so that even more steel customers can benefit from our efficiencies. Therefore, I suggest you buy from Nucor if you want a lower price from the larger steel companies."[9]

A few months later, Nucor announced a price increase in its merchant-quality bars and small structural steel pieces. Nucor was encouraged to boost its merchant quality bar and small structural prices by a 50-percent increase in its mill order backlog since mid-December 1975. It was able to increase its backlog despite increased competition from large integrated producers, who began meeting prices charged by Nucor and other minimills late in 1975.[10]

Nucor's announcement was followed a week later by similar announcements from a majority of its competitors. "Most other minimills don't want to follow Nucor, but they're being forced to follow," one source said. What led to the increases, it appeared, was the fact that there were recent increases in scrap prices and indications that Japanese mills were raising their prices as well.[11]

Efficient, aggressive competitors, such as North Star Steel Company, based in St. Paul, Minnesota, did not follow Nucor's lead. North Star announced in April 1976 that it would increase the price on its concrete reinforcing bars and merchant-quality bar products by $25 per ton. James Conway, then vice president of sales, said North Star would no longer meet Nucor Corporation's merchant-quality bar prices, which were as much as $30 per ton lower. This announcement indicated that the steel market still had a lot of strength, Iverson was quoted as saying. There was plenty of work for the minimills, it appeared, including the three operated by Nucor.[12]

Encouraged by this strength, Nucor officials decided the time was right to both boost prices and increase capacity for merchant bar products. On June 1, 1976, prices rose an additional $10 to $20 a ton. Shortly thereafter, more than $9 million was earmarked to build the first domestic

Below: Once reheated, billets move from the reheat furnace to the roughing mill, where they are formed into usable shapes. (Photo courtesy of *Iron & Steel Maker.*)

The billet heating sequence is shown from top to bottom. In 1976, with its focus on efficiency and automation, Nucor's total labor cost per ton of steel was $45, compared to the industry standard of $110. (Photo courtesy of *Iron & Steel Maker.*)

steel mill that would directly link a continuous billet caster to a bar mill at its Darlington, South Carolina plant.[13]

However, the price increase was short-lived. Demand dropped at the same time other minimills reduced their own prices. In September 1976 Nucor announced a price decrease on its bar products, cutting base prices by $15 per ton for all its product lines effective October 1, 1976. Iverson said in an interview that the across-the-board price reductions, which averaged more than 7 percent, were in response to special price protection deals reportedly offered by other domestic minimills, and reflecting the lowest demand since July 1975.[14]

But by the end of the year, steel and steel scrap prices had bottomed out. Iverson predicted that prices would probably increase by early 1977 and was confident that sales would climb. In a speech to financial analysts in New York in November 1976, Iverson said that the company's major competitors were no longer foreign steel, whose energy and labor costs were rising more quickly than Nucor's. He predicted that Nucor's sales in 1976 would reach $170 million, compared to around $121 million for 1975.[15]

But Big Steel was still complaining about imports. Bethlehem Steel noted in its 1977 Annual Report that the weak worldwide demand for steel put pressure on other nations to export their steel product or reduce employment. Many foreign companies, the report asserted, chose not to reduce their workforce, instead opting to sell steel in the United States below their production costs.

"The overall impact of imports on the American steel industry has been severe," Bethlehem maintained. "A number of steel companies were forced during 1977 to make permanent cutbacks in raw steelmaking capacity and in workforce levels. While not the sole reason, steel imports were certainly a factor in the formulation of Bethlehem's plan to permanently reduce capacity."[16]

The Trigger Price System

In 1977, total steel imports soared to an all-time high, more than 20 percent of the market by year's end. In December 1977, President Jimmy Carter announced a program to address some of the problems facing the domestic steel industry. The key to the administration's program was the institution of the Trigger Price System. It was a system that outlined trigger — or reference prices — for steel products entering the United States. The prices were supposed to be based on the production costs of the most effective Japanese producers. The trigger system kicks in to prevent prices from falling below a certain point, in order to help prop up domestic steel prices.

Many steel companies, including Nucor, disapproved, arguing that the system might actually encourage additional imports into the west.

"Trigger pricing gives a bonus to the foreign steel producers for keeping his employees at work and, in effect, penalizes the American steel producer for doing so," asserted Kaiser Steel in its 1977 Annual Report. "The company also thinks the trigger-price mechanism provides a quasi-legal status for most steel producers in the world to dump steel in the U.S. markets at the trigger price level."[17]

Iverson also opposed the initiative on the grounds that it amounted to government-controlled price-setting.

"The trigger prices originally instituted in 1978 are supposed to provide fast relief against dumping of foreign steel," Iverson said in a 1981 speech.

> *"In actuality they result in price-setting by the government. ... The real hazard in the trigger price system is that manufacturers outside the United States, or United States manufacturers who move outside, use the cheaper steel available and then export into the United States a wide variety of products at lower cost than domestic manufacturers because of our higher steel prices."*[18]

Trigger prices, Iverson contended, would probably stall the rebuilding of the steel industry, since they would distort prices and artificially prop up inefficient domestic mills which he believed should be closed anyway.

"The main reason I'm opposed to them is that I don't feel companies which produce steel at costs lower than this country should be denied access to our market," Iverson said in another interview, adding that his worst fear was that trigger prices might result in greater imports of finished goods and encourage domestic firms to set up offshore plants.

> *"If the trigger price system gets out of hand — and with a government bureaucracy, that's not unlikely — then a company could install manufacturing operations in other countries and ship back to the United States. In the long run, trigger prices could seriously injure the economy of our country."*[19]

Expansion and Success

In spite of the climate of the late 1970s, however, Nucor Steel continued to grow and prosper. In 1978, all employees received the following letter from Iverson:

> *"To Fellow Employees: Our company has a policy that all employees should share in the company's success. As part of this policy, the*

An aerial view of the minimill in Plymouth, Utah.

Above and below: Scenes from the interior of the Plymouth plant, where billets are formed from scrap metal. In spite of see-sawing steel prices, Nucor surpassed its own expectations. Bonuses as high as $500 were given to all employees.

company contributes about 10 cents out of each dollar of earnings to the employees' profit-sharing plan. Our earnings this year are exceptionally good. Provided these earnings continue, the contribution to the profit-sharing plan for this year will be substantially higher than in previous years. Many of us remember recent years in the past when we had problems operating in our normal levels of production because of poor economic conditions. In recognition of those difficult years and the loyalty and hard work which have made this year's performance possible, the directors have authorized an extraordinary payment. On August 15, all full-time employees who have been with the company 90 days or longer will receive $500. I hope this payment will be a benefit to you and your family. Save it, spend it or invest it wisely. By working together, your efforts have made Nucor the finest company I know."[20]

Focusing on Core Strengths

By 1979, 99 percent of Nucor's sales were from its primary business, the manufacture of steel and steel products. Sales had increased 167 percent in five years, from $160.4 million in 1974 to $468.6 million in 1979.[21] Company officials knew it was time to focus solely on what had made Nucor a success. The company had already sold off its Nuclear Division in 1976 for $171,000. At the time, there were 19 contracts out, 11 with the U.S. Navy, for a total book value of $376,470, all of which would be paid to Nucor. In the end, the Nuclear Division no longer fit Nucor's plans.[22]

That left only one non-steel-related division: Research Chemicals. By the end of 1979, Research Chemicals accounted for only one percent of the company's sales. It was easy to see that its days were numbered, but Nucor would hold onto it for a little longer.

In the late 1970s, Nucor embarked on a major expansion program of its Florence and Norfolk plants. New facilities were also in the works. In 1979, construction began on a new 400,000 tons per year mill in Utah. "We're pushing hard on expansion," Iverson said in a 1979 interview. "We want to run when we're hot."[23]

In 1979, Nucor had entered the cold-finish business, starting up a facility in Norfolk, Nebraska, and adding another one in Darlington, South Carolina, in 1981. Together the two plants produced more than 80,000 tons per year of cold-finished steel products which are used extensively for shafting and machined precision parts. The cold-finish process draws steel through a die, creating a product with excellent surface finish and more accurate dimensions. Nucor's Cold Finish Division produced rounds, hexagons, flats and squares in carbon and alloy steels. The market for cold-finished steel did not fluctuate as greatly as markets for other kinds of steel, explained Donald Holloway, general manager of Norfolk since 1977.

Since cold-finished steel could be used for either buildings or equipment, it could ride out the inevitable swings in either industry. "We have gotten pretty big with equipment manufacturers," he said. "It can be in farm equipment, electric motors, a wide variety of products. Even during a downturn, people are still buying washing machines and refrigerators. So our business fluctuates a little, but not that much."[24]

On January 1, 1979, Keith E. Busse was named a vice president of the corporation. Busse, also general manager of the Vulcraft Division in St. Joe, Indiana, had joined Nucor in 1975.

By December 1979, Nucor employed 3,100 people, mainly in its steel divisions.[25] Nucor had finally hit the big time. Merrill Lynch was highly recommending Nucor's stock and in 1978 offered a glowing description of the company in a research report issued to its brokers.

"The historic growth pattern that Nucor Corporation has achieved is very impressive, especially in light of the fact that Nucor is a producer and fabricator of steel and that the track record of the steel industry has been spotty at best in recent years," the report read.

"Because of its ability to generate good profits while selling at relatively low prices, Nucor is in an excellent position to increase market penetration and to accumulate capital for future growth."[26]

The glow of molten steel pouring into this ladle lights up the interior of the Plymouth, Utah minimill, built in 1981.

CHAPTER NINE

IN THE SPOTLIGHT

1980–1984

"We just do two things well. We build plants very economically, and we operate them very efficiently. ... All we want to do is build on that."

— Ken Iverson, 1980[1]

NUCOR STEEL MARCHED into the decade of the eighties full of confidence. It had finally broken into the ranks of the *Fortune* 500, ranking at number 481 by the end of 1979. A 40-percent increase in sales that year allowed it to move up 81 spots from its ranking of 562 the previous year. Ken Iverson, still considered a maverick in the steel industry, was the focus of increasing press coverage, and was invited to speak at influential gatherings and industry conferences. With many executives within the steel industry complaining about foreign competition and asking for help from the federal government, Iverson's can-do attitude and irrefutable results represented a refreshing change.

As media attention increased, Nucor's stock continued to climb. "People are finally beginning to realize we exist," was the only explanation one Nucor Corporation executive could give for Nucor stock's performance in the first six months of 1980. On July 15, 1980, Nucor's stock rose to 59⅜, its highest price so far. Only a week earlier, Nucor set what was then a 52-week high when it closed at 51¾. William Staton, who headed the research department of Charlotte-based Interstate Securities Corporation, noted that when the stock market as a whole dropped sharply, Nucor stock dropped only modestly.

Amazingly, given Nucor's presence in Charlotte, many of the city's residents passed up an investment opportunity with Nucor. Staton surmised that local investors were wary of Nucor because the "company's earning growth has been so dramatic that everybody kept thinking it couldn't go on."[2]

Two things occurred in June 1980 that would spark even greater public interest in Nucor Corporation.

"If Japan Can Do It ... Why Can't We?"

On June 24, 1980, NBC television broadcast a special entitled "If Japan Can Do It ... Why Can't We?" The broadcast, anchored and written by NBC news correspondent Lloyd Dobyns, studied the problems of American productivity and what was being done to improve it. "What makes the Japanese so interesting," Dobyns said in the broadcast, "is that they can show us what's wrong with the system in this country."

The Japanese, according to the report, used what they called a quality circle system, basically

Keeping a firm hand on costs, Nucor's minimills were a bright spot in an otherwise bleak time for the American steel industry.

a method of statistical control. They believed a company must have complete quality control over the production process from beginning to end. American productivity was down, the program pointed out, because of declines in innovation, spending on research and development, capital investment and personal savings. Despite the depressing news, there was one American company that stood out, one that was productive. That company was Nucor. The special examined Nucor's production process, its plants and its incentive program.[3]

A number of executives wrote Iverson letters of congratulations after the show aired. "I saw your interview on the NBC White Paper Report last week," wrote Tyler E. Glenn, Jr., of the Charlotte-based advertising company The Down's Group, Inc. "You did a super job as spokesman for 'little' steel. If 'big' steel could get its act together like Nucor, increased productivity would rival that of its Japanese competitors. The big guys should take lessons from Nucor."[4]

In 1980, Ken Iverson was named Best Chief Executive, following an NBC broadcast that put Nucor in the spotlight.

More praise arrived from J.R. Oden, Jr., president of Malone Freight Lines, Inc., in Birmingham, Alabama.

> *"We think your program should be a guide to other industrial firms in the United States to show what can be done to not only increase production, but also to produce a quality product. I think that it is very significant that your quality control is such that our Japanese competition wanted to see how to do it. Congratulations on proving that 'American Know How' is still working in this country."*[5]

The second thing that happened in June 1980 was that Iverson was named by *The Wall Street Transcript* as the 1980 Best Chief Executive in the specialty steel and minimill category. The staff at *TWST* selected the top CEO based on interviews with industry executives, leading financial analysts, money managers,

1980: NBC airs a program on Nucor, hailing the company's competitiveness.

1980: Ken Iverson named Best Chief Executive in the specialty steel and minimill category.

1980: Nucor's stock continues to rise, reaching 59⅜ for the first time.

1981: Minimill in Plymouth, Utah, comes on line.

trade journalists, members of the academic community and various other professional sources. Said one analyst:

> *"Iverson has used the newest technology available in the world to make his minimills. He has what we call a small electric furnace shop. Nucor is the lowest-cost producer in the United States and probably in the world. Iverson has used this new technology by putting it into small regional plants which can serve a limited market. He has done very well by any financial measure. This is the outstanding company in the industry."*[6]

Iverson wanted his company to be up there with the "big companies." And he believed he had the formula to do so without experiencing Big Steel's problems. He explained to *TWST* that Nucor was different from the competition in three ways.

> *"First, we build our plants more economically than other people. We are actually a kind of do-it-yourself organization. We build our own continuous casters. We build our own reheat furnaces. We build our own cooling beds. We even now build our own mill stands. This gives us a distinct advantage regarding capital costs in the construction of a mill.*
>
> *"Secondly, the big difference between our facilities and many of the other steel facilities is that the average age of our facilities is about four years. So we are not handicapped with old facilities or old equipment or the problem of making them environmentally acceptable.*
>
> *"The third area is, of course, that we rely very heavily on productivity incentives. We have extremely good productivity from our people. We really don't differentiate between management people or anybody else. We all have the same hospitalization, the same vacation, the same insurance program, the same holidays. We don't allow names on parking places. We don't have executive dining rooms. We don't have hunting lodges or fishing lodges. We don't have any company cars. We don't have any company airplanes. Sometimes I get tired of riding economy class, but everybody else has to.*
>
> *"We are a pretty simple company when you get down to it. All of our growth has been internally generated. We just do two things well. We build plants very economically, and we operate them very efficiently. ... All we want to do is build*

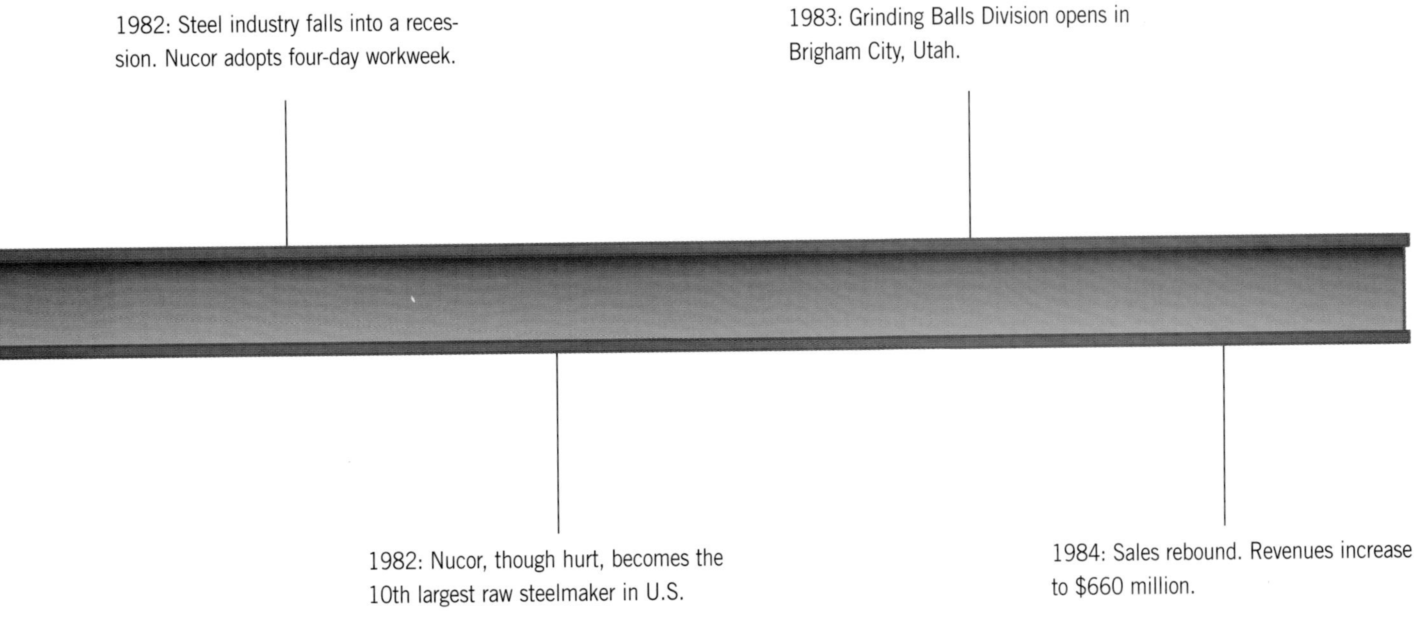

on that. We like the steel business, and we like the steel products area. ... We are going to try to stick to our knitting."[7]

Another key to the company's success was its decentralized management. With a corporate staff of only 22 employees, decisions were pushed down the management chain. Executives of other companies often asked Iverson how to streamline their own corporate structures. They were reluctant to fire people who had been with the company a long time, and they wanted advice. "Whenever I hear that, it galls me," Iverson said. "Why didn't they do it before? Why did they let it get so big and cumbersome in the first place?"[8]

Sam Siegel likes the philosophy of British historian Northcote Parkinson, who explained in the 1950s that the number of administrators in an organization tends to increase because officials hire assistants, who in turn create work. "We need to have people who do not need to be supervised, because then you need more people to supervise them," said Siegel.[9]

As James Coblin, who became personnel manager in 1985 would explain: "It's easier to stay thin than to be heavy and lose weight." He added, "I sympathize with companies that are trying to downsize and change their structure. It's difficult. If they want a Nucor system, it's best to start from scratch and hire new people. But if they're trying to change their culture, usually it doesn't work."[10]

Prosperity and Expansion

Nucor experienced record profits in 1980 and 1981.[11] It was also a time for expansion. In late 1980, Nucor expanded its Jewett, Texas mill from 250,000 tons to about 600,000 tons. In late 1981, the mill in Norfolk, Nebraska was expanded, increasing capacity from about 500,000 tons to 600,000 tons per year. And in mid-1981, Nucor opened a new 400,000 ton-per-year steel mill near Plymouth, Utah, enabling the company to further penetrate the western regional market.

The Plymouth facility was John Correnti's first project with Nucor. He would eventually become Nucor's president, chief executive officer and vice chairman. Arriving from U.S. Steel, Correnti described the feeling of liberation he experienced during the Plymouth construction.

"It was great fun because so much could be done so much faster than at U.S. Steel. There, you had a flock of engineers in Pittsburgh and a purchasing department in Pittsburgh. At Nucor, if you wanted to know who was going to purchase such-and-such, you looked in the mirror. If you wanted to know who was going to design such-and-such, you looked in the mirror."[12]

Remarkably, the plant was built in a year.

"In construction, I learned that time is money. The capital equipment you buy is so expensive that my philosophy has always been that once it arrives on the site, you are losing money every day until it's running and producing and giving you a revenue stream. So you've got to go like crazy and build the mill fast."[13]

The company's steel mills by then covered most of the American market. Darlington, South Carolina, served the Northeast and Southeast. Norfolk, Nebraska, served the Midwest. Jewett, Texas, served the Southwest and Southeast, and Plymouth, Utah, served the West and Southwest.

By 1982, the company's six Vulcraft divisions were producing in excess of 475,000 tons per year of steel joists and joist girders. About 70 percent of the steel produced by the steel mills was sold to outside customers. The company had embarked on an ambitious five-year product expansion, producing a wider range of grades and sizes of angles, rounds, channels, flats, forging billets and special small shapes. The products were used in farm equipment, oil and gas equipment, mobile homes, transmission towers, bed frames, hand tools, automotive parts, highway signs, building construction, machinery and industrial equipment.

In 1983, Nucor established a Grinding Balls Division in Brigham City, Utah, to produce steel

Right: Billets are rolled in continuous mills as cooling water is sprayed on the hot bar at the Plymouth minimill.

DANIELI
3
4

grinding balls which are typically sold to the mining industry for use in processing copper, iron, zinc, lead and other ores. This division would enter a competitive market where price, not quality, was the main criteria, noted Ladd Hall, general manager of the Vulcraft Division in Brigham City, Utah. Hall arrived at Nucor in 1981, and moved around the company before returning to his home state of Utah. He described the grinding ball process.

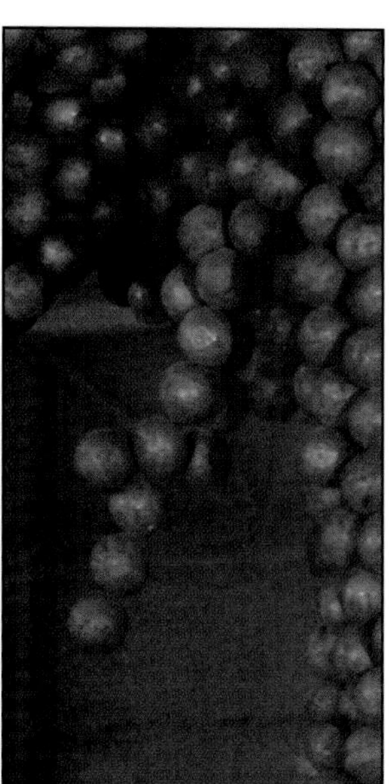

"We take a high-carbon rod, and we get all of that material from Plymouth, and heat it with electrically fired induction heaters, and then cut it into slugs of eight to 10 inches. The slugs are forged — actually slammed — together into a round ball anywhere from one to five inches. That product is further processed through a heat-treating furnace and is slow-cooled and sent out to our customers."[14]

As successful as the Plymouth plant would prove to be, getting things organized took time, recalled Daniel DiMicco, who joined Nucor as a chief metallurgist at the Plymouth plant in 1981 and has since become vice president and general manager of Nucor-Yamato. He noted that the plant hadn't reached its potential until certain processes were worked out.

"The major problem was that there was a tremendous lack of organization when it came to coordinating between the melt shop and the rolling mill, the inventory and the semi-finished billet yard. One of the biggest contributions we made was getting the bloom yard to operate efficiently. The bloom yard is one of those no man's land. Nobody really wants to have to bother with it, but it's the equivalent of the human heart of the plant. Everything flows through that area, the intersection of one process and another."[15]

Recession

But the steel industry was about to enter its darkest era in nearly half a century. America, already in a recession, was sinking in even deeper. In 1982, demand for steel dropped sharply, prompting massive layoffs at steel plants throughout the United States. In 1977, more than 30,000 people were employed at six U.S. Steel companies along the Monongahela River in Pennsylvania. By

Top: Nucor entered the grinding balls business in 1983, opening a plant in Brigham City, Utah.

Right: The rolling line keeps the billets moving through the mill stands at the Plymouth, Utah minimill.

1982, less than 10,000 remained employed in those plants. Employment continued to fall in the steel industry to 242,000, the lowest figure since the early 1930s. By 1984, one-third of the nation's steelworkers were unemployed.[16]

Inland Steel reported a net loss of $118.7 million on sales of $2.8 billion. Bethlehem Steel posted a record loss of $1.5 billion. U.S. Steel had already started to divest many of its steel assets. By late 1981, after merging with Marathon Oil, U.S. Steel had preserved less than 24 percent of its assets in the steel business.[17] Half of the American steel industry's capacity was idle in 1982. Between 1982 and 1983, the nation's steelmakers lost a staggering $6 billion collectively.[18]

Even Nucor was affected by the recession. Sales of $486 million in 1982 were 11 percent lower than in 1981, and net earnings of $22.2 million were 37 percent lower than the $34.7 million in 1981.[19]

Further exacerbating the situation, steel imports into the United States climbed to a record 26 million tons by 1984, prompting steelmakers to clamor for passage of the Fair Trade in Steel Act of 1984, which would limit imports to 15 percent of domestic consumption for five years. In 1985, the Reagan administration agreed to negotiate voluntary restraints.[20]

A 1981 report from the congressional General Accounting Office found several reasons why American companies were buying foreign steel. "The companies interviewed frequently cited, as reasons for buying foreign steel, unavailability or restricted sources of certain steel mill products domestically, and lack of dependability or slowness of U.S. companies' delivery systems," said Fred Lamesch, vice president of the American Institute for Imported Steel, Inc., speaking at the General Electric Biannual Steel Symposium in 1981. "GAO found that, though a number of buyers give lower prices as the main reason for purchasing foreign steel, many of them are attracted by other factors, with better marketing services and attitudes a major consideration."[21]

Meanwhile, Nucor was surviving the downturn without laying off a single employee. "Layoffs aren't in our plan," Sam Siegel told *The Wall Street Journal* in 1982. "And we'll do everything we can to prevent them." That strategy could keep costs up slightly, he added, "but we think it's worth it."[22]

However, the company was forced to reduce the workweek to four days for its employees in an effort to save money. The company also froze wages for its nearly 3,500 employees. In some cases, weekly productivity actually went up because employees wanted to increase their bonus to compensate for the lost wages of the fifth day. But the incentive plan, so attractive to Nucor's employees, had a negative side. Less work meant less money for everyone. "In a downturn, hourly workers may earn about 20 to 25 percent less than in good economic times," Iverson said in 1984. "Department heads earn 30 to 45 percent less, while compensation to corporate officers may drop as much as 60 to 70 per-

cent. I think in 1980 I earned $430,000. In 1982, I earned $108,000."[23]

With other companies abandoning the steel industry, Nucor was able to increase its market share in the steel joist area.

While 1982 was not Nucor's best year in terms of sales, there was some good news. The company became the 10th largest raw steel producer that year, with production of 1.2 million net tons of steel, jumping from 16th in 1981. The number one company was U.S. Steel, with 12.1 million tons. Nucor was the first minimill to make the top-10 list.[24]

Sales rebounded in 1983 and 1984. Net sales of $543 million in 1983 were 12 percent higher than in 1982. Sales of $660 million in 1984 allowed the company to post net earnings of $44.5 million.

In late August 1984, Nucor restructured the company's pricing policy by eliminating quantity discounts and lowering total prices by an average of $15 a ton. For example, before the new schedule, Nucor's price for 2-inch-by-2-inch-by-¼-inch angles in orders of 600 tons or more from Eastern mills was $269 a ton, while the price for orders of 20 tons was $289 a ton. The new price for at least 20 tons was $246.[25]

A survey by American Metal Market revealed that most competing minimills were planning to follow Nucor's move in order to remain competitive. But executives were reluctant to drop prices. One Eastern service center executive, who asked not to be identified, complained that Nucor's move was "an attempt to control the minimill industry," which he said would have an overall negative influence on the market.

> *"I just think it's bringing the market further down," he continued. "Who wants to see prices go down any more than they have? We're trying to firm up the market."*[26]

But Nucor maintained that it lowered its prices in an effort to meet import prices. It was easy to understand why. Total steel imports for July 1984 were up 91 percent over 1983, 420,103 tons compared with 219,799 tons.[27]

Nucor was no longer competing with big U.S. steel mills. Major mills had first ignored the minimill threat. "We were sort of viewed as a flea on the elephant," Iverson said. But the major mills eventually yielded some product lines to the minimills, considering the minimill threat contained, largely because of the minimills' inability to produce flat rolled and heavy structural steel. Integrated steel makers, like U.S. Steel and Bethlehem Steel, were starting to produce more sophisticated products that the minimills could not produce.

"Minimills have largely passed the phase of displacing tonnage from integrated producers," said Frank W. Luerssen, president and chief executive officer of the Inland Steel Company. An executive from another major steel company added, "We're concentrating on the more sophisticated products where they can't compete, and we've dropped the inefficient product lines to them."[28]

Nucor, at the time one of about 50 minimill operators, now faced increased competition from other minimills. "We're now head-to-head against much tougher competition," Iverson said in an interview. "It was no contest when we were up against the integrated mills. Now we are facing minimills who all have the same scrap price, the same electrical costs and the same technologies."

Left: Vulcraft steel joists.

As the eighties progressed, Nucor's steel deck was used in the construction of countless high-rise office and apartment buildings.

CHAPTER TEN

FORGING ALLIANCES

1984–1986

"The reason that Nucor is successful is because we don't know that we're not supposed to be. ... We don't tell our people what they can't do. We challenge them to do it, and they do it. We're actually amazed every day by the stuff our people will do."

— Joe Rutkowski, 1996[1]

NUCOR'S RAPID RISE in the world of steel had been remarkably free of the common impediments that had plagued other companies in the steel industry. The company had no unions. There were scant environmental problems and no suffocating fixed expenses. Press reports were generally favorable.

But in 1984, Nucor's directors dropped a bombshell when they determined that employees at plants in Norfolk, Nebraska, and Grapeland, Texas, might have assisted various importers to conceal violations of the Department of Commerce's Trigger Price Mechanism during the period between 1979 through 1982.

These trigger price regulations prohibited importers from selling below prices that at times exceeded competitive market prices. Nucor employees, of course, were accustomed to seeking the best possible prices in their steel purchase negotiations. Nucor, unbeknownst to corporate headquarters, purchased steel below the trigger price. According to a confidential memo concerning the incidents, one of the Nucor people involved was an officer at the plant level. The plant received inflated invoices or sent documents that enabled importers to demonstrate that they were complying with the trigger price regulations. According to the document, during the period in which the incidents occurred the spread between Nucor's purchase price and the trigger price "may have aggregated as much as a million dollars." However, the estimate was never finally determined.

It wasn't hard for Iverson and Nucor's board of directors to decide how to handle the incident. They notified the U.S. Department of Justice, which had already begun an investigation, that they would cooperate fully with the government. Nucor wanted the problem solved, and it wanted to do it properly. In the end, no wrongdoing was discovered.

Sam Siegel also contacted attorney Chick Abeles, asking him to examine the government investigation of possible violations of the steel trigger price system and to advise Nucor of possible guidelines for an internal investigation to coincide with that of the Department of Justice.

The Justice Department began an investigation of one importer whose sales to Nucor accounted for a portion of the suspect trade. The department also dispatched investigators to the plants to interview employees. A grand jury was convened in Houston, Texas, and Nucor agreed to testify in exchange for immunity from potential prosecution.

As the steel industry recovered from the recession, Nucor began to search for new markets and new products. Eventually, the company would produce steel plating.

On October 19, 1984, a Justice Department attorney confirmed its grant of immunity to individual Nucor employees and the corporation itself.[2]

In October 1984, Nucor was notified that the United States Customs Service's District Director in Houston had elected not to assess penalties against Vulcraft or Nucor Corporation. "The district director's decision is based upon the fact of the cooperation of Vulcraft, Nucor Corporation, Kenneth W. Atkins and Larry A. Roos, and the fact that Vulcraft and Nucor were not importers of record for steel products."[3] Nucor has similarly cooperated when contacted regarding other investigations concerning the steel industry. For example, on January 24, 1984, Richard B. Smith of the Federal Trade Commission wrote Iverson requesting documents and other information about Nucor for 1983. Siegel promptly gathered the materials, responding to Smith exactly one month later. He noted in a letter to Smith that Nucor "has not been involved in, and has no knowledge of, any collusive pricing activities. We have a policy of minimizing contact with competitors." As a result of this policy, Nucor was not even a member of the two big steel industry organizations, American Iron & Steel Institute, and the Steel Bar Mills Association.[4]

Changes at the Top

In 1986, Iverson was asked at the company's annual meeting if he had contemplated a successor. "I've thought about it for a long time," he responded. "I've decided that at some point in time I would probably bring in one of the officers of the company and let him serve as the chief operating officer of the day-to-day business, which would allow me more time to devote to research and development or to outside relations of the company. We would not be creating another management layer, which I'm very much opposed to," Iverson continued. "But we might be able, under that system, to divide up the responsibilities of the office that I serve and therefore do a more effective job in planning for the future and operating efficiently."[5]

A short time later, Dave Aycock was elected president and chief operating officer of Nucor. Aycock's promotion reinforced the company's assertion that there was no limit to how far a Nucor employee could rise in the company. Aycock had started at the Vulcraft Division in Florence in 1954 as a welder, earning an hourly wage. Without benefit of a college education, he

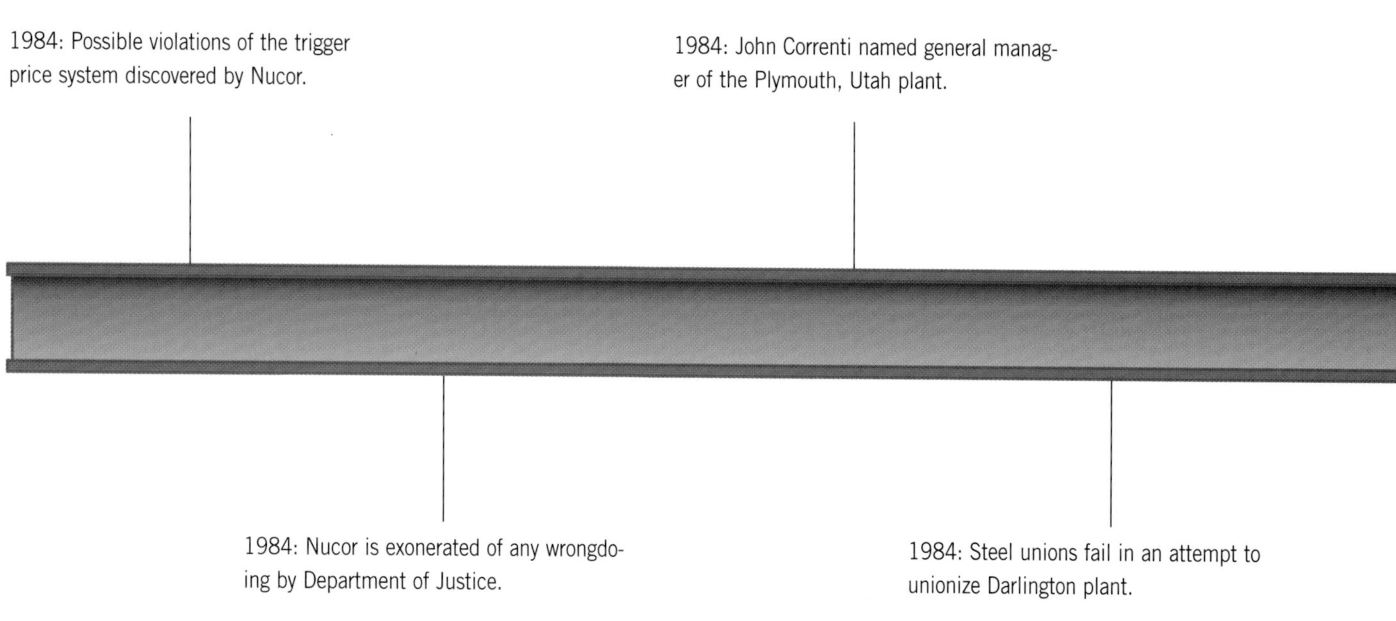

had risen to the top of the company through meritorious service.[6]

"I think Nucor is the way the United States of America was meant to be," said Joe Rutkowski, who would join the company in 1989 and serve as general manager of several Nucor plants. "If you work your ass off, good things come to you. If you do things properly and you're honest and hardworking and caring and committed and focused, the sky's the limit. You could be the president of the company."[7]

John Correnti, general manager of Nucor's Plymouth, Utah plant, would become president and chief executive officer of Nucor.

James Coblin, personnel manager since 1986, said Aycock's promotion was consistent with the overall philosophy of a company that always attempts to recruit and advance a certain kind of person.

> *"It is a person who is aggressive and goal-oriented. A dedicated, diligent person who has the ability to appear to be relatively reserved and laid-back. A down-to-earth person and a good listener, who makes time to listen and talk with employees. We take our very best department managers and make them plant managers, which are company officers. If you put all Nucor's officers in one room, you would be underwhelmed. They're just ordinary people by appearance. They don't require a lot of fanfare, but on the inside, they are very aggressive business people."*[8]

Promotions at Nucor tended to follow such criteria. For example, two year's earlier, in October 1984, John Correnti was named a vice president and general manager of Nucor's Plymouth, Utah plant. Correnti replaced Wilburn G. Manuel, who

1985: Business climate shows improvement for steel industry.

1985: Nucor operating four minimills, with 30 percent of the steel joist market.

1986: David Aycock elected president and COO of Nucor.

1986: Deal forged with Yamato Kogyo to build steel mill.

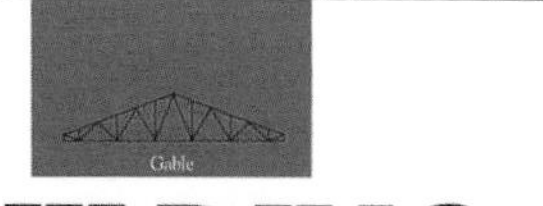

Requiring nonstandard girders, the University of Houston relied on Vulcraft to supply the right joists for its new Athletic/Alumni Center.

left to become general manager of a Florida Steel mill in Jackson, Tennessee.[9] Manuel had been the rolling mill manager at Darlington before becoming the general manager at Plymouth. Correnti, then 37, had joined Nucor in 1980 as construction manager for its 400,000-ton-per-year Plymouth plant.

The decision to move Correnti came as a result of Nucor's difficulties starting up the Utah minimill. Nucor had entered that market just as the steel industry as a whole was suffering a steep recession. Utah was an expensive mill, and it took Nucor a long time to make it efficient. As a result, the general manager quit and Correnti was brought in to effect changes. By 1985, costs were down and business was on the rise.

By 1996, the plant was producing 900,000 tons of steel a year with 345 people. "Over the years, our plant has had a reputation of adopting new technology," said Jay Bowcutt, its general manager. "We have a reputation of taking that technology and making it work. Not only making it work, but making it highly productive."[10]

Formula for Success

The prolonged national recession contributed to labor concerns, and in 1984, an attempt was made to unionize the Darlington plant. Representatives of the United Steelworkers of America and the Teamsters were invited to the plant by workers upset about working conditions during the recession. They had complained of two work-rule changes that came at a time when their wages were already threatened by a shorter workweek. The first complaint was that they would no longer be paid for cleanup work at bonus pay rates. The second was that management had reduced the work crews without trimming the work loads.

Union organizers went to the Darlington plant and began handing out invitations to a Saturday afternoon barbecue, where employees could listen to music and learn about the union. But most employees did not want to be involved with the union. In fact, some workers began shouting at the organizers and throwing sand at them. The union attempt quickly faded away.[11]

Nucor's incentive programs were so generous that the company remained comfortably union-free in a heavily unionized industry. Coblin, who had worked at General Electric and Ingersoll-Rand, developed a theory of opposites to explain the difference between Nucor and other companies. "The language of Nucor managers was the dead opposite of the language that I heard at GE," he said. For example, Nucor managers were constantly cautioning employees to slow down or take a break when necessary, while management at other companies was more likely to tell workers that their breaks were over and they needed to get back to work.

> *"I remember thinking that Nucor had found something out. If they can be 100 percent non-union in a heavily unionized business, with few managers and supervisors, and the supervisors they have are periodically slowing employees down rather than having to speed them up, they're onto something in the way of motivating hourly employees."*[12]

Coblin described another incident that confirmed his "theory of opposites." Workers

Vulcraft supplied more than 560,000 square feet of steel floor deck to The Ball Park, in Arlington, Texas, home of the Texas Rangers.

WITH VULCRAFT ON DECK, THIS BALL PARK BECAME A BIG HIT.

A classic ball park look with all the modern conveniences. That was the big challenge facing designers of The Ball Park in Arlington, home of the Texas Rangers. Today, the grand baseball stadium is complete, a monument to a difficult assignment superbly accomplished.

Vulcraft composite deck in combination with normal weight concrete.

One key design decision was the choice of structural steel and composite deck rather than cast-in-place concrete. Such a method was compatible with the steel framing spans. And, since the deck acted as a form for pouring the concrete, it saved valuable time and labor expense.

Installing composite deck is faster and easier than poured-in-place concrete.

It was the general contractor who, upon review of the project, immediately suggested Vulcraft supply the composite deck. His faith in the company was confirmed when Vulcraft not only came through with a competitive price, but also demonstrated their expertise at every stage of the deck's manufacturing. What's more, Vulcraft took the extended schedule of individual deliveries in stride by meeting every deadline with the exact materials required.

Upon its completion, more than 560,000 square feet of Vulcraft composite steel floor deck had gone into The Ball Park in Arlington, not to mention 93,000 square feet of roof deck. If you have a project that demands the experience of a seasoned player, contact Vulcraft or see Sweet's 05300 VUL for more information on a complete range of steel decking. Because when you have Vulcraft on deck, you can count on your project being a home run.

VULCRAFT
A Division of Nucor Corporation

PO Box 637, Brigham City, UT 84302, 801/734-9433; PO Box 100520, Florence, SC 29501, 803/662-0381; PO Box 169, Fort Payne, AL 35967, 205/845-2460; PO Box 186, Grapeland, TX 75844, 409/687-4665; PO Box 59, Norfolk, NE 68702-0059, 402/644-8500; PO Box 1000, St. Joe, IN 46785, 219/337-1800. Architect of Record: HKS, Inc.; Design Architect: David M. Schwarz/Architectural Service; Sports Architect: Howard Needles Tammen & Bergendoff; Structural Engineer: Walter P. Moore and Associates; Associate Structural Engineer: Datum Engineering, Inc.; General Contractor: Manhattan Construction Co.; Steel Fabricator: Owen of Georgia.

In 1986, Nucor agreed to a joint venture with the Japanese company Yamato Kogyo. Ken Iverson is sitting on the right, Sam Siegel is standing at the far right and David Aycock, wearing no jacket, is standing left of him.

at the Jewett, Texas, facility approached the supervisor there, asking him to fire a new employee. They argued that the man was not pulling his weight and was jeopardizing the bonuses for the entire team. The supervisor refused to fire the man, saying he had only been on the job for 30 days and deserved more time. After another month, the workers again asked the supervisor to fire the man, and the supervisor again refused. After a third month, when the workers made the same request, the supervisor fired the man.

> *"The crew was overheard shuffling away saying to themselves, 'Damn Nucor management, they drag their feet. They finally did what they should have done three months ago.' To me, that's a beautiful story because it illustrates the dead opposite of what would happen at most other companies, where the employees would come to the new guy and say, 'Management's going to fire you. We're not going to let them get away with this. We're going to write a grievance and protest this, and we're going to get your job back.'"*[13]

Rick Campbell, in 1997 a plant manager at Nucor Fastener in Arkansas, noticed the differences soon after he was lured from competitor Florida Steel in 1980.

> *"Florida Steel was a union shop, and the employees always seemed to be disgruntled about something. It was a straight hourly rate, so there was no incentive for them to produce at other than the most leisurely pace they could, while a corporate hierarchy pushed paper around. But Nucor was a company that was rewarding people who worked with their hands as well, if not better, than people who pushed the paper. My paycheck was half of what they were taking home. That's when the incentive program was explained to me."*[14]

In many ways, the supervisors at Nucor considered themselves servants to the hourly employees, since their job was to make life easier for the hourly workers, said Joe Rutkowski, the general manager of Nucor Steel in South Carolina. Rutkowski joined Nucor in 1989 as general manager of the cold-finish plant in Norfolk, Nebraska. After 18 months he transferred to Plymouth, Utah, and in 1992 he moved to Darlington, South Carolina.

> *"The reason that Nucor is successful is because we don't know that we're not supposed to be. ... We don't tell our people what they can't do. We challenge them to do it, and they do it. We're actually amazed every day by the stuff our people will do. The only thing we ask is that they do it safely."*[15]

One such person is Hank Carper, who joined Vulcraft in 1976 and later became supervisor of the Cold Heading Department at Nucor Fastener. He thinks it's great that ideas and solutions come from employees instead of from management.

> *"When I was at Vulcraft, a lot of changes came from people on the line. Nobody from the office would come out and tell us how to do things. Instead, the people tell management how to do things, and management says, 'We'll try it.' Then, after they see that the job is made easier, everybody is more productive, and the idea is implemented. They don't mess around about that. What the employees want, they will get, as long as it benefits the people on the lines."*[16]

Signs of Recovery

By 1985, the steel industry began to recover from the recession that had subdued the market for years. Nucor continued to expand both its product line and its bottom line. In 1984, the company's steel products consisted of steel joists that were used in shopping centers, manufacturing buildings, office buildings, schools, churches,

The Nucor-Yamato plant was the first steel minimill in the United States to manufacture wide-flange beams with a depth of 40 inches.

hospitals, and to a lesser extent in high-rise buildings or single-family dwellings. In 1984, Nucor had more than 30 percent of the total national market for steel joists and produced 424,000 tons of steel joists, up some 28 percent over the 331,000 tons produced in 1983.

The second steel product produced by Nucor was steel decking, corrugated sheets that were often installed over the tops of joists, then covered with insulation, tar and gravel to create roofs. Nucor had four plants producing decking, which in 1984 produced 118,000 tons, up 24 percent over the 95,000 tons produced in 1983. Three of Nucor's plants produced cold-finish bars that were used in shafting, hydraulics, pumping and shock absorbers. In 1984, Nucor produced 90,000 tons, compared to 62,000 in 1983. In 1985, Nucor installed facilities at its cold-finish plants that would allow them to produce another class of cold-finish bars, known as turned, ground and polished.

By 1985, Nucor was operating four minimills, all of the same basic design. They all used scrap, electric furnaces, continuous casting and in-line rolling. Nucor's steel mills were producing angles, channels, rounds and forging billets. In Utah, the plant produced reinforcing bar. The mills also produced some specialized alloy steel, along with a small amount of special bar quality steel. In

Above: A casting strand tender inside the Nucor-Yamato plant.

Below: The meltshop inside the Nucor-Yamato plant.

1985, Nucor became the eighth-largest steel producing company in the United States.

At the 1985 annual meeting, Iverson painted an optimistic picture of the steel industry, despite the intense competition. Nucor's orders were up 16 percent. The plants in South Carolina and Utah, Iverson told stockholders, were doing "exceptionally well." He explained that with a voluntary quota system in effect, the Japanese had retreated from the West Coast, where Nucor experienced a 30- to 40-percent increase in orders.[17]

In the first quarter of 1985, Nucor's profits were up 91 percent over those of 1984. Other minimills did not fare as well. Chaparral Steel experienced a $3 million dollar loss in 1984. Northwest Steel & Wire had reported losses for the last five or six quarters. Another competitor, Soule in California, which manufactured reinforcing bars, was closed down.

Nucor ended the year with net sales of $758.4 million, up from $660.2 million in 1984. Net earnings were up by $12 million to $58.4 million, compared to $44.5 million the previous year.

Nucor-Yamato

In 1986, Nucor signed a letter of intent with the Japanese company Yamato Kogyo to study the feasibility of building a steel mill to produce medium and large structural shapes, including wide-flange beams with a depth of 24 inches. If the concept succeeded, Nucor would be the first minimill to manufacture I-beams of that size. At the time, 24-inch I-beams were produced only by Bethlehem Steel, United States Steel and Inland Steel, three of the largest integrated producers.

As was often the case with Nucor, another company would provide the technology and Nucor would fine-tune it into reality. Yamato Kogyo would furnish the technology to cast a beam close to the finished size, dramatically reducing the number of rolling passes required in production. Nucor would supply both the melting and materials-handling technologies, in addition to managing the mill, which would be built in Blytheville, Arkansas. The project was estimated to cost $200 million, with Nucor owning 51 percent and Yamato Kogyo owning 49 percent.[18]

John Correnti, who had moved from U.S. Steel to build Nucor's minimill in Utah, was appointed general manager of the unique and challenging project. Correnti and others, including John Doherty and Ladd Hall, traveled to Japan to discuss the joint venture. Correnti recalled that their Japanese counterparts found it hard to accept Correnti's assertion that the plant could be up and running within 18 months. "Ladd could speak Japanese, having spent time there on a church mission," Correnti said. "After the meeting, I asked him, 'Well, Ladd, what do they think?' He answered, 'John, they think you're nuts.'"[19]

According to LeRoy Prichard, engineering manager of the project, the plant was constructed in record time. "It was a great experience working with John and getting that plant on line," said Prichard, who also arrived from U.S. Steel.[20]

Correnti recalled that the plant was designed to process 650,000 tons of steel, but in its second year it was already pushing one million tons. The plant was expanded, and by 1996 it was producing 2.3 million tons, making it the largest structural steel mill in the world.

"The Japanese were so impressed, but it wasn't easy for them to accept our type of management style. For example, a melter would sometimes come up to me and say, 'John, do you know how many tons we did today?' I'd ask how many and he'd tell me. I'd say, 'Great. Let's do more tomorrow.' My Japanese counterpart would ask who that was. I'd say, 'Oh, that's a second helper on a crew.' In Japan, a second helper in a crew would no more come up to the head of the company than he would fly to the moon."[21]

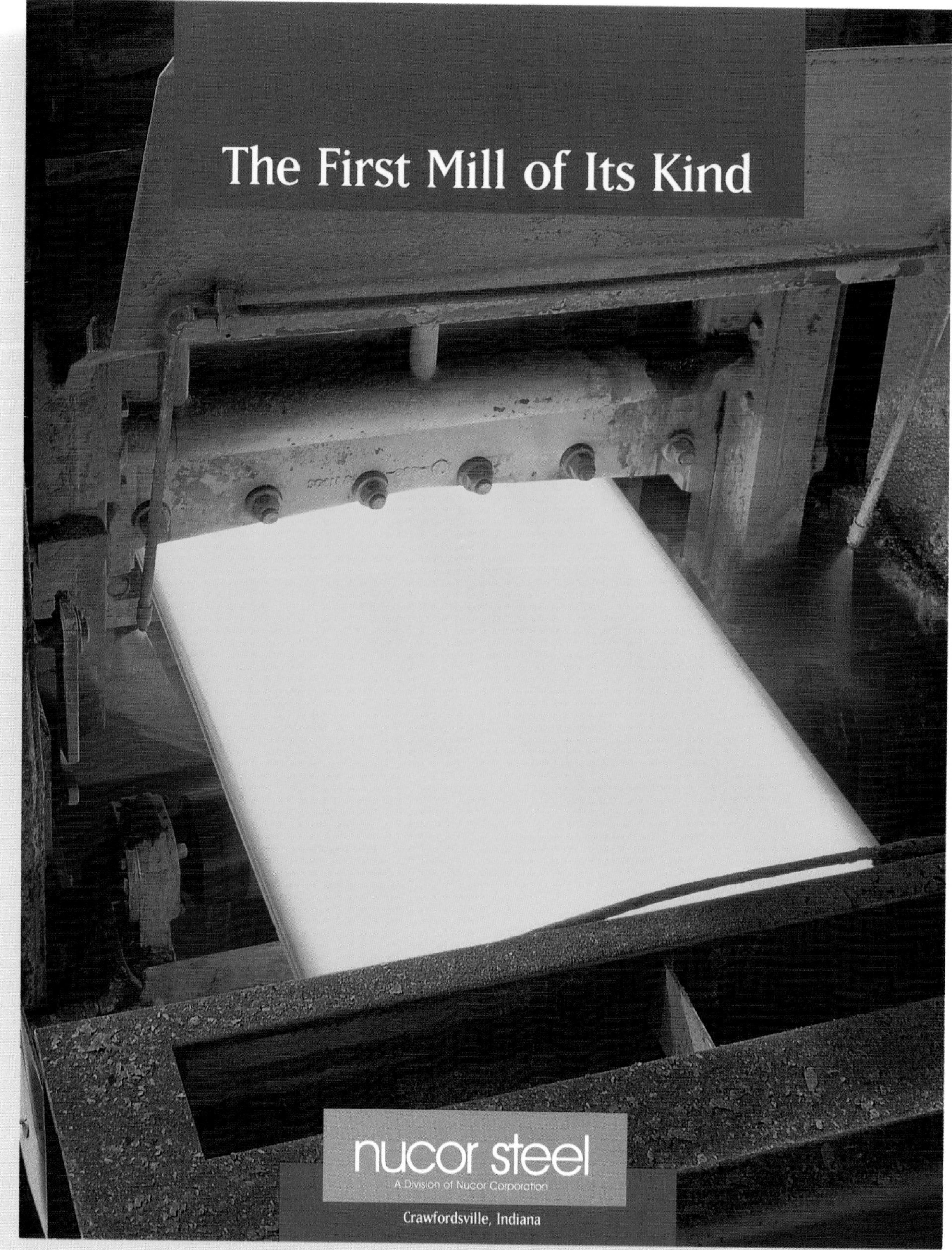

With its unique thin-slab continuous casting process, Nucor's steel mill in Crawfordsville, Indiana, was unlike any other mill in the world.

CHAPTER ELEVEN

CRAWFORDSVILLE
1986–1989

"It's the type of major development in steel technology that comes along once every 50 years."

— Ken Iverson, 1984[1]

CRAWFORDSVILLE, Indiana, was typical of any number of Midwestern towns in the 1980s. Farmland stretched for miles and silos dotted the landscape. With a population of just over 13,000, Crawfordsville served as the seat of Montgomery County. In 1987, Crawfordsville's principal industries were a Norcote Chemical plant, California Pellet and an R.R. Donnelly & Sons printing plant.

Crawfordsville, with its rural setting, was the place where Nucor would launch its most ambitious project to date — a mill to produce hot-rolled and cold-rolled sheet steels using a new thin-slab process that would yield flat-rolled steel at low capital cost. This project was critical to Nucor because flat-rolled steel was the largest single product area in the steel industry. Flat-rolled steel sheets made up the bodies of automobiles, steel cans, refrigerators, stoves, washers, dryers, pipes, culverts, and sidings and decks for buildings. In 1988, as Nucor began building its thin-slab caster, 40 million tons of the 96 million tons of steel consumed in the United States that year were flat-rolled products.

By casting steel in thin slabs, Nucor could bypass some of the most expensive machinery in a steel mill. Normally, steel was cast in thick slabs and then rolled until it was thin, as Ken Iverson explained at a stockholders' meeting in 1989.

"To give you an idea of what the difference is, let's talk about the conventional way of making flat-rolled products. The conventional way is to cast a slab of metal that's eight to 10 inches thick, then use a breakdown mill to reduce it until it's about an inch and a half thick. Then it goes to a finishing mill, where it passes through maybe six stands until it's only a tenth of an inch thick, and then it's coiled up into what's called a hot band. What we're doing is casting a slab only two inches thick that will be 52 inches wide. It will come out and go through a soaking (tunnel) furnace, then go through four finishing mills and directly be reduced from two inches to a tenth-of-an-inch through controlled cooling. Then it is coiled up.

"We eliminate the breakdown mill, the capital cost of the breakdown mill, the energy and labor cost associated with that. It should provide us the savings of $50 to $75 a ton in producing this, compared to the conventional method of making flat-rolled products."[2]

There would also be a reduction in the number of employees needed for the new mill.

Welcome NUCOR Corp.

Representatives of the small rural community of Crawfordsville held a reception in December 1986 to welcome Nucor.

Integrated mills at the time required between 50 and 60 workers per shift, not including maintenance personnel, to handle everything from casting to coiling. By contrast, Nucor's process would require only 12 people to do the same amount of work. The company estimated that the total labor cost at the Crawfordsville plant would be less than two man-hours per ton, including maintenance and administration. The total labor-plus-benefits cost was expected to be less than $50 per ton of steel in a product that would sell at an average of about $400 per ton.

If Nucor were to succeed, said *The Wall Street Journal* in 1987, it would signal "a new frontier in the battle for the few glowing embers still largely controlled by the integrated steelmakers."[3]

In the early eighties, thin-slab casting was little more than an unattainable steelmakers' dream. Mike Delaney, outside counsel for Nucor, as was his father before him, recalled that the government had commissioned a study to look into the technology, hoping it would cure the ills of Big Steel.

> *"Thin-slab casting is something that people have dreamed about but never thought possible. Even at the time that Nucor decided to do it, the U.S. government was going to fund a study, because certainly no private company would have the resources or the ability to do this. They were going to fund it so all the steel companies could get together and work on their technology. It would be for a five-year period, and then the results would be made public, and hopefully someone would be able to benefit from it. When Nucor announced it was going to do it, the government study just went down the tubes."*[4]

Iverson had been investigating the possibility of producing flat-rolled steel since 1983. Nucor had even attempted to develop a process internally that would be capable of casting a thin slab. A German company, SMS Concast, was also working on such a process, and Nucor had been monitoring its efforts for several years. SMS Concast developed the process first, and by 1985 the company was in operation with a prototype pilot plant in West Germany.[5]

Representatives from Nucor traveled to Germany to observe the compact strip production plant. "You could tell right away that the concept was going to work," said Rodney Mott,

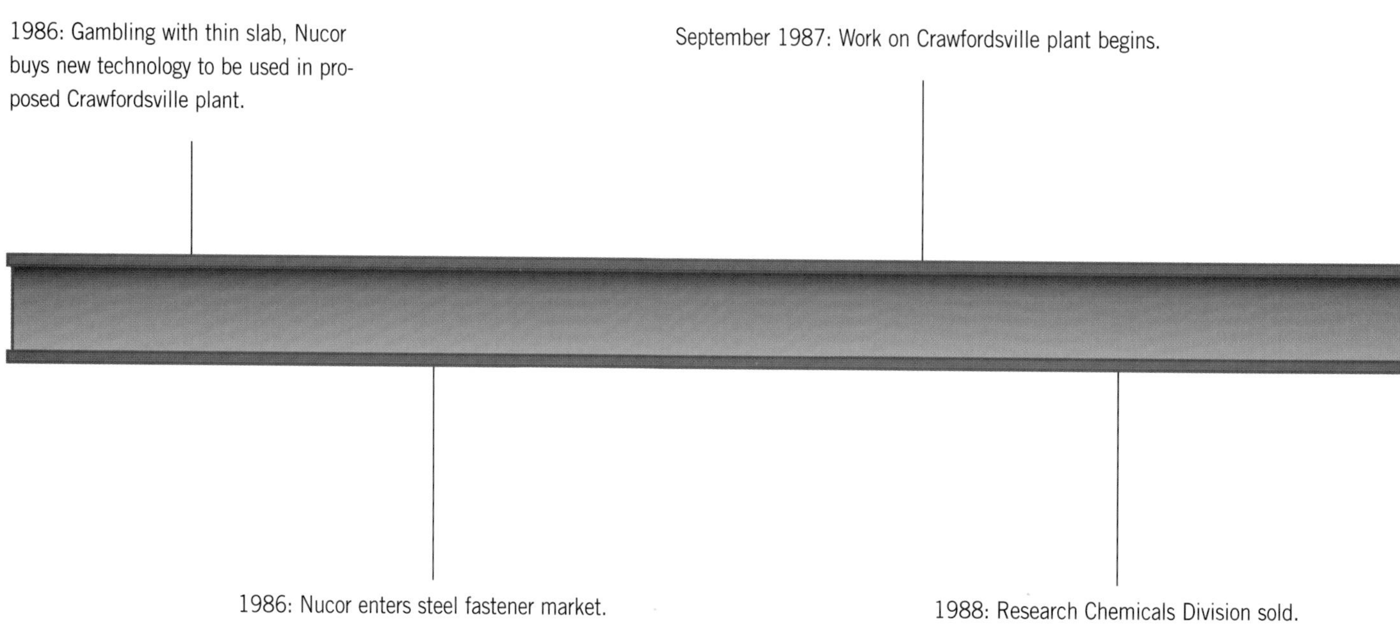

one of Nucor's representatives on the trip. After Mott helped establish the Crawfordsville facility, he helped establish the Hickman plant before becoming vice president and general manager of Nucor Steel in Berkeley County, South Carolina. In 1995, he was named Plant Manager of the Year for the entire steel industry.[6]

Even though Nucor executives were confident that the compact strip production would work, the financial commitment was daunting, admitted Delaney.

"What they had in Germany was a little tinker toy operation, a prototype," he said. "Who would have thought you could possibly do that on a commercial basis, and worse than that, who would have risked doing it? Yet, I can tell you that Nucor enthusiastically jumped on it. 'This is what we need to do.' You know, you lose sight of the risk-taking."[7]

Negotiating with Nucor for the technology was a bewildering process for the very formal Germans. They expected the process to take at least a year. But executives at Nucor knew what they wanted, and they had no intention of dragging out the discussions. The negotiations were swift. Nucor was the only company that was willing to gamble on the unproved SMS technology. None of the big steel companies were interested because they didn't believe that the thin-slab casting method developed by SMS was workable. SMS was so eager to sell the equipment that it even offered Nucor a money-back guarantee if the machines failed.

After placing its order for the compact strip production plant with SMS near the end of 1986, Nucor proposed an ambitious timetable. The schedule called for an initial cold-rolling, based on purchased hot band, to begin in September 1988; start-up of the electric furnace and casting machine for initial hot-run and debugging phase by March 1989; and start-up of the reheating furnace/hot rolling mill complex in April 1989.

Construction of the Crawfordsville facility would cost Nucor $270 million. At critical junctures during the development process, as much as 25 percent of Nucor's assets would be tied up in the project. "Thin-slab was a big gamble," said Corporate Controller Terry Lisenby, recruited by Nucor in 1985. "It would have been a serious wound had it not worked."[8]

Heading up the development phase was Keith Busse, an Indiana native who had joined Nucor in 1972 as controller of the St. Joe plant. In 1979, he

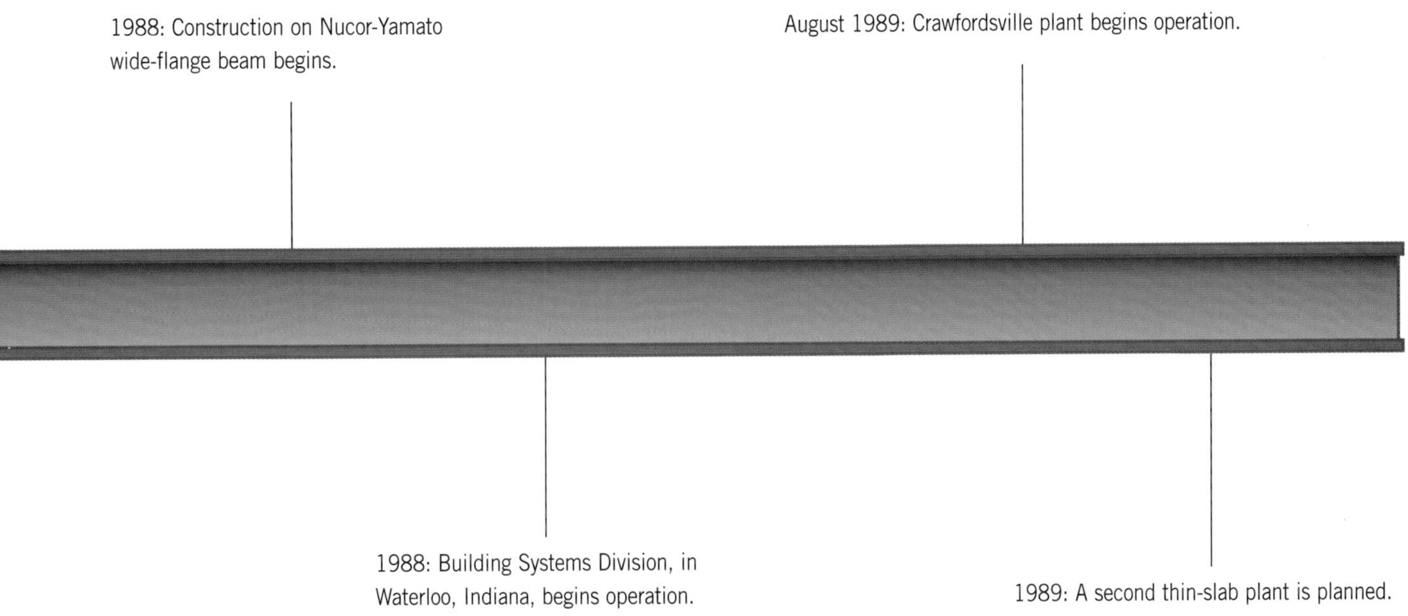

was named a vice president and general manger of the St. Joe plant. When Crawfordsville was complete, he was to become its new general manager.

In a 1988 interview, Busse was asked what would happen if the project failed. "At Nucor, no one talks of failure," he replied. "The possibility of failure is very remote."[9]

Outside of Nucor, however, industry observers were less confident that this novel form of steelmaking would succeed. The steel industry was intensely interested in what Nucor was doing in Crawfordsville. Many observers doubted that the company would succeed. "It'll take some time for Nucor to make inroads into flat-rolled steel," John Jacobson, a steel economist, told *The Wall Street Journal*. Other industry officials, the *Journal* reported, expected that Nucor would penetrate only markets for lesser-quality grades of sheet steel.[10]

John Ferriola, general manager of the Nucor Steel plant in Norfolk, Nebraska, was manager of maintenance at Bethlehem Steel when both the Crawfordsville project and Nucor-Yamato were under construction. He said Bethlehem executives were convinced the projects would spell the end for Nucor.

"We used to have these informal meetings. The general manager would sit there and tell us that [Nucor's projects] were good news for us, that Nucor was going to learn the hard way how these things are done. He said, 'That mill will never succeed, and it will bring Nucor down with it.' I remember sitting there, while he talked, thinking, 'Right. Non-union shop with a great incentive program. Yeah, that sounds like it's doomed to me.'"[11]

In 1991, Ferriola went to work for Nucor. "When I hooked up with Nucor, suddenly half my time that had been spent dealing with management or union issues was focused on what I was actually paid to do, contribute to the bottom line."

With so much at stake, nerves were frayed. To those watching Nucor's every move during the project, it was unnerving to realize that of the 23 people selected to be on the Crawfordsville development team, only four were from within the Nucor organization. The remaining 19, with one exception, had never been involved in building a steel mill before. The exception was Kris McGee, the site construction manager who had worked at U.S. Steel previously, and had considerable experience in steel mill construction.

Rodney Mott recalled the difficulties of trying to establish a plant with an entirely novel process. "There would be breakdown after breakdown. You couldn't make the equipment stay together. Still, we'd just rally the guys and try again. But behind closed doors, we would say, 'God, what if this doesn't work?'"[12]

But after a period of frustration, things began to fall into place. In June 1989, Nucor was ready to test the mill. The continuous casting unit was scheduled first for testing. In July, the hot-strip mill and the cold-rolling mills were tested. The steelmaking unit consisted of two 150-ton, eccentric-bottom-tap and two shell electric furnaces, each with a ladle refining station.

The magazine *American Metal Market* described the operation in a 1989 report on the Crawfordsville project. The steel was to be tapped at about 2,900 degrees Fahrenheit approximately every 100 minutes, then raised to a temperature of 2,950 degrees in a ladle-refining furnace. Some 125 tons of steel would be tapped, leaving a liquid heel of 25 tons in the furnace. A vacuum degassing unit would also be included and could be used on about 20 percent of the steel.

The liquid steel would be poured into a tapered, funnel-shaped, 30-inch-deep water-cooled copper mold via a ceramic nozzle, to within four inches of the top of the mold.

The caster had an adjustable-width mold, so the thickness of the slab could be either 40 millimeters or 50 millimeters. The 52-inch-wide slab would exit the machine at a speed which ranged from a minimum of 2.5 meters per minute to a maximum of seven meters per minute. After the slab left the casting machine, it would enter a 525-foot-long slab-heating tunnel furnace. The slab would then be heated to a uniform temperature within eight to 10 minutes. Energy consumption per ton was expected to be approximately 0.6 million BTUs, versus 2.0 for many facilities in the steel industry.

At the terminus of the heating furnace was a high-pressure descaling unit and a shear, which would be used when there were cobbles (severe

THE BAR MILL

AFTER FORMATION in the melt shop, the billet goes to the rolling mill, an amazingly versatile process where the semi-finished steel is made into the final product. The billet enters a large furnace, heated by natural gas and air burners. The slab is reheated to somewhere between 2,100 and 2,300 degrees Fahrenheit, traveling through the furnace on a firebrick-lined bed. The billet then goes to the roughing part of the mill, a set of rolls that massage the shape of the billet to roughly resemble its shape when finished. The billet enters the mill at about 50 feet a minute, increasing speed as it passes through each part of the mill until reaching 1,300 to 2,000 feet per minute. The finished bar exits the last mill stand at a temperature of about 1,900 degrees. After the bars are cut to customer length, they are allowed to cool and then are bundled and identified.[1]

deformities) on the sheet. The four-stand hot strip mill was to have a capacity of about 2 million tons per year, which meant that the steel would spend less time in the hot strip mills (about three to four minutes) than it would in the slab heating furnace (about 20 minutes).

The hot strip mill contained the latest in technology at the time, with automatic gauge controls, roll bending and continuous variable crown controls. The exit speed of the sheet from the fourth stand was expected to be about 1,500 feet per minute. Automatic roll changing would take approximately 12 minutes. The two downcoilers featured sophisticated computer controls and sensing devices on the hot strip mill. The single-strand cold-rolling mill included the same control features. A typical operation would reduce a hot-rolled sheet from 0.11 inches to 0.028 inches in five passes.[13]

In August 1989, the Crawfordsville plant began operation. There were still some bugs in the operation, however. Dimensionally, the plant could produce the steel accurately to within $^{1}/_{1000}$ of an inch from side to side, and to within $^{3}/_{1000}$ of an inch from end to end. From a metallurgical standpoint, it had excellent properties, as good as any in the world. But there were problems with the surface of the sheet. The plant was using a descaler, which projected water at the hot sheet at pressures of 3,900 pounds per square inch. (By comparison, tap water flows at around 40 to 50 pounds per square inch.) But some of the pumps were failing and the nozzles tended to clog. The scales weren't always removed, preventing the plant from producing a consistent Class One surface. To solve the problem, Nucor increased the number of pumps used, changed nozzles, and put filters on the nozzles.[14]

At the 1990 annual meeting, Iverson proudly showed shareholders the first automotive part to come out of the Crawfordsville plant. It was a bracket used to hold a radio in a Ford vehicle. The plant also produced brackets that held automobile starters and batteries.

Competitors were slow to embrace the new thin-slab casting technology. Even after Nucor solved the problem of scaling, many still believed that the quality of the steel would be inferior. A 1990 report by The Robinson-Humphrey Company, Inc., proved otherwise.

"Crawfordsville's quality has been excellent with over 90 percent of recent output being prime-quality metallurgically reflected in flatness and lack of edge cracking," the report stated. Still, the few problems Iverson had described at the annual meeting did have an effect on other steel companies, the report stated. "A variety of surface defects, however, are holding back

Crawfordsville's highly automated control room overlooks the five-stand finishing mill, which reduces the thickness of the slabs from two inches to .071 inches.

At the mill's laminar cooler, metal is sprayed from both the top and bottom, using 16 separate banks of water jets.

widespread product introduction and delaying the qualification process."[15]

At the end of 1991, the Crawfordsville mill was shipping more than 700,000 tons of finished products. In 1993, the plant would be expanded to allow production of 1.8 million tons per year.

But Nucor wasn't spending all its time on the Crawfordsville project during this period.

Stealing Back the Steel Fastener Market

In September 1986, Nucor entered the steel fastener business. At the time, imports controlled nearly 90 percent of this market in the United States. "It's really an effort to bring that business back home," Iverson said in a 1987 interview.[16] The mill was built in St. Joe, Indiana, at a cost of $25 million. With an annual capacity of 40,000 tons, the facility produced hex-head cap screws, hex bolts and socket-head cap screws. In the early nineties, the facility would be expanded and improved.

In December 1986, Nucor purchased Genbearco Manufacturing Company, Inc., in Wilson, North Carolina, from General Bearing Corporation. The company, which manufactured steel bearings and steel parts, became Nucor's Bearing Products Division. The division would evolve over the ensuing decade, and in 1995 Doug Jellison became its manager. By that time, the division could manufacture about 120 million parts a year, including a component called a hub inner ring, found in the wheel bearings of cars. The division supplied these rings for all General Motors passenger cars, about half of Chrysler's automobiles and a small percentage of Ford vehicles. Nucor bearings were also used in electric motors, washing machines, lawn mowers and many other devices with moving parts.

Although unusual for Nucor, steel for these parts was purchased from sources other than Nucor, said Jellison. "Right now, none of the bar mills produce the bearing-quality steel," he said in 1996. He added that the Norfolk, Nebraska mill was in the process of an upgrade that would produce the correct kind of steel within the next few years.[17]

The Research Chemicals Division Is Sold

During this period, the company's Phoenix-based Chemicals Research Division, which offered the most comprehensive line of rare earths from a single source anywhere in the world, accounted for less than 2 percent of Nucor's sales. On September 30, 1988, Nucor announced that it had signed an agreement to sell the Research Chemicals Division to Princeton, New Jersey-based Rhone-Poulenc, Inc. A subsidiary of Rhone-Poulenc SA in France, the company produced rare earths at plants in Lyon, France, Freeport, Texas, and Niihama, Japan. A company spokesman explained to American Metal Market in a 1988 interview that purchasing the Research Chemicals Division from Nucor would allow Rhone-Poulenc to expand into new areas.

Before the acquisition, Rhone-Poulenc had supplied the component ingredients for rare earths. In fact, Research Chemicals had been a customer of Rhone-Poulenc's. The divestiture, negotiated by Sam Siegel, represented a net gain of $40 million dollars for Nucor, more than five times the division's annual sales. It was ultimately a significant gain, considering that Nucor had acquired Research Chemicals for $50,000 in 1956.[18]

James Cunningham, who had run the division since 1966, moved to Rhone-Poulenc for three years before retiring.[19]

The Trade Deficit

The issue of U.S. protectionism re-emerged in late 1986 when the national trade deficit topped $176 billion. A public debate emerged between those favoring increased protectionist measures and those who opposed such measures. Iverson belonged to the latter group. Those in favor of protectionism included labor unions and the Democratic party. These groups cited a December 1986 study published by the Joint Economic Committee, which was produced by economists Barry Blueston of the University of Massachusetts and Bennet Harrison of MIT. The study found that 58 percent of the eight million new jobs the U.S. economy created between 1979 and 1984 paid less than $7,000 year. The study also asserted that the American middle class was shrinking.[20]

Iverson did not believe that a policy of protectionism was the answer. He believed that America should look within, rather than to foreign competition, for the solutions to its trade deficit, as he explained in 1987.

"In the long run, I believe this protectionism can have a devastating effect on our economy. The protectionists' point of view does have the support of some powerful constituencies. Manufacturers who would rather lobby than fight, labor unions whose ranks have thinned in recent years, and politicians looking for campaign issues and public attention.

"The United States trade deficit will not shrink much unless the imbalance between American spending and production is corrected. With a huge trade deficit of $170 billion in 1986, this will not be easy and will not be

Above: Jessie Barnes, a chucker operator in Nucor's Bearing Products Division, in 1996.

Right: John Newcomb stresses the importance of quality in the Bearing Products Division as he trains operator Joey Webb.

accomplished overnight. We need a trade policy that not only reverses national overspending but one that also holds protectionist pressures at bay."[21]

As the debate raged, Nucor continued to improve its own ability to compete with both foreign and domestic steelmakers.

In 1988, construction began on Nucor's joint venture with Yamato Kogyo on a wide-flange beam plant being built near Blytheville, Arkansas. With a port on the Mississippi River, the mill was expected to service the entire market area east of the Rockies. Nucor hoped to win a full 20 percent of that market.

The Building Systems Division began operation that year as well. This division, based in Waterloo, Indiana, offered a unique service to contractors by supplying metal buildings and metal building components. General Manager Harry Lowe was recruited in 1990 to run the division, which he said is different from all other areas of Nucor.

"You take a piece of raw material, iron ore or whatever you want to call it, and then send it through the steel mill, where they would make a usable shape out of it. In conventional construction, the product would then go to a company like Vulcraft, and they would create a shape that would become part of a building. The product is then sold to a fabricator who combines the columns and beams and the rest into a building which is then sold to a contractor, who sells it to a customer. Well, we're basically like the fabricator, one step further along from Vulcraft, one of our biggest suppliers. We sell an entire building to a contractor, who then erects it for the customer."[22]

After a slow start in 1988, the division produced more than 45,000 tons of buildings and building components in 1996. Total Nucor sales in 1987 reached a record $851 million, 13 percent higher than in 1986.

Nucor's total capital expenditures in 1988 exceeded $300 million, and in 1989 they exceeded $200 million. But Iverson was confident that the investments would pay off, as he explained to *The Wall Street Transcript*. "Once these projects are completed, they will generate large amounts of cash so that we should pay off any debt that we have within a relatively short period of time, three to five years."[23]

A Second Thin-Slab Mill

Once Crawfordsville was operational, plans for a second thin-slab mill were soon in the works. In 1992, Nucor Steel completed construction and began operation of a second sheet mill that would produce more than 1 million tons per year of hot-rolled sheet steel products. The plant, located near Hickman, Arkansas, would ship some 900,000 tons of finished steel in its first five months of operation.

D. Michael Parrish, a Nucor employee since 1975, became vice president and general manager of Hickman. He noted that the highly automated facility produced 2.1 million tons of steel each year with only 345 employees, a remarkably low man-hours per ton ratio of .37. Parrish said the incredible efficiency was the result of automation, Nucor's aggressive incentive programs and careful hiring.[24]

Nucor managers had the luxury of choice when employment notices were posted. David Chase, department manager for the Hickman project, said he received more than 2,500 applications for 250 jobs. "People were coming from as far away as Chicago and Houston. People from local industry were willing to leave their jobs and go to work for Nucor."[25]

"They're very interested in the bonus system, and want to contribute any way they can to try to benefit from those higher pay wages. One very important feature we look at is how a person will fit personality-wise with the kind of people we're trying to hire. In other words, although we interviewed people who were valedictorians of their high school class, many didn't fit our organization, so we couldn't hire them. ... I look for someone who shows a little bit of initiative to go beyond just a high school education to better themselves, be it some kind of technical training or two-to-four-year college."[26]

Nucor's steel mill in Hickman, Arkansas, was the second one to use the thin-slab technology that had been pioneered in Crawfordsville. Here, a 50-millimeter slab emerges from the caster and passes through the withdrawing-straightening unit before moving to the soaking furnace.

CHAPTER TWELVE

Passing the Torch

The Nineties

"When you open up the history books, our grandchildren, 30 years or 40 years from now, are going to open it up to Steel in America, and they're going to see two names there and two pictures. They're going to see Andrew Carnegie, father of the integrated industry, and Ken Iverson, father of the American minimill. That's just the way it's going to be."

— John Correnti, 1996[1]

NUCOR'S CRAWFORDSVILLE gamble paid off almost immediately. Following a minor sales slump in 1991 caused by a slowing economy, both sales and earnings bounced back. Sales remained comfortably over the $1 billion mark.

But as Nucor continued to post strong earnings, it also attracted some unpleasant publicity.

On May 10, 1991, *The Wall Street Journal* published a story headlined, "Hazardous Duty: Nucor Steel's Sheen is Marred by Deaths of Workers at Plants — Efficient Mill Stresses Output Over Safety, Some Claim; Executives Defend Record." The story alleged that Nucor's worker death rate since 1980 was the highest in the steel industry, more than double the industry average. Ten Nucor workers had died in plant accidents since 1980, the story noted, while National Steel Corporation, with nearly twice as many production workers, had five worker deaths.[2]

A week earlier, *The Charlotte Observer* had quoted Joseph Kinney, a Chicago safety advocate who had founded the National Safe Workplace Institute in 1987, as saying that Nucor was a "large company that's involved in a dangerous enterprise, and safety is not a major concern." Since 1980, according to the article, Nucor's death rate was 23.4 annual deaths per 100,000 workers, compared with the steel industry average of 10.5 deaths per 100,000 workers, as calculated by the American Steel and Iron Institute. Citing statistics from the United Steelworkers Union, the article said that Nucor, then ranked number seven among steel companies, had the worst rate of the top-10 steelmakers.[3]

In a June 1991 letter to Kinney, Iverson chastised Kinney's statistics. Iverson told Kinney that he had incorrectly classified Nucor as a foundry instead of a steel mill. "The lost-time injury rate per 100 workers, as reported by the Bureau of Labor Statistics, is 24.4 for metal fabricators, compared with 15.5 for steel mills. As you can see, between 1980 and 1990 three of the Nucor employee fatalities occurred in steel mills. The balance occurred in metal fabrication divisions or our trucking division."[4]

Iverson also noted that Nucor had 20 percent fewer administrative employees than companies with which Nucor competed. Nonadministrative employees tend to have higher accident rates than administrative employees who work in offices. In

In 1995, Nucor joined the state of South Carolina in a recycling partnership that has since become a model for other states. Nucor tax attorney Billy Moore was so impressed with the legislation, which Sam Siegel was instrumental in crafting, that he had copies of the bill encased in plastic blocks.

addition, Nucor had built six new facilities from scratch between 1980 and 1990. Safety was always a larger problem during the construction and start-up of new plants. Further, several of the fatalities attributed to Nucor were trucking accidents not related to plant operations.[5]

According to Nucor records, the fatalities at Nucor plants, starting in 1980, were: a Vulcraft driver killed during a highway accident in which alcohol was involved; a painter/longspan who was struck by a structural roof truss when it fell from a trailer; a worker at Vulcraft-Texas who was struck by joists while removing them from a trailer; a shipper/loader trainee at Vulcraft-Texas, who was run over by a forklift; a Vulcraft-Indiana driver killed in a trucking accident while transporting products to a Nucor customer; a shipping and receiving administrator at Vulcraft-Utah, who was struck by cold-finished steel bars in the shipping department; a lead mill adjuster at Nucor Steel-South Carolina, who was electro-

A worker at Nucor Steel in Utah watches as steel moves through a rolling mill.

1991: Nucor's safety record becomes an issue in *The Wall Street Journal.*

1991: Nucor-Yamato plant expands.

1991: David Aycock retires from the presidency. John Correnti becomes president and COO.

1992: Iron Carbide plant in Trinidad is announced.

Ken Iverson proudly accepts the National Medal of Technology from President George Bush in 1991, at a ceremony in the Rose Garden. The award was given to honor Iverson for his innovations in steelmaking technology.

cuted by a floor fan that was not grounded; and a shipping employee at Vulcraft-Utah, who was pinned by cold-finished steel bars in the shipping department when defective strapping on a bundle of steel broke.

The accidents were not related to the fast pace of the production teams, said James Coblin, head of personnel. "It's typically in down times when you have accidents, or when you're working real slow and you don't have enough orders. But when you're really getting the tons out and everybody is getting big bonuses, we're not having accidents."[6]

Coblin noted that "one fatality is unacceptable. We've had 10 and we're working on it. But day to day, our overall record is very good, and we're striving to improve it."[7]

Keith Busse, who oversaw construction of the Crawfordsville plant, was furious with *The Wall Street Journal* article and subsequent publicity. "I think it's a lousy, highly prejudiced, biased article," he said. "This is a witch hunt from the top on down." Busse claimed that company detractors, including organizations with ties to unions, were behind the articles.[8]

1994: Nucor and rival U.S. Steel enter joint-venture agreement to develop iron carbide steel.

1995: Ken Iverson steps down as CEO; Correnti succeeds him.

1995: Nucor announces plan to build third hot- and cold-rolled sheet steel plant.

Other large steel industry companies were not immune from the issue. *Iron Age* reported in May 1991 that serious violations by the USS Division of USX Corporation resulted in a record $3.25 million payment in fines for what OSHA called "repeated and willful" acts violating safety standards at the company's Clairton and Fairless Works.[9]

According to popular radio commentator and columnist Paul Harvey, other steel companies were uncomfortable with the continuing success of Nucor.

> *"There is no more thrilling story in contemporary American industry than the David and Goliath story of Nucor Steel. Conspicuously uncomfortable are the steelmaking giants whose cumbersome bureaucracy and antiquated machinery inhibit modernization. Also, Nucor employees, more efficient, make more than other steelworkers. So they have no use for a union. So Nucor is an embarrassment both to traditional Big Steel and to the Steelworkers Union."*[10]

Harvey then raised the safety issue. "There is an organization based in Chicago called The National Safe Workplace Institute. I understand this institute is largely funded by the union," Harvey wrote. "Which may help explain how that institute zeroed in on Nucor as being an unsafe place to work."[11]

Executives noted that the company's excellent rating with insurance companies was proof that it did not have a safety problem. In 1995, Wausau Insurance Companies awarded Nucor a Certificate of Merit for its recent safety record.

Most employees felt privileged to work at a company that offered unlimited opportunity. Sam Huff, who joined the Grapeland Vulcraft facility as a rigger in 1969, rose through the ranks to become vice president and general manager of Nucor Steel in Jewett, Texas, in 1995. "I do not have a college education," he noted. "I was fortunate to have the world's best steel company build

The reversing cold-rolling mill in Crawfordsville, Indiana.

a facility in my hometown, where I could start in an entry-level job and advance as far as my skills and efforts would take me. I never imagined I could reach the general manager level."[12]

John Correnti

On March 1, 1991, H. David Aycock, who had started at the Vulcraft plant in South Carolina in 1954 as a laborer, announced his intention to retire at the end of June 1991 as Nucor's president and chief operating officer. John D. Correnti was named his successor, and Sam Siegel was elected vice chairman of the board of directors and chief financial officer. Terry Lisenby was named a vice president and corporate controller.

Another potential candidate for promotion had been Keith Busse. After Correnti got the nod, Busse left in 1991 with plans to start his own minimill company, Steel Dynamics, Inc., in Butler, Indiana. In 1997, Busse was featured in a *Business Week* cover story as one of the nation's top 25 entrepreneurs.

"The steel industry hasn't typically been a hotbed of entrepreneurialism, but ex-Nucor exec Keith Busse has his year-old company, Steel Dynamics, Inc., off to a fast start. Busse's low-cost minimill began making steel far more rapidly — and profitably — than a slew of other Nucor wannabes. Now, after a successful IPO that raised $150 million, Busse plans to build up a full line steelmaker with costs well below old-line rivals."[13]

The control booth at the Hickman, Arkansas, mill.

Above and right: Nucor Wire used a completely revolutionary process to cast steel directly into wire.

Correnti was called by Iverson in December 1990 for a meeting at the Charlotte airport. At the time, Correnti was in charge of Nucor-Yamato Steel Company in Blytheville, Arkansas.

"He was at the gate waiting for me. We went into the USAir club, where we grabbed a cup of coffee and sat down. He said, 'John, Dave Aycock has decided to retire. I'd like you to come in and be the president and chief operating officer of Nucor Corporation.' It stunned me. I guess I aspired to it, but I thought it might be some time later in my career. He said, 'What do you think about that?' I said I was speechless. And I really was."[14]

Correnti had started his career in the steel industry with U.S. Steel following his graduation from Clarkson University. Sent to Texas to help build uranium plants, his turning point came when his assignment was almost completed. The company had offered him several options, all of which would mean leaving Texas at a time when he wanted to remain.

"I met Dawn and fell in love. Now there's Texas, and then there's the rest of the United States. She said, 'Well, if you want to marry me, you'd better look for a job in Texas. I'm not going to Gary, Indiana, or anywhere else.' So a friend of mine got me in touch with a headhunter."[15]

The headhunter set up an interview with Nucor Personnel Director John Savage, who advised him that Nucor was searching for talent to build a minimill in Utah. Naturally, that defeated the whole purpose of changing jobs, and Correnti politely declined. Nucor officials remained persistent. "I told Nucor that it sounded like a wonderful company, but I wanted to stay in Texas." Nevertheless, Correnti was persuaded to meet Ken Iverson in December 1979.

"I really liked Ken, but I explained my situation. I said, 'Well, Ken, I've fallen in love with this girl, and she really wants me to find a job in Texas so she could still see her family.' He said he understood."[16]

Several days later, Correnti was offered a job with a salary of $36,000 a year. He had been earning $21,000 at U.S. Steel. "The point I'm trying to make is, you can't convince people but you can bribe them. I said to myself, 'I can fly Dawn back and forth from Salt Lake City to San Antonio every weekend making that kind of money.' So that's how my career got started with Nucor."[17]

Correnti had been general manager of construction at the minimill in Plymouth, Utah, before building the joist plant at Brigham City. Upon completion of the joist plant, he became its general manager. He was also general manager of the steel mill at Plymouth before being named Nucor's president and chief operating officer. Although Nucor had no executive committee, Correnti, Iverson and Siegel would go out to lunch every day. Iverson and Correnti usually had soup, and Siegel usually had a baked potato.

In 1991, Nucor moved its modest location across from Phil's Deli (which Nucor executives fondly referred to as the executive dining room) to Charlotte's fashionable South Park. The new facilities doubled Nucor's office space, with 10,000 square feet in the Arnold Palmer Building at 2100 Rexford Road.[18]

In March 1991, Nucor-Yamato Steel Company announced it would expand its Blytheville, Arkansas, plant at a cost of more than $150 million. The mill would add an additional ladle furnace and an additional rolling mill. At completion, it would produce large sections of steel, up to 40 inches in depth and 260 pounds per foot. The mill would also be equipped to handle a higher percentage of cut-to-length requirements than the existing mill.

At the Crawfordsville plant, performance was even greater than anticipated. The mill made a ton of sheet steel in 45 man-minutes, versus the three man-hours the best big steelmakers had achieved. In 1992, construction was under way for another such mill in Hickman, Arkansas.

Even the Grapeland Vulcraft facility, which had been in a slump since 1986, was thriving once again. The plant's production had peaked in 1985 at about 112,000 tons and 11 production lines, said General Manager James Darsey. "Then the oil boom hit and a savings and loan crisis and a few other things. The economy, in general, was very poor in this area." By 1996, the steel joist plant had 7 production lines with a capacity of about 90,000 tons.[19]

On September 16, 1991, at 10:30 a.m., Ken Iverson received the National Medal of Technology

At only 65,000 square feet, Nucor Wire in Lancaster, North Carolina, was considered a midget mill.

SUPPORT CAN BE BEAUTIFUL.

It's not surprising that Brown & Root's employees think the exposed joists in their fitness center are an attractive part of the building's design. But it's a bit unusual when the accountants often comment that those steel joists are absolutely gorgeous. That's because those Vulcraft arched chord joists cost them half as much as the originally specified rolled I-beams would have cost. Half as much.

You see, Vulcraft is the largest supplier of steel joists in the country, including more than a dozen nonstandard designs, more than anyone in the industry. We've been making nonstandard joists for years and with our expertise as well as our large inventory of steel, we make them quickly and economically. What's more, the earlier we get involved in the design stages, the better for the project. Because our experienced engineers can assist the project's designers and bring the end product in more quickly and at less cost than could be done with traditional methods. Just like we did for one of the country's largest contractors, Brown & Root. And if we can do it for them, we can most certainly do it for you.

With Vulcraft nonstandard joists you expand your design possibilities with all the benefits of steel joist construction: they're lightweight and easy to erect like standard joists and can be delivered when you need them. Consider Vulcraft joists for your next project, no matter how large or small. Because our support comes in all sizes and styles, too. See Sweet's 05100/VUL or contact any of the plants below.

VULCRAFT
A Division of Nucor Corporation

PO Box 637, Brigham City, UT 84302 801/734-9433; PO Box 100520, Florence, SC 29501 803/662-0381; PO Box 169, Fort Payne, AL 35967 205/845-2460; PO Box 186, Grapeland, TX 75844 409/687-4665; PO Box 59, Norfolk, NE 68702-0059 402/644-8500; PO Box 1000, St. Joe, IN 46785 219/337-5411. General Contractor: Brown & Root; Steel Fabricator: Palmer Steel Supplies, Inc.

Even as the company focused more attention on its steel mills, the Vulcraft divisions continued to provide high-quality joists at low prices.

from President George Bush in a special Rose Garden ceremony. The citation for the award read:

> *"For his concept of producing steel in minimills using revolutionary slab casting technology that has revitalized the American steel industry."*

Iverson was the first steel industry executive to win the medal, the nation's highest award for technological achievement. He was one of 13 individuals and businesses to earn it for 1991. "I am very proud to accept this award on behalf of all 5,500 Nucor employees," he said. "Our most valuable asset is a workforce that can rapidly solve the processing problems and make technology work."[20]

Revolutionary Wire Technology

At the end of 1991, Nucor announced that it had signed a licensing agreement with Gradic Wire AB of Stockholm, Sweden, which would make Nucor the exclusive North American producer of direct cast wire using a patented technique called G-casting. The G-casting technique was a totally new process for casting steel, faster than anything that had ever been done before. The process employed a master wire that ran with the outflowing melt, solidifying in a cooling zone to form the new wire. Low initial investments and high yields meant that production costs were far less than with conventional wire production methods.[21]

Established in Lancaster, North Carolina, Nucor Wire occupied only 65,000 square feet, about one-tenth the size of Nucor's other mills, and was known as a midget mill. With a melt shop, a hot mill and a cold finishing facility, the mill was devoted exclusively to producing stainless steel wire. Five-millimeter stainless rods were cast at the unheard-of rate of 200 feet per minute. That wire was then hot-rolled down to a width of about .080 inches.

"There's never been a hot mill that rolls to that small of a size," said T.W. "Bill" Baugh, who became general manager of Nucor Wire in 1994. "We do all of this in an oxygen-deprived environment, so we use no picklers or acids, and basically it's a zero-discharge facility. It's another one of those technologies that we have made work when everybody in the industry said it would never work."[22]

Baugh said the inventor of the process, Sven Eckerot, traveled from Sweden to see his invention in action. "He went around the plant with his mouth agape the entire time. He was thrilled. We rarely invent things, but we are very good at perfecting them."[23]

Ambitious Goals

While Nucor's fortunes continued to rise, the industry in aggregate was in decline. *The Washington Post* devoted a series of four articles to the issue of unemployment among steelworkers. The series began with the story of a man who lost his job at USX's massive Fairless Works facility in 1991, after working as a mill mechanic for 25 years. A year later, according to the article, 80 percent of the 1,960 workers laid off from that plant remained unemployed.[24]

Big Steel was prepared to fight back, according to a 1992 article in *The Wall Street Journal.* The big companies had witnessed Nucor's achievements, and U.S. Steel told *The Wall Street Journal* that it was prepared to build a minimill of its own by the end of the decade with technology that would exceed its minimill rivals. The company's Gary, Indiana, facility would be expanded with coal-injection technology that would do away with coke ovens, and new coating techniques and forming characteristics would be used in its high-end products.

Iverson was mindful of Big Steel's determination and believed that a stiffer challenge from the integrated companies was yet to come. "There isn't any reason why an integrated mill couldn't put in a

The fastener plant in St. Joe, Indiana, allowed Nucor to gain a leadership role in the competitive fastener business.

thin-slab caster using much of the same equipment they have," Iverson said. "They could do it with a lot less capital cost than it took us."[25]

Iron Carbide

In late 1992, the company announced plans for construction of a 320,000-ton-per-year facility to produce iron carbide in the Republic of Trinidad and Tobago. The plant was developed through an agreement with Iron Carbide Holdings, which provided the technology. It was Nucor's first venture outside the United States, and, like many Nucor projects, it was revolutionary in concept. It was also unusual because of the permanent tax-free status negotiated by Sam Siegel.

"If Nucor succeeds in producing the high-carbon metallics at $110 per ton, iron carbide will revolutionize the metallics outlook for electric-furnace steelmakers — and give them a new weapon in their competition with blast-furnace steelmaking," said *New Steel* magazine.[26]

The facility was completed in 1994, and after some adjustments and delays, the first boatload of iron carbide was shipped to the United States in April 1996. The challenge was the natural result of using an untried technology. "Our biggest surprise was that even though a lot of the parts looked correct on paper, we had to figure out how they all worked together," explained Gus Hiller, general manager of the facility.[27]

Above, below and next page: Interior shots of Nucor's fastener facility in Conway, Arkansas.

"We have had a tremendous amount of difficulty with the mechanics of the process," noted LeRoy Prichard in 1996. He had joined Nucor in 1989 as manager of New Steel Technology, in charge of evaluating alternatives to iron. "We aren't out of the woods yet, but we have learned a great deal."[28]

Using iron ore and natural gas, the plant produced an iron carbide that looked like dull black sand. It was shipped to Nucor's mills, where it was injected into the molten steel to boost the iron content.[29]

Trinidad was chosen because of the price and availability of natural gas, the proximity to a source of iron ore and the availability of shipping, said Hiller. Other factors were a stable government and an educated population.[30] The plant employed about 65 people, mostly under the age of 25 except for Hiller and John Scheel, the production manager. The highly automated facility required four shifts of nine people, plus some administrators and engineers.

Even the youngest recruits were given tremendous amounts of responsibility. Reginald Kercelus, who had recently graduated from the University of the West Indies, was hired as a mechanical engineer trainee. Soon, he found himself involved in the facility's construction. "I was flying from state to state, looking at equipment and going to design meetings. It was a hell of an experience for the first year and a half," he recalled. At age 24, he became a shift superintendent.[31]

In an ironic twist, longtime rivals Nucor Steel and U.S. Steel announced a joint venture in late 1994 to develop a new technology to produce steel directly from iron carbide. The cooperation was not too surprising, as a number of Nucor workers had migrated from U.S. Steel over the years. Following a feasibility study of the process, the idea was to construct a demonstration plant to develop and evaluate the commercial feasibility of the new process. The plant would be built near Nucor's thin-slab sheet-steel mill in Hickman, Arkansas, and the iron carbide for the demonstration plant would come from Nucor's Trinidad facility.[32]

Forging a Stronger Future

Sales topped $2 billion at the end of 1993, bringing earnings to $123.5 million. Correnti's plans for the future were ambitious. His number one goal, he told *The Business Journal* in Charlotte, was to make money. His second goal was to move Nucor up from the nation's fourth-largest steel producer to first place by the year 2000. *The Business Journal* cited industry sources that agreed the goal was attainable.[33]

Becoming number one seemed like a very realistic goal to people at Nucor. "There is no doubt in anybody's mind," said Hamilton Lott, Jr., general manager of the Florence joist facility. "Nucor has been so focused on being the best and growing at a rapid pace that it just seems natural," agreed Doug Jellison, who joined Nucor in 1990 and is now general manager of the Bearing Products Subsidiary.[34]

Analysts were recommending Nucor stock with enthusiasm. *The Wall Street Journal* reported in June 1994 that minimills were the stars of the steel industry, coming at a time when the steel market was at its strongest in decades. "A strong case could be made to just buy Nucor and not worry about the rest of the industry," said

John C. Tumazos of Donaldson, Lufkin & Jenrette. Tumazos noted that Nucor had delivered 83 percent of the steel industry's growth in shipments since 1988, and predicted that the company would continue to lead.[35]

In 1995, Nucor placed seventh in a "hidden value index" produced by CDB Research & Consulting, ahead of such companies as Coca-Cola, Intel and Walt Disney. The index measured eight nonfinancial attributes, including employee relations, customer satisfaction and loyalty, brand equity, ability to innovate, ability to reduce costs, ability to increase productivity, ability to avoid regulatory problems and ability to increase revenue. Nucor's customer satisfaction and loyalty were particularly noted.[36]

In early 1995, Nucor announced it would build a third steel mill to produce hot-rolled and cold-rolled sheet steel in Berkeley County, South Carolina. The new mill would use the same thin-slab process used in Nucor's Crawfordsville and Hickman plants. Following its completion in 1997, the Berkeley County plant would establish Nucor as the second-largest steel producer in the United States.

The company continued to invest heavily in its quest to become the top steelmaker. In 1995 and 1996, Nucor planned to spend $825 million in expansion, hundreds of millions of dollars more than the next nearest competitor, Ipsco Steel, which would spend $294.6 million. Despite less capital spending, Nucor's competitors were ambitious. Atlantic Steel Industries planned an on-line billet-weighing system for a six-strand billet caster. Ipsco and Tuscaloosa Steel planned to increase capacity, while Tuscaloosa and Oregon Steel planned to streamline operations.

North Star Steel, forming a joint venture with Australian steelmaker BHP, entered an agreement to develop a new mill that would utilize a medium-slab caster to produce slabs 3.7- to 4-inches thick. North Star President Robert Garvey explained that the medium-slab caster was chosen because the steel quality would be higher

Scrap metal before it is converted to steel. Nucor, which uses recycled steel, is the largest recycler of scrap metal in the United States.

than with a thin slab. Ipsco also intended to install a medium-slab caster.

In the meantime, Birmingham Steel led the minimills in spending on bar and rod. The company's largest project was a $175 million facility for melting and casting in Memphis. Birmingham also drew up plans to build a new rod and bar mill for its American Steel & Wire subsidiary.[37]

Controversies

As Nucor grew, it attracted more controversy. In 1995 the Nucor Corporation was fined almost $120,000 in South Carolina for violating safety and pollution laws at two plants there. Five years earlier, Nucor had been fined $185,000 by the Arkansas Department of Pollution Control and Ecology for violating air pollution laws. It was the fifth-largest fine in Arkansas history. Iverson defended Nucor's record, noting that most of the pollution fines involved paperwork violations. He added that steel work was "hard, hot, dirty, dangerous, skilled work." South Carolina Labor spokesman Jim Knight said the fines were not unusual for a steel plant. "It's a high-hazard industry to begin with, so it's typical for investigators to find serious violations when they go in," he said.[38]

But later that year, Nucor drew criticism from the nation's largest pension fund for nominating a board of five white men. The New York-based Teachers Insurance and Annuity Association-College Retirement Equities Funds, which held 1 percent of Nucor's stock, asked Nucor to adopt a policy saying it would seek qualified women and minority candidates. The TIAA-CREF's proxy statement appeared on Nucor's 1995 proxy statement.[39]

Forbes watched with amazement as the episode unfolded. "One of Nucor's lucky shareholders is TIAA-CREF. This $142 billion institutional behemoth owns 912,900 Nucor shares and has a handsome profit on them. Is TIAA-CREF proposing a vote of thanks? Quite the contrast. The pension fund is trying to force Nucor to change its ways." *Forbes* pointed to Thomas Jones, who became president of the teachers' retirement fund in 1993, as the man behind the attack on Nucor. Jones had become famous in the 1960s as a black power radical and was one of the leaders in an armed takeover by black stu-

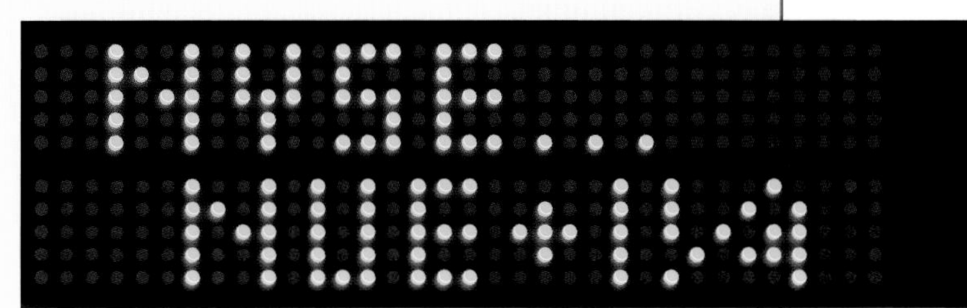

The Little Stock That Could...

This poem was written March 4, 1993 by Joe Urey, who handled advertising for Nucor.

From someone who knows little
'bout the market,
I'd like to give you a tip.
Put a small amount, twenty years ago,
In Nucor, and let 'er rip!

For years I paid no attention
To share price or growing P/E.
I put stock splits from Sam in a shoe box,
Then something occurred to me.

Could this really be growing?
Could my little stake get plump?
Should I pay more attention
When Standard & Poors takes a jump?

So I flicked on my calculator,
Scanned the pages of *WSJ*,
And looked for that NUE number
That occurred at the close yesterday.

Holy smokes, I was so happy!
Those numbers gave me a thrill.
I'd heard of growth and appreciation,
But I thought that took some skill.

I've simply been sitting like a chicken,
Idly hatching its nest.
And out pops a baby fortune ...
Nucor, you guys are the best.

Nucor's cold-finish mill in Darlington.

dents of the Cornell University (Iverson's alma mater) student union building in Ithaca, New York. His message not only to Nucor but to other companies with white male boards, was to set a timetable for putting women and blacks on their boards, or he would make it an issue.[40]

Also blamed for putting the issue in the spotlight was John H. Biggs, chairman and CEO of TIAA-CREF, who happened to be white and who strongly supported Jones' stance. Biggs' and Jones' attacks on Nucor ruffled the feathers of more than a few stockholders. One, Dr. James D. Hlavacek, now a member of Nucor's board of directors, sent a scathing letter to Biggs in April of 1995. "Based upon recent articles in *The New York Times* and *Fortune* and the Nucor stockholder proposal you were responsible for, I am appalled at your attack on Nucor, one of the high performing and most socially responsible companies in the U.S," he wrote. Biggs had a TIAA-CREF retirement annuity of more than $265,000, and he owned an additional $50,000 in Nucor stock. Hlavacek, an author of best-selling books on management, threatened TIAA-CREF with reprisals in his next book.

"If you don't stop this foolish and personal crusade against Nucor, my new book in 1996 will devote at least one page to your shallow understanding of a well-run, for-profit organization," Hlavacek wrote.[41]

When the referendum was put to a vote, stockholders overwhelmingly rejected the proposal.

On a more positive note, Nucor joined forces with the state of South Carolina in 1995 to bring recycling to the state through tax incentives, largely through the efforts of Sam Siegel, who was instrumental in crafting the legislation. Because the company converts scrap metal into steel, it has become the largest recycler in the United States. As a result, the tax incentives, the largest in the history of the United States, have amounted to more than $250 million in savings for Nucor.[42]

Ken Iverson Steps Down

Iverson's health became cause for concern after he underwent heart surgery to replace an aorta. As a child, Iverson had suffered from scarlet fever that had left him with a heart murmur. During a routine physical examination, Iverson's doctor recommended that he have the condition thoroughly evaluated before he had a heart attack. Iverson contacted a cardiologist immediately, and a few days later underwent major surgery in Houston, Texas.

Ever since the surgery, there had been speculation that he would step down as chief executive officer. On December 6, 1995, Nucor announced that John Correnti had been named CEO. Correnti, until then president and chief operating officer, would also become vice chairman. Iverson, then 70, would retain his title of chairman, but the day-to-day operations would now be overseen by Correnti. Sam Siegel, the company announced, would remain vice chairman and chief financial officer.

Business Week noted some differences between the two men in a 1996 article.

> *"Correnti is regarded as harder-driving than the genial Iverson, and he preens a bit more in the limelight. He made friends with then-Governor Bill Clinton when the company was negotiating plant sites in Arkansas. And he continues to meet with Clinton, talking steel and politics at the White House. 'I'm one of the Republican Friends of Bill,' Correnti said in the interview."*[43]

Taking the reins of the company, Correnti was faced with an enviable problem: how to encourage growth — which reached $3.6 billion in 1996 — while maintaining the unique culture that had achieved such success. "There's no doubt, as you get bigger it becomes tougher and tougher," he said in a recent interview. "But you cannot isolate yourself from your employees. As a matter of fact, the most fun I have is when I visit the plants twice a year."

> *"I walk through that plant and its office and shake everyone's hand and shoot the breeze. I want them to know if they have a problem, they can pick up the phone or write a letter and communicate with someone who is not a nameless, faceless stranger who's pulling the strings. The issues are simple. Number one: What does a person care about? How much money they can make. Number two is job security. If I bust my ass and I work hard and do a good job, am I going to have a job tomorrow? Number three, are you going to treat me fairly, and with dignity and respect? Number four, if I think I'm getting screwed or a lousy deal, where do I take my complaint? Responding to these issues is how we remain non-union. That's why we have some of the highest-paid steelworkers in the world, but yet have one of the lowest labor costs of anybody in the world."*[44]

"My goal is to keep Nucor growing," he said in 1996. "We're not going to grow at 25 to 30 percent like we have the last three or four years, but we're going to continue to grow at 15 to 20 percent and we're going to do it the way we always have. Through green field sites, building our own, training our own, establishing our own culture in those plants."[45]

The management changes gave rise to several complimentary retrospectives about Iverson's career. Iverson, wrote *The Pittsburgh Post-Gazette*, had been "to his generation of steel men what Andrew Carnegie was to his."[46]

Correnti was confident that he could lead Nucor, but he was the first to admit that "no one is ever going to fill Ken Iverson's shoes."

> *"Not John Correnti and not somebody who follows me. When you open up the history books, our grandchildren, 30 years or 40 years from now, are going to open it up to Steel in America, and they're going to see two names there and two pictures. They're going to see Andrew Carnegie, father of the integrated industry, and Ken Iverson, father of the American minimill. That's just the way it's going to be."*[47]

NOTES TO SOURCES

Chapter One

1. George Mays, *R.E. Olds: Auto Industry Pioneer*, William B. Eerdmans Publishing Company, Grand Rapids, Michigan, 1977, pp. 13-17.
2. *Ibid.*
3. *Ibid.*, p. 96.
4. *Ibid.*, p. 114.
5. C.B. Glasscock, *Motor History of America or The Gasoline Age*, Floyd Clymer, 1937, pp. 28-29.
6. *Ibid.*, p. 33.
7. Unpublished history compiled by Sam Siegel.
8. *Motor History of America*, p. 52.
9. *Ibid.*, p. 86.
10. *Ibid.*, p. 322.
11. *Ibid.*, pp. 323-324.
12. Siegel history.
13. *Ibid.*
14. *Ibid.*
15. *Ibid.*
16. Richard Preston, *American Steel*, Prentice Hall Press, New York, New York, 1991, p. 54.
17. Reo Holding Corporation, notice and proxy statement, August 29, 1955.
18. *New York Herald-Tribune*, December 21, 1955. Section 3, p. 12.
19. *The New York Times*, December 22, 1955.
20. Nuclear Corporation of American, Organizational Manual, 1956.
21. Nuclear Corporation of America, 1959 Annual Report.
22. Nuclear Corporation of America,1958 Annual Report.
23. *Ibid.*
24. Financial Statements and Schedules for Annual Report on Form 10-K, years 1956-1960.
25. *Ibid.*
26. *Ibid.*

Chapter Two

1. Sam Siegel, interviewed by the author, September 11, 1996. Transcript, p. 12.
2. Prospectus, Nuclear Corporation of America, Inc., October 23, 1961, p. 10.
3. Richard Preston, *American Steel*, Prentice Hall Press, New York, New York, 1991: pp. 62-66.
4. Siegel interview, p. 12.
5. *Ibid.*, pp. 4-5.
6. *Ibid.*
7. Articles of Incorporation, Vulcraft Corporation, June 12, 1946.
8. Mabel Bristow, interviewed by the author, p. 3.
9. H. David Aycock, interviewed by the author, September 13, 1996. Transcript, p. 2.
10. *The Wall Street Journal*, September 6, 1962, p. 20.
11. Madge DeFosset, interviewed by the author, October 7, 1996. Transcript, p. 10.
12. *Ibid.*, p. 8.
13. Ideal Communications, Inc., Vol. 1, No. 3, August 1992, p. 6.
14. Memo, Purdue University, semi-annual newsletter for the Purdue School of Mechanical Engineering, Spring 1988.
15. *American Steel*, p. 58.
16. Ideal Communications, Inc., Vol. 1, No. 3, August 1992, p. 6.
17. Ken Iverson, interviewed by the author, September 11, 1996. Transcript, p. 8.
18. *The Wall Street Journal*, September 6, 1962, p. 20.
19. Ken Iverson interview, p. 13.
20. *Vulcraft News*, company newsletter, September 1962.
21. Aycock interview, p. 4.
22. *The River Ran Red*, a documentary film on the Homestead Steel Strike of 1892, produced by Steffi Domike and Nicole Fauteux, 1992.
23. Western Union Telegram from the Teamsters Union to Vulcraft, August 31, 1964.
24. Memo from Ken Iverson to Vulcraft truck drivers, dated September 2, 1964.
25. Memo from Ken Iverson to Vulcraft employees, Florence, South Carolina, dated September 2, 1964.
26. *Ibid*
27. The Teamsters Coloring Book, published by the Communications Workers of

America, AFL-CIO
28. Nuclear Corporation of America, Analysis of Sales and Earnings, 1961 through 1968.
29. *Ibid.*

Chapter Three

1. Ernest Delaney, interviewed by the author, September 12, 1996. Transcript, p. 8.
2. Minutes of a Special Meeting of the Board of Directors, Nuclear Corporation of America, January 28, 1965.
3. Richard Preston, *American Steel*, Prentice Hall Press, New York, New York, 1991, p. 66.
4. *The Evening American*, Phoenix, Arizona, May 2, 1965.
5. Minutes of a special meeting of the board of directors, Nuclear Corporation of America, May 27, 1965.
6. *American Steel*, p. 67.
7. Minutes of a special meeting of the Board of Directors, Nuclear Corporation of America, May 27, 1965.
8. *New York Daily News*, July 24, 1968, p. 8.
9. Minutes of a special meeting of the board of directors, Nuclear Corporation of America, July 8, 1965.
10. Telegram from Sam Siegel to Harold G. Shelton, July 30, 1965.
11. Press release from Nuclear Corporation of America, August 12, 1965.
12. Press release from Nuclear Corporation of America, August 24, 1965.
13. Ernest Delaney, interviewed by the author, September 12, 1996. Transcript, p. 8.
14. James Cunningham, interviewed by the author, October 9, 1996. Transcript, p. 6.
15. Letter to employees from Iverson, November 1, 1965.
16. *Management Review*, August 1992, p. 25.
17. Betsy Liberman, interviewed by the author, September 11, 1996. Transcript, pp. 3-4.
18. Ken Iverson, interviewed by the author, September 11, 1996. Transcript, p. 21.
19. *Management Review*, August 1992, pgs. 25-26.
20. Ken Iverson, interviewed by the author, September 11, 1996. Transcript, p. 25.
21. *American Steel*, p. 72

Chapter Four

1. Betsy Liberman, interviewed by the author, September 11, 1996. Transcript, p. 2.
2. Ken Iverson, interviewed by the author, September 11, 1996. Transcript, p. 20.
3. A Study of Nucor, by Professor Frank C. Barnes, University of North Carolina at Charlotte, 1984.
4. Rose Daniel, interviewed by the author, October 7, 1996. Transcript, p. 2.
5. *Ibid.*
6. Liberman interview, p. 2.
7. Nuclear Corporation of America, Analysis of Sales and Earnings, 1961-1967.
8. A talk by F. Kenneth Iverson, president of Nucor Corporation, before the New York Society of Security Analysts, March 29, 1973, *The Wall Street Transcript.*
9. *Ibid.*
10. *Ibid.*
11. Nucor Corporation, a case study by Judy Lapkin, Harvard Business School, 1975.
12. Nucor, a case study by Frank C. Barnes, University of North Carolina at Charlotte, 1984.
13. Nuclear Corporation of America, 1966 Annual Report.
14. Press release from Nuclear Corporation of America, April 3, 1967.
15. Nuclear Corporation of America, 1967 Annual Report.
16. James Campbell, interviewed by the author, September 12, 1996. Transcript, p. 13.
17. Press release from Nuclear Corporation of America, October 20, 1967.
18. Nuclear Corporation of America, 1967 Annual Report.
19. *Ibid.*
20. Nuclear Corporation of America, Analysis of Sales and Earnings, 1961-1967.
21. Nuclear Corporation of America, 1967 Annual Report.

Chapter Five

1. *Arizona Republic*, December 10, 1972.
2. Minutes of the Board of Directors, NCA, August 16, 1966, New York City.
3. Harvard Business School, case study on Nucor, by Judy Lapkin, 1975.

4. Feasibility Study and Analysis of Capital Requirements and Operations, prepared by Nuclear Corporation of America, April 18, 1967.
5. Rod Hernandez, interviewed by the author, October 7, 1996. Transcript, p. 2.
6. *The Wall Street Journal*, January 12, 1981, p. 1.
7. Press release from the South Carolina State Development Board, July 10, 1968.
8. Donald F. Barnett and Robert W. Crandall, *Up from the Ashes: The Rise of the Steel Minimill in the United States*. Brookings Institute, 1986, p. 18.
9. Donald F. Barnett and Louis Schorsch, *Steel: Upheaval in a Basic Industry*, Ballinger Publishing Company, Cambridge, Massachusetts, 1983.
10. Paul A. Tiffany, *The Decline of American Steel: How Management, Labor and Government Went Wrong*, Oxford University Press, 1988, New York, pp. 144-146, p. 163.
11. *Up From the Ashes*, p. 5.
12. Feasibility Study and Analysis of Capital Requirements and Operations, prepared by Nuclear Corporation of America, April 18, 1967.
13. Feasibility Study and Analysis of Capital Requirements and Operations.
14. Press release from the South Carolina State Development Board, July 10, 1968.
15. Text of a speech given by F. Kenneth Iverson, July 10, 1968, Darlington, S.C.
16. Nuclear Corporation of America company literature on file.
17. *33 Magazine*, December 1970, p. 2.
18. John Doherty, interviewed by the author, October 8, 1996. Transcript, p. 2.
19. *Ibid.*
20. E. Michael Delaney III, interviewed by the author, September 12, 1996. Transcript, p. 17.
21. *The News and Press*, Darlington, S.C., July 11, 1968, p. 2B.
22. Brochure produced by Morgardshammer, Sweden, 1967.
23. Nuclear Corporation of America, company files.
24. Nuclear Corporation of America, 1969 Annual Report.
25. *33 Magazine*, December 1970, pgs. 63-64.
26. *American Steel*, p. 76.
27. *33 Magazine*, December 1970, p. 64.
28. Press release from Nuclear Corporation of America, March 31, 1970.
29. *Arizona Republic*, Phoenix, Arizona, December 10, 1972.

Chapter Five Sidebar

1. Joseph Rutkowski, information and comments, January 29, 1997.
2. *Ibid.*
3. Webster's New World Encyclopedia, Prentice Hall, New York, New York, 1993. p. 1,053.
4. Joseph Rutkowski, information and comments, January 29, 1997.

Chapter Six

1. Memo from H. M. Crapse to employees, M & S Steel, Fort Payne, Alabama, January 8, 1968.
2. *Ibid.*
3. *Ibid.*
4. Copy of the petition filed by M & S Steel Company against the Ironworkers of America, January 25, 1968.
5. Letter from M & S Steel attorney, John E. Tate to Louis Leipsitz, National Labor Relations Board representative, March 18, 1968.
6. Letter from John E. Tateto Louis Leipsitz, NLRB, March 11, 1968.
7. Copy of an Order withdrawing Notice of Hearing and Dismissing Petition, August 6, 1969, signed by Walter C. Phillips, Regional Director, NLRB, Atlanta, Georgia.
8. *The Wall Street Journal*, January 12, 1981, p. 19.
9. John Savage, workshop on NCA philosophy, Phoenix, Arizona, May 1982.
10. Jerry DeMars, interviewed by the author, October 7, 1996. Transcript, p. 3.
11. James Ronner, interviewed by the author, October 11, 1996. Transcript, p. 5.
12. Donald Holloway, interviewed by the author, September 11, 1996. Transcript, p. 11.
13. Hamilton Lott, interviewed by the author, September 10, 1996. Transcript, p. 21.
14. Richard Preston, *American Steel*, Prentice Hall Press, New York, New York, 1991, p. 82.

15. *The Nucor Story*, published by Nucor Corporation, undated, p. 9.
16. *Reader's Digest*, August 1985, pp. 113-114.
17. John A. Savage, former Manager of Personnel Services, Nucor, adaptation of a presentation given at the spring meeting/workshop of the Council on a union-free environment, Phoenix, Arizona, May 16-19, 1982.
18. Gene Harris, interviewed by Karen Nitkin, February 19, 1997. Transcript, p. 5.
19. Sam Huff, interviewed by the author, September 11, 1996. Transcript, p. 8.
20. Ken Iverson, interviewed by the author, September 11, 1996. Transcript, p. 26.
21. Michael Dunn, interviewed by Karen Nitkin, March 17, 1996. Transcript, p. 6.
22. Employee handbook, Nuclear Corporation of America, 1969.
23. Employee handbook, Nuclear Corporation of America, 1970.
24. Robert Foster, interviewed by Alex Lieber, February 20, 1997. Transcript, p. 7.
25. Vulcraft Division, Florence, South Carolina, rates of manufacturing department, May 27, 1968.
26. *American Steel*, p. 83.
27. Nuclear Corporation of America, 1968 Annual Report.
28. Nuclear Corporation of America, 1969 Annual Report.
29. Nuclear Corporation of America,1968 Annual Report.
30. *American Steel*, p. 86.
31. Dick Giersch, interviewed by the author, October 2, 1996. Transcript, p. 6.

Chapter Seven

1. Nucor Steel, a case study by Judy Lapkin, Harvard University, 1975.
2. Donald F. Barnett and Robert W. Crandall, *Up from the Ashes: The Rise of the Steel Minimill in the United States*. Brookings Institute, 1986, p. 39.
3. "Steeling Against Inflation," Report to the Annual Meeting of the Steel Service Center by Peter F. Marcus, Mitchell, Hutchins Inc. May 10, 1977.
4. Press release from Nuclear Corporation of America, December 28, 1971.
5. Press release from Nucor Corporation, July 12, 1972.
6. A talk by F. Kenneth Iverson, president of Nucor Corporation, before the New York Society of Security Analysts, March 29, 1973, *The Wall Street Transcript*.
7. Joe Urey, interviewed by the author, September 11, 1996. Transcript, pp. 4-5.
8. Donald B. Thompson, "Steel Stalks Dollars as Shortage Looms," *Industry Week*, April 9, 1973, pp. 36-37.
9. *Ibid.*
10. Nucor Steel, a case study by Judy Lapkin, Harvard University, 1975.
11. Press release from Nucor Corporation, March 8, 1974.
12. Speech given by Kenneth Iverson before the American Institute for Imported Steel, December 7, 1981.
13. *Ibid.*
14. *33 Magazine*, December 1970, p. 65.
15. A talk by F. Kenneth Iverson, president of Nucor Corporation, before the New York Society of Security Analysts, March 29, 1973, *The Wall Street Transcript*.
16. *The Wall Street Journal*, August 9, 1973, p. 26.
17. *Ibid.*
18. Wally Hill, interviewed by Alex Lieber, February 26, 1997. Transcript, p. 3.
19. *The Charlotte News*, May 7, 1975, p. 8C.
20. Ken Iverson, interviewed by the author, September 11, 1996. Transcript, p. 32.
21. E. Michael Delaney III, interviewed by the author, September 12, 1996. Transcript, p. 5.
22. *World Herald*, Omaha, Nebraska, January 26, 1975.
23. *The Carolina Financial Times*, January 27, 1975.

Chapter Eight

1. "Nucor to Hold Steady Line on Prices," *American Metal Market*, September 19, 1975, p. 1.
2. "World Steel in the 1980s," a report by Rev. William T. Hogan, S.J.,*Center Lines*, published by Steel Service Institute, Vol. XIV, August 1981.
3. H. David Aycock, interviewed by the author, September 13, 1996. Transcript, p. 18.
4. Donald F. Barnett and Robert W. Crandall, *Up from the Ashes: The Rise of the Steel*

Minimill in the United States. Brookings Institute, 1986, pp. 36-37.
5. "The Steel Industry: An American Tragedy," a report by Faulkner, Dawkins and Sullivan, February 22, 1977.
6. "Nucor Meets Foreign Steel Prices," *American Metal Market*, July 24, 1975, p. 1.
7. *Ibid.*
8. "Nucor to Hold Steady Line on Prices,"*American Metal Market*, September 19, 1975, p. 1.
9. Open letter to steel customers from Kenneth Iverson and Nucor, advertisement in *American Metal Market*, December 22, 1975, p. 3.
10. "Nucor Hiking Merchant Bar, Small Structurals," *American Metal Market*, February 12, 1976, p. 1.
11. "Distributors Doubtful Merchant Quality Bar Prices Can Be Firmed in Market," *American Metal Market*, February 20, 1976, p. 1.
12. "North Star Ups Price of Rebars," *American Metal Market*, April 1, 1976.
13. "Nucor Moving with Plan to Link Continuous Caster with Bar Mill," *American Metal Market*, May 26, 1976, p. 1.
14. "Nucor to Cut Prices $15 on Bar Products," *American Metal Market*, September 24, 1976, p. 1.
15. "Steel and Scrap Prices Bottom; Hikes Loom in First quarter of 1977," *American Metal Market*, November 22, 1976, p. 1.
16. Excerpt from the 1977 Annual Report of Bethlehem Steel, reprinted in The Steel Industry of America report, 1978.
17. Excerpt from Kaiser Steel Corporation's 1977 annual report, reprinted in The Steel Industry of America, 1978.
18. Speech by Kenneth Iverson before the American Institute for Imported Steel, December 7, 1981.
19. Revived Triggers May Hinder Industry's Progress: Iverson," *American Metal Market*, October 4, 1980, p. 6.
20. Letter to employees of Nucor Corporation, from F. Kenneth Iverson, August 15, 1978.
21. Nucor Corporation, 1979 Annual Report.
22. Purchase agreement between Nucor Corporation and Nuclear Research Corporation, November 9, 1976.
23. "Nucor Outlook for '79: Profit," *The Wall Street Journal*, August 29, 1979, p. 7.
24. Donald Holloway, interviewed by the author, September 11, 1996. Transcript, p. 8.
25. Securities and Exchange Commission, Form 10-K 1979 Annual Report.
26. Research report prepared by Merrill Lynch, February 2, 1978.

Chapter Nine

1. "TWST Names Iverson Best Chief Executive Steel Industry," *The Wall Street Transcript*, June 30, 1980, pp. 58, 379.
2. "Nucor Corp. Stock Soars to New High," *The Charlotte News*, July 16, 1980, p. 13A.
3. NBC White Paper Special, "If Japan Can Do It ... Why Can't We?", broadcast June 24, 1980.
4. Letter from Tyler E. Glenn, Jr., to K. Iverson, July 1, 1980.
5. Letter from J.R. Oden, Jr., to K. Iverson, July 21, 1980.
6. "TWST Names Iverson Best," pp. 58, 379.
7. *Ibid.*
8. Ken Iverson, interviewed by the author, September 11, 1996. Transcript, p.35.
9. Sam Siegel, quoted in "Barebones Finance," *CFO magazine*, November 1991.
10. James Coblin, interviewed by the author, September 13, 1996. Transcript, p. 28.
11. Nucor Corporation, 1981 Annual Report.
12. John Correnti, interviewed by the author, September 13, 1996. Transcript, p. 10.
13. *Ibid.*, p. 11.
14. Ladd Hall, interviewed by the author, October 14, 1996. Transcript, p. 8.
15. Daniel DiMicco, interviewed by the author, October 9, 1996. Transcript, pp. 5-6.
16. "Jobs and the Jobless in a Changing Workplace," *National Issues Forum*, 1984, p. 5.
17. Revived Triggers May Hinder Industry's Progress: Iverson," *American Metal Market*, October 4, 1980, p. 7.
18. *Ibid.* p. 6.
19. Press release from Nucor Corporation, "Nucor Reports 1982 Results Return on Stockholder's Equity Was 10%," February 22, 1983.

20. "Jobs and the Jobless in a Changing Workplace," *National Issues Forum*, 1984, p. 21.
21. "Steel Imports Protect American Metalworking," speech by Fred Lamesch, V.P., American Institute for Imported Steel, Inc., New York City, October 14, 1981.
22. "Nucor May Be Ripe for New Recommendation After Removal From Buy Lists Sparks Sell-Off," *The Wall Street Journal*, June 7, 1982.
23. "Ken Iverson: Simply the Best," *American Way Magazine*, 1985.
24. "Top 15 List of Steel Producers Changes; Nucor Becomes No. 10," *American Metal Market*, February 23, 1983, p. 2.
25. "Nucor Pricing Move Forces Center and Minis into Competition," *American Metal Market*, September 14, 1984, p. 1.
26. *Ibid.*
27. *Ibid.*
28. "Is Climate Cooling Off at Nucor?", *The Charlotte Observer*, August 7, 1983, p. 5B.

Chapter Ten

1. Joe Rutkowski, interviewed by the author, September 10, 1996. Transcript, p. 8.
2. Confidential memo from attorney Chick Abeles, Washington, D.C. firm of Wald, Harkrader & Ross, to Sam Siegel, November 9, 1984.
3. Letter from Barry Blyveis, U.S. Justice Department attorney, to Michael D. Ridbery, attorney advising Nucor, October 19, 1984.
4. Letter from Sam Siegel to Richard B. Smith, Federal Trade Commission, February 24, 1984.
5. Transcript from Nucor's 1984 Annual Stockholders Meeting.
6. *Reader's Digest*, August 1985, p. 114.
7. Rutkowski interview, p. 43.
8. James Coblin, interviewed by the author, September 13, 1996. Transcript, p. 7.
9. "Manuel Leaves Nucor to Head Fla. Steel Div.", *American Metal Market*, October 2, 1984.
10. Jay Bowcutt, interviewed by the author, October 31, 1996. Transcript, p. 5.
11. Coblin interview, p. 20.
12. *Ibid.*, pp. 10-11.
13. *Ibid.*, p. 12.
14. Rick Campbell, interviewed by the author, October 10, 1996. Transcript, p. 3.
15. Rutkowski interview, p. 8.
16. Hank Carper, interviewed by Alex Lieber, March 7, 1997. Transcript, p. 4.
17. Transcript from Nucor's 1984 Annual Stockholders Meeting.
18. *Ibid.*
19. John Correnti, interviewed by the author, September 13, 1996. Transcript, p.17.
20. LeRoy Prichard, interviewed by the author, October 16, 1996. Transcript, p. 4.
21. Correnti interview, p. 17.

Chapter Eleven

1. "Technology: Major Advance in Steel Seen," *The New York Times*, February 16, 1984, p. D2.
2. Transcript from Nucor's 1989 Annual Stockholders Meeting.
3. *The Wall Street Journal*, January 8, 1987, p. 6.
4. E. Michael Delaney III, interviewed by the author, September 12, 1996, p. 18.
5. "The Odds Are With Nucor's Venture," *American Metal Market*, September 18, 1989.
6. Rodney Mott, interviewed by the author, September 12, 1996. Transcript, p. 21.
7. Delaney interview, p, 18.
8. Terry Lisenby, interviewed by the author, September 12, 1996. Transcript, pp. 7-8.
9. "Nucor's Strategic Project," *Management Journal*, 1988, pp. 15-16.
10. *The Wall Street Journal*, January 8, 1987, p. 6.
11. John Ferriola, interviewed by the author, October 9, 1996. Transcript, p. 2.
12. Mott interview, p. 6.
13. "Steelmaking at Crawfordsville," *American Metal Market*, September 18, 1989, p. 22A.
14. Transcript from Nucor's 1990 Annual Stockholders Meeting.
15. Report by Robinson-Humphrey, 1990.
16. "Small Steelmakers Finding Profitable Market Niches," *The Wall Street Journal*, January 8, 1986, p. 6.
17. Doug Jellison, interviewed by the author, October 10, 1996. Transcript, p. 3.
18. "Nucor Division Eyed by Rhone-Poulenc," *American*

Metal Market, October 6, 1988, p. 2.
19. James Cunningham, interviewed by the author, October 9, 1996. Transcript, p. 4.
20. "Protectionism Can't Protect Jobs," *Fortune*, May 11, 1987. pp. 121-128.
21. "The Myths of Protectionism," Speech to the American Metal Market Association, New York, New York, June 23, 1987.
22. Harry Lowe, interviewed by the author, October 15, 1996. Transcript, p. 4.
23. Transcript of an interview of Ken Iverson with *The Wall Street Transcript*, November 30, 1988.
24. D. Michael Parrish, interviewed by the author, October 9, 1996. Transcript, p. 3.
25. David Chase, interviewed by Karen Nitkin, March 4, 1997. Transcript, pp. 7-8.
26. *Ibid.*

Chapter Eleven Sidebar

1. Joseph Rutkowski, information and comments, January 29, 1997.

Chapter Twelve

1. John Correnti, interviewed by the author, September 13, 1996. Transcript, p. 37.
2. "Hazardous Duty - Nucor Steel's Sheen Is Marred by Deaths of Workers at Plants," *The Wall Street Journal*, May 10, 1991, p. 1.
3. "Celebrated Nucor Has High Death Rate," *The Charlotte Observer*, May 5, 1991, p. 1A.
4. Letter from Ken Iverson to Joseph A. Kinney, June 11, 1991.
5. Company literature from Nucor Corporation: Background on Safety Practices and Policies, 1991.
6. James Coblin, interviewed by the author, September 13, 1996. Transcript, p. 23.
7. Coblin interview, p. 24.
8. "Story Infuriates Nucor Manager," *Journal Review*, Crawfordsville, Indiana, May 11, 1991, p. 1.
9. "OSHA Is Out to Cooperate," *Iron Age Magazine*, May 1991, p. 26.
10. "The David and Goliath Tale of an American Steel Company, Paul Harvey column, *Los Angeles Times Syndicate*, 1991.
11. *Ibid.*
12. Sam Huff, in a letter to the author, dated September 6, 1996.
13. "The Best Entrepreneurs," *Business Week*, January 13, 1997.
14. Correnti interview, p. 37.
15. *Ibid.*
16. *Ibid.*
17. *Ibid.*, p. 9.
18. "Nucor Move Breaks the Mold," *The Business Journal* Charlotte, North Carolina, April 15, 1991, p. 1.
19. James Darsey, interviewed by the author, October 7, 1996. Transcript, p. 4.
20. Press release from Nucor Corporation. "Nucor's Iverson Receives National Medal of Technology," September 16, 1991.
21. T.W. "Bill" Baugh, interviewed by the author, October 10, 1996. Transcript, p. 4.
22. *Ibid.*, p. 5.
23. *Ibid.*, p. 10.
24. "The American Dream: Fired Up and Melted Down," *The Washington Post*, April 12, 1992, p. 1A.
25. "Minimill Inroads in Sheet Market Rouse Big Steel," *The Wall Street Journal*, March 9, 1992, p. B1.
26. John Schriefer, "Carbide, at Last," *New Steel magazine*, July 1996.
27. Gus Hiller, interviewed by the author, October 11, 1996. Transcript, p. 5.
28. LeRoy Prichard, interviewed by the author, October 16, 1996. Transcript, p. 10.
29. *Ibid.*, p. 6.
30. Gus Hiller interview, p. 10.
31. Reginald Kercelus, interviewed by Karen Nitkin, February 18, 1996. Transcript, p. 2.
32. Press release from the Nucor Corporation, "Nucor Signs Letter of Intent For New Steelmaking Process," October 12, 1994.
33. "Man of Steel," *The Business Journal*, September 19, 1994, p. 1.
34. Doug Jellison, interviewed by the author, October 10, 1996. Transcript, p. 12.
35. "Steel," *The Wall Street Journal*, June 29, 1994.
36. "Digging for Hidden Value," *FW's Corporate Finance*, Summer 1995.
37. "Major Mills Broaden Their Reach," *New Steel*, September 1995, pp. 30-44.

38. "Nucor Corporation's South Carolina Plants Hit With Fines," *The Post and Courier* Charleston, South Carolina, January 31, 1995, p. 1A.
39. "Nucor Disputes Criticism That Board Lacks Diversity," *The Business Journal*, April 10, 1995, p. 1.
40. "Diversity Hucksters," *Forbes*, May 22, 1995.
41. Letter from Dr. James D. Hlavacek, Managing Director of Market Driven Management, to John H. Biggs, April 19, 1995.
42. Sam Siegel, interviewed by the author, March 11, 1997.
43. "From Blueprints to Grand Design: Ex-engineer John Correnti Now Must Recast Nucor," *Business Week*, January 8, 1996, p. 24.
44. *Ibid.*, pp. 28-29.
45. Correnti interview.
46. "Nucor at Middle Age Seeks to Re-energize Itself," *Pittsburgh Post-Gazette*, October 1, 1995, p. C1
47. Correnti interview, p. 37.

INDEX

T

U

V

W

XYZ

THE LEGEND OF

NUCOR

CORPORATION

WHEN HE CONCEIVED THE design of the first Oldsmobile in the late 1800s, Ransom E. Olds could never have guessed that his venture into automobile manufacturing would lead to the growth of a state-of-the-art, world-class steel company.

The amazing thing about Nucor's strategy for success is that it is so simple: give employees a stake in the company's growth; focus on the business at hand; keep red tape and bureaucracy to a bare minimum. Revenues of $3.6 billion in 1996 prove the soundness of these ideals.

A unique bonus system throughout Nucor links productivity directly to paycheck. Managers are not required to prod for improved performance and efficiency; employees are self-inspired. Supervisors have the task of providing the tools and the environment. The rest is left up to the workers, who frequently find ingenious ways to boost productivity. Executives at Nucor's headquarters do not expect to be consulted before many of these ideas are implemented. In fact, the entire multibillion-dollar corporation runs with an executive staff of only 23.

When F. Kenneth Iverson became president of then-Nuclear Corporation of America in 1965, he took the helm of a company that was on the verge of bankruptcy. In 1968, he took a huge gamble when Nuclear Corporation built its first minimill, simultaneously taking on both Big Steel and foreign steel. In the seventies and eighties, Nucor reaped profits while Big Steel suffered from foreign competition and obsolete technology.

Iverson relinquished the post of chief executive officer in 1996 and was succeeded by John Correnti while Iverson continues as chairman. With a deeply embedded culture of efficiency, innovation and mutual respect, Nucor will continue to follow the road to its inevitable place as the nation's number one steelmaker.

Jeffrey L. Rodengen

About the Author

Best-selling author Jeffrey L. Rodengen has been a producer, director and nationally syndicated columnist. Today, he is best known for his unprecedented works on the evolution of American industry.

Jeff was born in Minnesota and now lives in Fort Lauderdale with his wife, award-winning photographer Karine Rodengen, and their twin children. Among Jeff's current and forthcoming titles are:

The Legend of Chris-Craft

IRON FIST: *The Lives of Carl Kiekhaefer*

Evinrude-Johnson and The Legend of OMC

Serving the Silent Service: The Legend of Electric Boat

The Legend of Dr Pepper/Seven-Up

The Legend of Honeywell

The Legend of Briggs & Stratton

The Legend of Ingersoll-Rand

The Legend of Stanley: 150 Years of The Stanley Works

The MicroAge Way

The Legend of Halliburton

The Legend of York International

The Legend of Amdahl

The Legend of AMD

The Legend of Applied Materials

The Legend of Echlin

The Legend of Goodyear: The First 100 Years

The Legend of AMP

The Legend of Cessna

The Legend of Pfizer